The Color of Mind

D1566648

The History and Philosophy of Education Series
Edited by Randall Curren and Jonathan Zimmerman

The Color of Mind

Why the Origins of the Achievement Gap Matter for Justice

DERRICK DARBY AND JOHN L. RURY

The University of Chicago Press
Chicago and London

The History and Philosophy of Education Series is published in cooperation with the Association for Philosophy of Education and the History of Education Society.

The University of Chicago Press, Chicago 60637
The University of Chicago Press, Ltd., London
© 2018 by The University of Chicago
Published 2018
Printed in the United States of America

27 26 25 24 23 22 21 20 19 18   1 2 3 4 5

ISBN-13: 978-0-226-52521-1 (cloth)
ISBN-13: 978-0-226-52535-8 (paper)
ISBN-13: 978-0-226-52549-5 (e-book)
DOI: 10.7208/chicago/9780226525495.001.0001

Library of Congress Cataloging-in-Publication Data

Names: Darby, Derrick, 1967– author. | Rury, John L., 1951– author.
Title: The color of mind: why the origins of the achievement gap matter for justice / Derrick Darby and John L. Rury.
Other titles: History and philosophy of education.
Description: Chicago: The University of Chicago Press, 2018. | Series: History and philosophy of education series | Includes bibliographical references and index.
Identifiers: LCCN 2017028628 | ISBN 9780226525211 (cloth: alk. paper) | ISBN 9780226525358 (pbk: alk. paper) | ISBN 9780226525495 (e-book)
Subjects: LCSH: African Americans—Education—United States. | Educational equalization—United States. | Academic achievement—Social aspects—United States. | Discrimination in education—United States. | Social justice—United States.
Classification: LCC LC2731 .D37 2018 | DDC 371.829/96073—dc23
LC record available at https://lccn.loc.gov/2017028628

♾ This paper meets the requirements of ANSI/NISO Z39.48-1992 (Permanence of Paper)

CONTENTS

What School Leaders Need to Know

Anna Julia Cooper, an African American educator and scholar writing more than a century ago, recounted a shameful episode. A black woman was admitted to a prestigious art school based on glowing reviews of her sample drawings. When she reported to register for classes, the astonished superintendent, who "had not dreamed a colored person could do such work," rescinded her admission. Not only did this "shrivelling caste spirit" taint art in America, as Cooper laments, but the presumption of black inferiority also stained education more broadly at the time.[1]

Had this aspiring artist been admitted, superior artistic talents would not have spared her the indignity of being denied acceptance as a social equal. So, not surprisingly, given the caste spirit of the times, some people thought it better for a black student such as her to attend a racially segregated school, where her equal dignity would be respected. But it is hardly clear that this would have been an ideal solution. It is likely not one that the student would have preferred, given her application to the white school. Facing the doubts of others about their intellectual and creative abilities because of race haunted many black students in the past, and unfortunately such doubts remain pertinent today. If black people are to be educated within racially diverse schools, and achieve at levels comparable to white peers, we must debunk doubts about their intelligence, character, and conduct.

In 1935, when W. E. B. Du Bois asked, "Does the Negro Need Separate Schools?," America was still firmly in the clutches of Jim Crow.[2] Although education was widely regarded as a great equalizer, supposedly creating a level pathway to achievement and attainment, racial segregation of schools placed blacks and whites on separate and unequal tracks. In addition to engineering black-white inequalities in educational outcomes, Jim Crow schooling sent the pernicious message that blacks were not equals to whites in intelligence, character, or conduct. And, as the story above suggests, even very talented African American students were subject to the indignity of condemnation on these grounds. We coin the term *Color of Mind* to describe this racial ideology. History shows that the Color of Mind and school practices pertaining to the manner, location, and content of instruction have worked in tandem to deny blacks in America a proper education. Philosophy dictates that confronting the Color of Mind and its manifestation within racially diverse schools today is an imperative of justice.

The historical evidence we supply in this book shows that the Color of Mind has served to rationalize racially exclusionary school practices and unequal educational opportunities, and the effects of these, in turn, have worked to sustain this racial ideology. This makes the Color of Mind and educational inequality mutually reinforcing. It should come as no surprise, therefore, that Du Bois seriously entertained the thought that blacks might get "a proper education" in "Negro schools," where contact between students, and between teachers and students, was based not on unequal social relations and beliefs about black inferiority and white superiority but on "perfect social equality."[3] We argue that the Color of Mind is the rotten foundation of black-white educational achievement gaps and educational opportunity gaps in the United States. Tackling both the educational inputs (related black-white opportunity gaps) and the outputs (achievement gaps) requires overcoming this noxious racial ideology.[4] Du Bois was prescient in appreciating this.

Dignitary Injustice

Cooper and Du Bois raised concerns about inequality that pose a question about justice. Does justice demand that persons be able to relate to one another as equals in social, political, and legal terms? We think that it does, and this conception will loom large in why we believe that the origins of the black-white achievement gap matter for justice. We contend that the achievement gap between blacks and whites must be viewed historically to appreciate how past and present educational practices and unequal educational opportunities sustain unequal social relations between black and white youth. This will help us think more clearly about how to rectify this distinctive form of injustice.[5]

We do not deal with all forms of injustice in this book. Philosophical problems of distributive justice, for instance, will be mentioned only in passing.[6] Instead, we focus on links between dignity, equality, and justice. For those who, like Du Bois, emphasize the ideal of standing in equal relations, injustice is present when practices, processes, or ways of treating persons render them unable to stand in relations of equality with other persons. So, for instance, when blacks are taken to be an "inferior" race and institutions such as schools are arranged in ways that send this message, as was the case during and long before the Jim Crow era, then this group suffers an injustice that assaults their dignity or worth. Failing to recognize the equal dignity of all persons, as happens when schools prevent blacks and whites from relating as equals, constitutes a distinctive form of injustice, which we call *dignitary injustice*. So, more precisely, this book is about why the origins of the black-white achievement gap matter for understanding the operation of dignitary injustice in schools.

Our focus on dignitary as opposed to distributive justice is linked to a very influential ethical ideal. Following Cooper's and Du Bois's leads, our primary justice concern is with African Americans not being treated with respect as equal persons or, to invoke an ethical ideal associated with philosopher Immanuel Kant, with not being afforded the dignity that all persons are owed.[7] Historically marginalized African American voices, including some that we highlight in this book, appeal to the dignity of humanity to critique racial injustice in education. Cooper was one such voice;[8] there were many others. This ideal has been enshrined as a core constitutional value in countries such as South Africa, which lists human dignity as a fundamental value, along with the right to have it respected and protected. More broadly, dignity has informed thought about the foundation for a decent society.[9] And recently, it has been viewed as essential for resolving social conflict and promoting social cohesion.[10]

To be sure, the concept of dignity—its meaning, value, and implications—is also a source of philosophical controversy. Still, given the role it has played in activist voices of African Americans such as Frances Ellen Watkins Harper, who also sought to improve black education more than a century ago, we utilize this ideal to explain why the Color of Mind has been a distinctive ethical problem—an affront to black dignity—and to argue that expelling it from schools is an imperative of dignitary justice. In many instances throughout the book, we let history dictate our points of focus philosophically. Harper, Cooper, Du Bois, and other African American voices of dissent do not offer full-blown theories of dignity. Nonetheless, anticipating contemporary theorists, these figures invite us to associate dignity with equal status. Moreover, as we demonstrate, they dislodge the view that this form of moral status, which calls for a certain kind of public recognition, should be conditional upon the arbitrary factor of racial membership. They presume, and rightly so, that all people are worthy of dignity without qualification.

Thus, by their deeds and words, these voices of dissent demonstrate that blacks should be regarded with the same dignity afforded whites. Blacks and whites should be considered as equal partners in a larger society of equals.[11] These African Americans teach us that having a shared dignitary status ensures that all persons, regardless of race, can look each other in the eyes as equals.[12]

From this ethical perspective, dignitary injustice results when laws, practices, or social arrangements constitute an affront to our equal status. The moral ideal of achieving social relations based on equal dignity is, therefore, essentially the same one that prompted Du Bois to suggest that it might be more readily attainable for black children in racially segregated schools. However deficient in resources "Negro" schools may have been, and such deficits were legion, Du Bois presumed that they would not be schools of dignitary injustice. Obviously, much has changed in America since 1935, and we are no longer living with the old Jim Crow. Yet Du Bois's concern about dignitary injustice in "mixed" schools remains distressingly relevant.

The influence of the Color of Mind also raises a justice concern about whether facially discriminatory school practices can be universally justified to American citizens, especially given the nation's long-standing commitment to equality of educational opportunity. There are also the well-documented benefits of education, and the many ways that schooling increasingly influences society.[13] But addressing this justice concern is not our principal task, even if there are ways of understanding dignitary injustice that can speak to this.[14] In this work, we follow the voices of dissent in associating it with unequal status, and utilize this formulation in our ethical assessment of sorting practices within racially desegregated schools. This is clearly not the only injustice at issue in public education today, but it takes center stage in our story.

School leaders today need to know that some of what goes on behind school doors—such as tracking, discipline, and special education practices—not only creates disparities in educational achievement between black and white students but also precludes them from relating to one another as equals. And since racially segregated education is inherently unequal and unlawful, as the US Supreme Court ruled in *Brown v. Board of Education*, concrete steps are needed to tackle dignitary injustice in today's racially desegregated schools. This, as we shall argue, requires that school leaders conscientiously attend to the mutually reinforcing relationship between the Color of Mind and school practices. This book combines history and philosophy to uncover the racist origins of the black-white achievement gap to argue that this relationship is a problem of justice, and to explain what must be done to address it. We also aim to vindicate ongoing efforts by social justice school leaders to create institutions based on perfect social equality, where dignitary injustice no longer prevails within K–12 schools.

The Concept of Race

Near the close of the nineteenth century, in the year following the Supreme Court's *Plessy v. Ferguson* decision ratifying "separate but equal" as a legal doctrine, Du Bois penned his now famous essay, "The Conservation of Races."[15] He begins by explaining why the American Negro was so keenly concerned with discussions about the origins, nature, and destinies of the races of humankind. "Most discussions of race" with which the Negro is familiar, Du Bois explains, contain "certain assumptions as to his natural abilities, as to his political, intellectual and moral status," which he felt were wrong.[16]

With this deft observation, Du Bois makes the point that race is *not* simply a matter of phenotypic differences in skin color, hair texture, or certain morphological features; rather, it essentially concerns an association between such characteristics and assumptions about cognitive ability, temperament, and moral status. And in the case of American Negroes, as Du Bois describes African Americans, it was the presumption of black inferiority in then prevailing conceptions of race that connected such physical markers with derogatory views about intelligence, character, and conduct. This was part and parcel of the Color of Mind racial ideology that underwrote the Supreme Court's decision in *Plessy*. It also served more generally to rationalize basic societal institutions that rendered blacks and whites unable to stand in relations of perfect social equality.

There are different ways of trying to undo all this. Du Bois famously did so by arguing for the conservation of races. That is, he did not deny that humankind is divided into different races with different characteristics such as color, hair texture, and language, though he notes that these physical characteristics are not exclusive to a particular race. But he defines a race as "a vast family of human beings, generally of common blood and language, always of common history, traditions and impulses, who are both voluntarily and involuntarily striving together for the accomplishment of certain more or less vividly conceived ideals of life."[17] With this conception of racial groups, Du Bois sought to situate the Negro race among the great races of humankind, with its own distinctive yet ongoing contributions to human history and future development. In offering this alternative perspective, which sought to elevate and affirm the dignity of the black race, Du Bois became a powerful and influential voice of dissent.

Contemporary philosophical work on race, especially regarding the nature and meaning of the concept, has been shaped by Du Bois's reflections, although engaging such debates is beyond the scope of our project.[18] On the race question, our objectives are limited to documenting instances of the disparaging racial ideology that Du Bois called attention to, and identifying the connections between this doctrine and schooling practices, noting how Harper, Cooper, Du Bois, and other voices of dissent gave the lie to it by their deeds and words.

To be sure, not everyone agrees with Du Bois's way of conserving the race concept, particularly insofar as it flirts with the controversial idea that races form some sort of natural division of humanity. Indeed, on the basis of evidence we discuss herein, most contemporary race theorists argue that race does not have a biological foundation and represents nothing more than a social construct, albeit one with dire consequences for African Americans as a group.[19] Philosophers have been particularly keen on making this point. While some of them debate the wisdom of conserving race in an imagined "nonracist" future, there is little doubt about the importance of racial disparities in education and along other indicators of welfare today. Even if we accept the proposition that race lacks validity as a biological category, our lived experiences suggest that it still matters profoundly, not only when it comes to tracking the unequal distribution of goods, resources, and opportunities, but when it comes to the impact of systemic practices and institutions on sustaining relations between blacks and whites that preclude them from relating to one another as equals.

Much historical work has been done on the construction of race as a social category in the United States, and on conceptions of black inferiority and their relationship to other matters such as crime and punishment.[20] We build on and contribute to this body of scholarship with a focus on schooling, by attending to nineteenth-century racist ideology, its philosophical antecedents, and its relationship to the education of African Americans during and long after the demise of black chattel slavery. In his important book, *Race: The History of an Idea in the West*, Ivan Hannaford argues that the concept of race dates to fifteenth-century Europe.[21] We do not start our story about the Color of Mind there, however. We begin with the racist ideology of antebellum America, but acknowledge the importance of racial views promulgated during the Age of Enlightenment (or Age of Reason) in Europe as well as views about slavery expressed in the classical world in shaping beliefs about race and race differences in and well beyond this period.

Anyone skeptical about the concept of race, and wanting to move beyond it, may criticize research on the black-white achievement gap more generally. If race is a myth, they may ask, why bother examining a problem in terms that serve only to perpetuate race and racial differences?[22] Alternatively, others may ask, why not focus on class instead of race, and address income and wealth gaps that contribute to differences in academic achievement? The historical record is clear, however, on the role of *racial* beliefs in creating and perpetuating unequal schooling for blacks and whites. It is against this backdrop that we discuss the black-white achievement gap. For good or bad, Americans still keep track of race-based distinctions for various purposes, including documenting, measuring, and explaining differences in educational achievement. And these circumstances clearly do not warrant eschewing the discourse of race, or attending to social class instead of race in considering the achievement gap. Instead, they demand confronting it head on.

Achievement and Opportunity Gaps

Kids vary in measures of educational achievement, but white students typically have better test scores than black ones, which is one familiar measure.[23] It is tempting to infer from this test score gap that white children are brighter than black children. Then, in the ensuing debate, someone will ask whether the purported differences in intellect are innate or due to family, neighborhood, or peer influences. Another option, which we pursue, holds that the black-white achievement gap stems from past and present injustices related to the interplay between the Color of Mind and school practices. The idea of differences in intelligence, character, and conduct between blacks and whites has a long history, and acknowledging this raises a number of questions we will answer.

However, we focus exclusively on the *black-white* achievement gap in the United States, though we realize that there are other forms of stratification in educational achievement and attainment that track gender, class, ethnicity, and other demographic characteristics.[24] Theories about differences between blacks and whites in intelligence, character, and conduct historically have exceeded other varieties of bigotry, and established "race" as a critical rationale for distributing and organizing educational opportunities. Indeed, race, more than class, ethnicity, or even gender, has played a prominent role in policies regarding the distribution of educational resources in America. As we will document, both inequality of educational opportunity and unequal social relations were socially engineered and enforced with episodes of planned and spontaneous racial violence, the legal authority of state-sanctioned racial apartheid policy, and decades of local exclusion and discrimination based on color and other phenotypic characteristics.[25] History reveals that myths about black inferiority and white superiority were at the center of an educational structure that systematically and purposefully allotted inferior and unequal schooling to African Americans. Indeed, it matters immensely for our investigation that Du Bois asked whether the "Negro" needed separate schools. He did not ask whether Native Americans, Latinos, children of immigrants, poor children, or English learners needed separate schools.

Our argument would be richer and more complex if it dealt with instances of educational achievement gaps unrelated to the black-white racial binary. But the book would be much longer. Moreover, taking up test score and other achievement gaps between Latinos and whites, English learners and native speakers, social class and gender differences would also obscure a critical point that we want to stress, and for which we provide ample philosophical and historical evidence. It is that race in the United States historically became associated with certain undesirable qualities of mind, character, and conduct first and foremost with regard to people of African descent who have certain phenotypic characteristics. And, as our argument shows, this racial ideology had consequential implications for education well before the antebellum era that have persisted into the present. Thus, in lieu of offering a comprehensive treatment of nonracial achievement gaps, we identify scholarship in our notes that addresses achievement gaps between other demographic groups. Our hope is that future historical treatments of these other gaps might benefit from our more narrowly focused study of the historical origins of the black-white achievement gap.

A further way to complicate our story would be to attend to differences in education, schooling, and disparate educational achievement *within* the black community. On this score, some observers note differences between native-born black Americans and recent black immigrants from the Caribbean, Latin America, Africa, and other places. Although it is certainly important to register the complexity and diversity of the black experience in the United States both historically and in the present moment, we will forego adding this additional layer of complexity to our analysis. For one, black immigrant groups constitute less than 9 percent of the black population today, and were an even smaller portion during the periods of history we consider. They were less than 4 percent in 1980.[26] So, as a distinct group, black immigrants hardly have affected the interplay between racial ideology and schooling practices that constrained educational opportunity and perpetuated the dignitary injustice that we explore. Second, because this group is relatively small and understudied, there is limited evidence about their distinctive educational experiences and outcomes. And lastly, the evidence that we do have suggests that black immigrant children do not on average experience higher levels of prosperity and status than their African American cohorts. In the words of a recent study, "Black immigrants are unlikely to have cultural attributes that give them a robust socioeconomic advantage in improving their children's welfare."[27] In short, children from these families fall prey to the Color of Mind in many of the same respects as their native-born counterparts.

Throughout this book, we will use "black-white achievement gap" and "racial achievement gap" interchangeably. But our nomenclature is certainly not meant to deny the existence or importance of nonracial achievement gaps. Nor do we suggest that everything there is to say about race is simply a matter of black and white.

What History and Philosophy Reveal about the Racial Achievement Gap

Economists and sociologists, who usually dominate discussion of the racial achievement gap, tell us that it is a persistent, quantifiable disparity in academic performance as measured by test scores, grade-point averages, promotion and graduation rates, and other such factors between certain groups of students. Social scientists use sophisticated statistical tools and varied data sources to document, explain, and propose interventions to close achievement gaps.

For instance, economist Roland Fryer has tested the hypothesis that black kids do worse than whites in schools because of pressure from peers who tease and reject them for "acting white." Known for innovative research on the black-white achievement gap, Fryer proposed cash and similar incentives to help them resist these "anti-achievement" influences. The hope, which was not fully supported by his findings, was that paying cash for grades would raise black student achievement and close the gap.[28] Many other strategies, some of which we discuss later, have been proposed, including "school choice" and the development of charter schools, along with greater school "accountability" and the use of standardized assessments.

Quantitative and qualitative social scientists have much to teach us about the racial achievement gap, but some aspects of the problem, rooted in history and philosophy, go beyond their expertise. When nineteenth-century Americans thought about "achievement gaps," many would have taken skull sizes to be relevant data points. Additionally, many thought anatomical and skin color variations were linked to behavioral dispositions as well. Our thinking about achievement gaps, and how to measure them, has certainly evolved since then. Today, achievement gap discourse is associated with scores on standardized tests along with other indicators of academic ability and performance, such as grades. Instead of measuring skull sizes, modern Americans look to social and economic status, opportunity gaps, and related factors to explain variation in academic achievement. However, as our story reveals, despite African American progress from enduring slavery to seeing an African American family in the White House, the conclusions we draw today about differences in intelligence, character, and conduct between blacks and whites often resemble those of the past.

In recent decades, Americans have kept track of various achievement gaps: between boys and girls; kids with wealthy families and those in poverty; disabled students and their nondisabled peers; and students who are English language learners and those who are native speakers, among others. However, the gap between black and white students has arguably received the most sustained attention from researchers and the public at large.[29] This is not surprising, given America's history of black chattel slavery, when it was often illegal to teach blacks to read. There also is the more recent history of state-mandated racial school segregation, when blacks attended inferior schools and were commonly educated for servitude. Under these utterly unequal circumstances, when blacks clearly did not have comparable opportunities for education, there could hardly be similar outcomes between them and whites on tests of academic achievement. Opportunity gaps produce achievement gaps. And it would be unreasonable to expect such inequalities in either opportunities or achievement to disappear overnight, or even soon after Jim Crow schooling was outlawed nationally in 1954.

Looking back at this appalling history from today's perspective, it may seem senseless to conclude that blacks performed worse on reading and math tests because of an innately inferior intelligence to that of whites, given inequalities in educational opportunity between them. Nevertheless, this is precisely what many Americans believed, and not just slaveholding Southerners. Indeed, at the time it was widely thought that humans could be divided into distinct races with dissimilar abilities and behavioral propensities, arranged in a natural order that had whites as the most advanced and blacks the least. Intelligence was deemed an important measure of distinction, but so were moral character and behavior, as Du Bois astutely noted in 1897.

We realize that contemporary policy reform in the United States has placed inordinate emphasis on standardized assessment, and acknowledge the need to also focus attention on inequality in educational resources and opportunities. A number of scholars have pointed out that while achievement gaps are most certainly linked historically to opportunity gaps, closing opportunity gaps should be our main focus.[30] They propose that focus should be shifted from the symptoms of unequal education, namely achievement gaps, to its causes—opportunity gaps. But we have several concerns about this suggestion.

It could be highly problematic to concede the language of achievement as a critical dimension of educational improvement. As some champions of the opportunity gap proposal such as Kevin Welner and Prudence Carter have suggested, systematic measurement of outcomes is "a key component in an evaluative feedback loop," which enables educators and policymakers to improve the educational experiences of marginalized students.[31] Beyond that, eschewing the concept of achievement, or other methodical assessments of academic outcomes, runs the serious risk of affirming the Color of Mind in popular perceptions, permitting deep-seated assumptions about racial differences in ability to persist or even grow. Similar efforts in the past to shift discourse away from IQ did not succeed in overcoming racist arguments regarding intelligence, which continue to surface, or foreclose parallel debates about academic achievement.[32] Such questions lie at the very center of racial ideology and cannot be sidestepped. Ultimately, to argue that contemporary achievement gaps reveal a dignitary injustice rooted in opportunity gaps of the present and the past, we must continue to consider educational outcomes as carefully and thoughtfully as possible.

Finally, as we noted earlier, addressing achievement as well as opportunity gaps requires addressing the Color of Mind, which is the flawed foundation of both racially unequal achievement outcomes and racially unequal opportunities. Turning our attention to opportunity gaps does indeed have the advantage of placing the spotlight on out-of-school factors such as poverty, housing, health, and safety, where we encounter gross racial disparities in opportunities to enjoy certain benefits and avoid certain burdens. But the story we tell here about the relationship between the Color of Mind and education clearly has applications to these factors. Racial ideology, we presume, is also the corroded foundation underlying racial disadvantage and racial inequality more generally. However, as we will argue later, school leaders cannot fix these out-of-school factors, though they can certainly do things to mitigate or enhance their effects. An important virtue, then, of focusing as we do on the racial achievement gap, which is also rooted in the Color of Mind, is that the dignitary injustice associated with this is something within their power and authority to address behind school doors. And given the evidence that most of the racial achievement occurs within, not between schools, taking action here can have a considerable impact on achievement outcomes, which are so consequential to the future life prospects of students.[33]

A Legacy of White Supremacy in Education

The Color of Mind is a caustic ideology that has buttressed white supremacy, understood both as a *descriptive* thesis indicating that whites are superior to blacks, and as a *prescriptive* thesis signaling that whites should dominate blacks or enjoy a more favorable allotment of societal benefits and burdens. Our historical analysis, focusing exclusively on education, shows that the Color of Mind and education have been connected and mutually supporting in ways that continue to sustain white supremacy in today's schools. So the present resembles the past, with the difference being that white supremacy is often sustained in contemporary institutional structures and practices despite less evidence of intentional discrimination, and where more educators operate with good intentions.

For much of American history, blacks were believed to be inferior to whites in cognitive ability, character, and conduct, though there was disagreement over whether nature or their unfortunate circumstances and culture were responsible. Today, kids in K–12 schools judged to have such deficiencies are sorted into lower-track classes, receive more punitive disciplinary measures, and are assigned to special education for the emotionally disturbed or learning disabled. As a consequence, many are marginalized and stigmatized, which has a profound impact on their academic achievement.

The Color of Mind and its relationship to the unequal education of African Americans shape our story about the origins of differences in achievement between blacks and whites and their pertinence for the present. They also shape our argument about why all this matters for tackling dignitary injustice within schools today, where everyday practices denigrate black intelligence, character, and conduct. This ideological perspective, found in the writings of Thomas Jefferson as well as later pro-slavery writings, served to rationalize separate and unequal education for blacks both during and long after slavery's demise. It was featured in nineteenth-century Southern schoolbooks, and even appeared in anti-slavery strongholds such as Boston, where school leaders asserted the Color of Mind to maintain school segregation over the objections of African American parents and their white allies.

Americans did not invent the Color of Mind. Many Europeans, including eighteenth-century philosophers David Hume and Immanuel Kant, articulated similar ideas, as we shall see. Far from being a relic of the distant past, however, the notion that blacks are inferior to whites in terms of intellect, character, and conduct continues to permeate American educational institutions and to inform public consciousness. As Lisa Delpit deftly observes, many people—including some African Americans—believe that "multiplication is for white people," that blacks embrace an "anti-achievement ethic," and that large numbers of black youth are suspended or expelled from schools for having "behavior" or "character" problems.[34]

Today's public discussion of the black-white achievement gap, which has been largely focused on social scientific research, has been inattentive to its historical origins, which reveal an enduring and evolving relationship between the Color of Mind and racially unequal schooling. To address this, it is necessary to consider how the idea of differences in academic achievement between blacks and whites was constructed, what purposes it served, and how it evolved. It means examining how the Color of Mind and its construction of the black-white achievement gap were contested, as well as how its supporters fought to sustain them. Perhaps of greatest significance for contemporary school leaders, it requires knowing how the Color of Mind persists in today's schools, and why doing something about it is an imperative of dignitary justice.

Our argument has several implications: (1) racial desegregation of schools falls short of what dignitary justice requires; (2) fixing the problems outside school such as poverty, crime, inequality, single-parent households, teen pregnancy, and the ghetto, though immensely important, is in itself insufficient to address the systemic structures within schools that also affect the black-white achievement gap; and (3) meaningful measures to close the black-white achievement gap do not require a massive windfall of resources.

Plan of the Book

The story we tell about the origins of the racial achievement gap and why they matter for dignitary justice will appeal to educators who make social justice a priority.[35] This is particularly true of committed, compassionate, and visionary school leaders, who are able to challenge unequal social relations in the classroom. They can make schools more equitable and equal by dismantling the systemic structures that sort, segregate, and stigmatize students. Their work with teachers and staff on curriculum and pedagogical practices can help foster a school climate of belonging that respects the dignity of all students and enables them to relate to one another as equals. And with these efforts, social justice leaders can contribute to improved student achievement, especially for historically marginalized black students, which can help mitigate the black-white achievement gap.

These school leaders will face many challenges, including working with other educators, teachers, parents, and school board members who disagree about root causes of the black-white achievement gap and why kids get sorted in schools, and are also uninformed about the enduring historical relationship between schooling and the messages this conveys about children's intellect, character, and conduct. To get them on board, school leaders need a historically informed justice-based argument for targeting sorting practices *within* schools that denigrate the dignity of black students and perpetuate the black-white achievement gap. The argument we offer in the chapters that follow demonstrates that these two problems—racial sorting within schools *and* messages of black inferiority and white superiority—must be tackled together, since they are mutually reinforcing.

Our argument summons America's racially unequal history of education and establishes its relationship to the Color of Mind, the black-white achievement gap, and contemporary school sorting practices to illuminate why they are unjust, who bears responsibility for addressing them, and what can be done to tackle these urgent problems. To present and develop this argument, we must answer a number of important questions: How was the Color of Mind constructed? How was it institutionalized in schooling? How did it contribute to black-white gaps in educational attainment in postbellum America? We address these questions in chapters 2 and 3, respectively.

Chapter 4 tells the story of how the Color of Mind was contested by voices of dissent. James McCune Smith, Frederick Douglass, Booker T. Washington, Frances Ellen Watkins Harper, Anna Julia Cooper, Mary Church Terrell, W. E. B. Du Bois, Mary McLeod Bethune, and Nannie Helen Burroughs were among the pioneering African Americans who brought dignity to black education in deed and word under dire conditions of dignitary injustice. It also charts the course of black-white achievement gap trends beginning in the early decades of the twentieth century, which was responsive to these efforts to support black education as well as others' efforts to stifle it.

In 1954, the US Supreme Court decision in *Brown v. Board of Education* declared racial segregation in schools unconstitutional. In chapter 5, we discuss the black-white achievement gap—how it widened and narrowed—leading up to and following this landmark ruling. We also describe how segregationist critics reasserted the Color of Mind to resist *Brown*, eventually agreeing with certain liberals that racial differences in intellect were cultural rather than innate. This "cultural turn" continues to shape how many Americans understand and explain the black-white achievement gap today.

There are conditions such as poverty, inequality, and residential segregation and other structural matters that educators do not have the capacity or authority to resolve, even though these problems surely do impact the black-white achievement gap. In chapter 6, we suggest that school leaders not be held accountable for these conditions, although they can certainly assist children who live with them. There we also raise concerns about the notion that doubling down on racial integration of schools is a sufficient response to dignitary injustice in education.

In our allegedly post-racial era, it is tempting to think that we have turned the corner on our nation's dark past and left the Color of Mind and its link to schooling behind. Sadly, this is not the case. Chapter 7 attends to how the Color of Mind thrives in schools today—and not merely in the hearts and minds of educators and students who may harbor implicit if not intentional racial bias, but also in systemic sorting practices behind school doors that sustain it. Here we supply a brief historical overview of tracking, school discipline, and special education practices along with a description of their ripple effects for students, schools, and society. In chapter 8, we consider competing philosophical and causal explanations for why we sort kids in schools, with a view toward arguing that agreement about such explanations is not necessary to demonstrate the dignitary injustice inherent in these sorting practices.

The final chapter addresses the ethical and practical implications of our historical evidence for understanding how contemporary school practices sustain the Color of Mind, and ultimately the black-white achievement gap. We argue that these problems are a dignitary injustice that twenty-first-century school leaders have a duty to address. We then offer some general prescriptions for how to best address the pernicious relationship between the Color of Mind and school sorting practices, foremost of which is adopting a Color of Mind Index to measure and assess school climate, and to hold schools and school leaders accountable for getting good results. Along with our prescriptions, we list some of the specific actions others have claimed are vital for achieving these results. Here our goal is not to endorse or even advocate for adopting these specific actions as a matter of educational policy and practice, but merely to provide concrete suggestions regarding steps that school leaders might take toward expelling the Color of Mind from their schools and combating dignitary injustice. Chapter 1, to which we now turn, reviews the important yet limited contributions that social scientists have made to our understanding of the racial achievement gap.

ONE

The Racial Achievement Gap

The nation's school report card, issued by the National Assessment of Educational Progress (NAEP), documents trends in student achievement. It offers a snapshot of how different age cohorts perform on standardized reading and mathematics tests. Over time, NAEP indicates whether the racial achievement gap between black students and their white classmates is narrowing and, consequently, whether we are making good on the promise of equal educational opportunity. It also helps us to assess whether major education reforms, such as No Child Left Behind, have achieved their objectives. However, although NAEP and other quantitative reports are useful resources for marking progress on standardized tests, they delineate the achievement gap in largely statistical terms.

Framing the Achievement Gap

Social scientists define achievement gaps as stable and statistically significant differences in the average performance of students at the same grade level but from distinct demographic or economic groups on standardized tests. Such gaps, typically presented in figures like the ones below, are calculated with national, statewide, and local datasets, and extend over varying intervals of time. The figures below show black-white differences in NAEP for reading and mathematics between 1973 and 2004, for seventeen-year-olds across the country. Basically, they indicate that the racial achievement gap—the difference between black and white scores—shrank by about 40 percent in less than two decades and then stabilized. Today, the gap remains about what it was thirty-five years ago. Data regarding the racial achievement gap can be parsed by gender and socioeconomic status, but gaps between black and white students, while reduced, continue to be evident when gender and

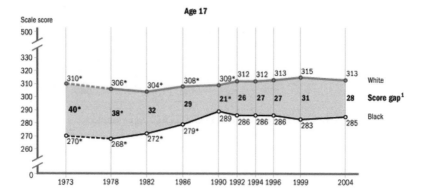

Figure 1. NAEP Scores in Mathematics for Black and White Students, 1973–2004
[1] Calculated as white average scale score minus black average scale score.
* Annual average scale score or gap significantly different from 2004.
Source: National Center for Educational Statistics, *NAEP 2004: Trends in Academic Progress;*
Three Decades of Student Performance in Reading and Mathematics (Washington, DC: Institute of
Education Sciences, US Department of Education, 2005), p. 33.

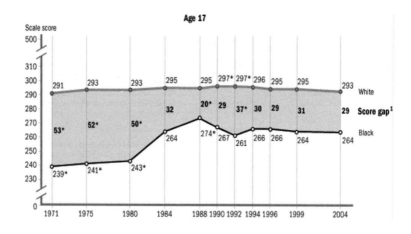

Figure 2. NAEP Scores in Reading for Black and White Students, 1973–2004
[1] Calculated as white average scale score minus black average scale score.
* Annual average scale score or gap significantly different from 2004.
Source: National Center for Educational Statistics, *NAEP 2004: Trends in Academic Progress;*
Three Decades of Student Performance in Reading and Mathematics (Washington, DC: Institute of
Education Sciences, US Department of Education, 2005), p. 42.

socioeconomic status are statistically controlled. Relatively affluent black males generally perform worse on standardized tests in math and reading than their white counterparts. In other words, contrary to the suggestion that social class or gender may matter more than race in terms of achievement differences, evidence of the black-white gap exists even when considering blacks and whites of comparable economic status, or males and females.[1]

These and similar data inform reports about where the nation stands on the achievement gap.[2] Although this gap is certainly not confined to major urban areas, it is particularly acute in places having large numbers of poor black and other minority students.[3] And despite considerable convergence in the racial achievement gap during the 1970s and 1980s, progress has stalled in the interim.[4] Moreover, disparities persist in school factors other than grades and test performance that affect academic achievement. A report released by the UCLA Civil Rights Project found that in 2012, black secondary students were more than three times more likely than whites to be suspended from school (23 percent of blacks and 7 percent of whites).[5] Other studies have found that the dropout rate for black high school students has been nearly double that for whites.[6] Such factors pose serious challenges to promoting black student achievement.[7] More than sixty years after the historic *Brown v. Board of Education* decision, substantial racial differences in educational accomplishment remain pervasive.

Explaining the Gap

In 1966, Congress authorized a study to assess equality of opportunity in schools. Led by sociologist James Coleman, it marked the beginning of systematic research on educational achievement by social scientists. Coleman investigated the effect of school resources on educational outcomes and determined that it was relatively modest. He found that family background was a stronger predictor of variation in student achievement (test scores) than levels of school funding, teacher characteristics, or other facets of institutions. Subsequent research corroborated these findings. Although more recent studies have found that Coleman underestimated the contributions of schooling to achievement differences, his report still gives credence to arguments against additional resources for institutions serving poor and minority students.[8] On the other hand, Coleman did help to focus new attention on families, and by extension the alleged "failures" and "deficiencies" of black kids, their parents, and their communities. The extensive tradition of social-scientific research flowing from this perspective has profoundly influenced studies of the racial achievement gap.[9] Researchers utilize a wide variety of data sources, yet the range of explanations for variation in achievement remains narrow.[10] And in the public mind, traditionally racist perspectives persist. In what follows, we sort prevailing explanations of the achievement gap into three broad categories, representing factors said to influence racial differences in academic performance. We also associate them with contemporary political viewpoints.

1. Is It Innate?

A requisite starting point is an explanation dating at least to the eighteenth century. Are black students coming up short in school when measured against white children because they are *innately* less intelligent? This is a controversial question today, but it has not always been so. Indeed, the view that black people are innately less intelligent than white people, and generally inferior to them, was once a widely shared belief.

Southern writers defended slavery by arguing that Africans were inherently unequal, or, as one put it, "an inferior species, or at least variety of human race." Even in the North, prominent anti-slavery minister William Ellery Channing could describe blacks in 1835 as naturally "affectionate, imitative and docile," a more affirmative yet still demeaning portrayal.[11] Such ideas were very slow to change. Nearly seven decades later, philanthropist Robert C. Ogden complained about the "childish characteristics" of African Americans, and declared that "a school of domestic training" was appropriate for their education in New York.[12]

Regardless of their views about involuntary servitude, most whites nonetheless believed that blacks were naturally mentally inferior to whites, and many thought the point beyond dispute. Indeed, near the end of the century in 1890, just six years before the US Supreme Court would uphold racial segregation as a principle of law in *Plessy v. Ferguson*, former Confederate soldier and US senator from Alabama John T. Morgan made the point this way: "The inferiority of the negro [*sic*] race, as compared with the white race, is so essentially true, and so obvious, that to assume it in argument, cannot be justly attributed to prejudice."[13] Such beliefs survived well into the twentieth century, and historically were associated with conservatives, or the Right.

It is tempting to think that such beliefs about black intellectual capacity are no longer influential. Yet occasionally, they still surface in public discourse. Moreover, research continues to uncover evidence of their persistence. According to survey data, from 1977 to 1996 the percentage of whites believing blacks to be innately less intelligent and capable of learning than whites dropped from 27 to 10. Interestingly, when the same survey did not attribute learning differences to genetic factors, the percentage doubting black intelligence increased dramatically to 53. Clearly, many whites still harbor doubts about black intellectual ability, even though far fewer accept genetic explanations for it. Thus, it is reasonable to agree with the study's conclusion: "There is little prospect that 'rumors of inferiority' will cease or that racial differences in estimates of students' potential will disappear."[14]

A variation of the inferiority argument has been to attribute black under-achievement not to innate racial differences in intelligence but to laziness or "shiftlessness," a lack of effort, motivation, or focus. The claim is that black kids generally don't do as well as whites on measures of academic achieve-ment because they fail to work as hard. Researchers who study racial ste-reotypes have observed correlations in public attitudes about race between traits such as "hardworking" or "lazy" and "intelligent" and "unintelligent." And they find that whites are more likely to view blacks as less intelligent or indolent. When assessed in 1990, nearly 65 percent of whites viewed blacks as less hardworking, while a little below 60 percent deemed them less intelligent.[15] In one sense, the appeal to laziness in explaining black under-achievement may seem to be an advance over genetic explanations; it ap-pears to be a less pessimistic racial stereotype, portraying underachievement as something that can be remedied. But appearances often are deceiving.

The shift from innate stupidity to laziness in explaining black under-achievement is hardly an advance. Both views perpetuate the presumption of black inferiority, no matter the ultimate explanation, and both are gener-ally associated with social conservatives politically. Indeed, the observed correlations between these traits in historically recent studies of racial atti-tudes suggest that they represent the same pernicious construct. Whether it is genes or lack of character, both explanations of black-white achievement differences imply that it is something endogenous to black kids that best explains why they do not perform better on tests.

2. Is It Due to Family Background?

As noted above, an important legacy of the Coleman Report has been a focus on family background as an explanation of the black-white achieve-ment gap. This is a common factor cited in social scientific discussions of the gap, focusing on a child's home life and key family characteristics such as the number of parents, along with their income, wealth, and education. It also includes parental behavior, such as how much they read to their kids and how discipline is handled at home, with some researchers noting racial differences in such activities.[16] Political scientist Robert Putnam offers telling accounts about how family background, especially parental socioeconomic status, remains a strong correlate of success in school and social mobility.

And although gender and race continue to pose special challenges, the interplay of financial resources, family structure, and parenting loom large in determining life prospects in this account. It is a valuable insight, but it is almost certainly not the whole story.

Putnam highlights kids from families of modest means, from single-parent households, or from broken homes in working-class and even ghetto neighborhoods. He argues that during the 1950s, poor white and black kids had much better prospects of achieving success than their counterparts today. But race was definitely a major factor. As one African American respondent, Jesse of Port Clinton, Ohio, recalled, "The hardest part [of growing up] was not being accepted as a human being."[17] Despite this, Putnam suggests that black children's "humble class origins did not prevent them from using their talents and work ethic to achieve great upward mobility, any more than comparably modest family backgrounds prevented [white children] from gaining success in life."[18] This speaks against the stereotype of indolent blacks, but success was not always due to talent and diligence. For kids rising up from humble beginnings, it was also about being rooted in circumstances that did not pose nearly insurmountable obstacles. Even if Jesse was fortunate in this regard, many other blacks certainly were not.

Putnam also describes the more recent case of a black youth who lived, off and on, with his mother in Atlanta and a grandfather in New Orleans. Verbal and physical abuse, alcoholism, and general neglect were norms in these households. Peers proved to be negative influences, and his neighborhoods were sites of everyday mayhem, factors that can raise stress levels and inhibit learning.[19] Even though he struggled in school, receiving bad grades and an expulsion for skipping class, he managed to graduate. His story shows how neighborhood poverty and vice can pose major obstacles to achievement. Success in this case was also far from simply being about inherent talent, work ethic, or willpower. Kids similarly endowed in these respects today, but placed in dramatically different neighborhood environments, are bound to have quite dissimilar routes to achievement.

While these insights highlight the significance of the family as a social institution, they also point to its limitations as an arbiter of success. Furthermore, this explanation of the achievement gap speaks to both conservative and liberal political viewpoints, with one emphasizing the importance of family responsibility, the other the power of the family's immediate social context. Many black communities have been ravaged by segregation, unemployment, mass incarceration, extreme poverty, and political neglect, although, as we argue in chapter 6, these are structural problems school leaders cannot fix. As sociologist William Julius Wilson and other scholars have demonstrated, countless families crumbled in the face of these developments, and their children suffered the consequences.[20] Whether this was due to irresponsibility, changing social and economic conditions, or the war on drugs, it has nonetheless contributed to the racial achievement gap.

3. Is It the Legacy of Discrimination?

Many people are skeptical about explanations of the achievement gap that focus on either black kids or their families. They suggest, rather, that the problem is the vast overrepresentation of black children among the most disadvantaged Americans. Liberals tend to hold this view. One cannot consider the achievement gap, they argue, without reflecting on the country's long legacy of racial discrimination.[21] And this requires attention to broader issues such as segregation, societal prejudice, and political contributions to racial differences in educational achievement and attainment. These are particularly daunting issues that direct attention far beyond the schoolyard. Moreover, their resolution will undoubtedly entail a radical redistribution of resources, which will require sweeping political change not likely to occur in the immediate future.[22] While social justice school leaders will also complain about these things, some will also rightly point out that these problems are beyond their power and authority. School leaders are responsible for what goes on inside the building, not outside it. Of course, they hope that a positive school experience which encourages achievement in a supportive climate will ameliorate the impact of adverse experiences students encounter at home, in their neighborhoods, and elsewhere outside school.

Educational researcher Gloria Ladson-Billings has called for a shift from discussing the racial achievement gap to considering an "educational debt" that stems from a long intervening national history of inferior schooling for African Americans.[23] Since parental education is such a critical factor in the achievement of successive generations of children, the unequal provision of schooling in the past still affects the success of black students today. Linda Darling-Hammond elaborates on this idea by calling for more attention to the "opportunity gap," or contemporary inequalities in access to educational resources. The endemic poverty of many predominantly African American communities, linked to a lack of jobs and residential segregation, often means that local schools are inadequately funded. Darling-Hammond points out that fiscal resources, good leadership, and thoughtful, committed teachers can have a significant impact on the lives of young people in such circumstances. Along with Ladson-Billings, she takes issue with the basic argument of the Coleman Report, which directed attention away from schools as educative agencies and money as an indispensable resource.[24]

These scholars certainly recognize the importance of family and community factors in achievement, but place structural and institutional factors in the spotlight.

The educational debt and the opportunity gap are products of history.[25] Shortchanging the educational experiences of one generation affects those that follow. Parental attainment is widely seen as the single most important determinant of kids' school success by social scientists.[26] Denying education over successive generations prevented the development of this vital resource in black communities. This is yet another dimension of Ladson-Billings's point about historically rooted disadvantage. We offer a more detailed account of the relevant history in subsequent chapters. This matters today for understanding racial differences in academic achievement, and for explaining how existing school practices that sustain the Color of Mind are profoundly unjust.

According to the US Supreme Court, actions or policies with seemingly unintentional racially disparate impact are not unconstitutional. For many observers, however, little argument is needed to link today's glaring racial disparities to past racial discrimination. For example, sometimes gross disparities in school funding exist between certain predominantly white and predominantly black school districts.[27] Even if such differences, on average, are much less dramatic than in the past, their continued presence suggests a pattern of discrimination. More telling is the long history of systematic exclusion of African Americans from predominantly white suburban school districts. Even if we accept the Coleman premise that funding levels have little bearing on achievement, it is clear that long-standing segregation and concentrated poverty certainly do. Such patterns are impossible to explain without taking account of the extensive marginalization experienced by black students in the United States.[28] This is a familiar refrain among liberals, or the Left.

Philosophically, it is not necessary to argue that today's racial disparities in education were intended to have certain discriminatory or injurious effects, only that they do have such an impact. This suffices to make them objectionable, and raises the question of potential remedies. It is impossible, of course, to go back in time and reverse the educational debt imposed by discriminatory policies in the past. But it is certainly possible to address unjust school practices contributing to the achievement gap today and promising to do so in the future if not addressed. This is why school leaders must take on the systemic practices pertaining to tracking, discipline, and special education that sustain the Color of Mind in their schools.

Closing the Gap

While the principal explanations of the gap—it's the black kids, it's their environment, or it's societal discrimination against them—have long been debated, it is possible to appeal to more than one. Indeed, it is likely that the complexity of the problem will demand such a multifaceted account. However, perhaps because public policies are shaped by political debates that often seek simplistic solutions to complex problems, remedies like cash for grades that focus on specific factors such as peer effects have proliferated. And explanations of the racial achievement gap that point the finger at blacks and their immediate environment persist despite contrary evidence.[29]

Proposals for closing the achievement gap are generally aligned with explanations for it. For example, where poor school-related choices—reflecting lack of motivation or peer influence—are taken to explain black underachievement, as Fryer speculated, interventions such as the controversial policy of paying students cash for better grades have been proposed. Those who place more emphasis on environmental differences have called for moving families out of the ghetto or for giving them "school choice" options to choose better schools. By the same token, those who focus attention on white opportunity hoarding, and take segregation to be a linchpin of unjust inequality, often advocate a robust form of school integration as a route to closing the achievement gap.[30]

A common feature of these solutions is the need for more monetary resources in addition to political will, both of which are in short supply these days. We believe there is a need for additional resources in schools serving high-poverty constituents, and the latter two options—choice and integration—are concerned with evading or overcoming obstacles in the larger social context of schools. But there is also a case to be made for putting the focus back on developments that occur behind school doors. This allows school leaders to address issues more or less subject to their control, which do not necessarily require a bounty of new monetary resources. Focusing on remedies for systemic school practices that sustain the Color of Mind fits the bill in this regard. And, as the case studies to be discussed later reveal, these practices can be addressed with committed and creative school leadership.

Education and Achievement with Dignity

Racial disparities in student achievement do not necessarily raise problems of justice. No reasonable theory of justice requires that educational outcomes be equal—after all, students do indeed differ in performance due to ability and effort. However, when there are systematic differences in educational outcomes such as test scores or grades patterned along racial lines, there is reason to fear that something is amiss.[31]

Unless we implausibly assume that a particular racial group just cannot make the grade due to innate deficiencies, racial patterns are presumptive evidence that environmental factors or systemic barriers inhibit more varied outcomes. Our argument that school practices sustaining the Color of Mind are unjust will draw primarily on normative considerations pertaining to dignity, or respect for persons as equals—though concerns about fairness, legitimacy, and the difference that formal education makes in access to competitive opportunities, social status, and social mobility are also grounds for taking issue with them.

As Robert Putnam discovered in his interview with Jesse, the African American who grew up in Port Clinton, Ohio, often the hardest part about growing up black and going to school is not being accepted as a human being or, to put it another way, as a person with equal dignity. Jesse's concern, which pinpoints the idea on which our social justice argument will rest, is associated with a moral imperative of Immanuel Kant's ethics—the imperative to respect the humanity of persons as ends-in-themselves, also known as *the formula of humanity*. This categorical moral imperative holds that human beings, regarded as persons, are "exalted above any price" and are "not to be valued merely as a means to the ends of others . . . but as an end in itself."[32] Human beings, so regarded, possess dignity (an absolute inner worth), which commands respect from others, and allows us to value ourselves as equals to all other persons in this regard.

Kant's being a champion of human dignity is, at first blush, somewhat paradoxical. Although he urges us to treat human beings as something with dignity and without a price, Kant is also widely regarded as one of the inventors of modern racism. His contribution to constructing the Color of Mind, which we consider in the next chapter, is hardly something we would expect from such an enlightened moral thinker.[33] Of course, the same can be said about Thomas Jefferson, the great American statesman, who espoused the ideal that "all men are created equal" while denying that blacks are indeed persons with equal dignity. He believed this not just of enslaved blacks but free ones such as mathematician Benjamin Banneker and poet Phillis Wheatley, whose compositions Jefferson judged "below the dignity of criticism."[34]

Dignity is an egalitarian notion, and so, in principle, applies to all human beings taken to have an absolute inner worth. However, when we attend to their thoughts about race and worth, Kant, Jefferson, and many others seemingly had a more qualified egalitarian sensibility, which dispels the irony of their beliefs about black people. For these thinkers, being human was no guarantee of possessing dignity; and for black Africans and their descendants, judged to be without inner worth, there was no paradox in using them as a mere means to serve the ends of others. Philosophers have long debated the measure of worth, and for some it has been a matter of intelligence. But purported differences in intelligence, as we will document, have long been associated with race.

For instance, early nineteenth-century poet, essayist, and philosopher Ralph Waldo Emerson, who was rather explicit about his qualified egalitarianism, held that innate differences in intellect made the crucial difference between who should lead and who should serve; and blacks, according to Emerson, were ordained by Providence to serve whites, given their allegedly diminished powers of mind. In his view, white supremacy was endorsed descriptively and prescriptively, such that presumed racial differences in intellect warranted differential racial treatment. His words express this clearly:

> I believe that nobody now regards the maxim "that all men are born equal," as anything more than a convenient hypothesis or an extravagant declamation. For the reverse is true—that all men are born unequal in personal powers and in those essential circumstances, of time, parentage, country, fortune. The least knowledge of the natural history of man adds another important particular to these; namely, what class of men he belongs to—European, Moor, Tartar, African? Because Nature has plainly assigned different degrees of intellect to these different races, and the barriers between are insurmountable.[35]

Obviously, school leaders cannot change societal racist beliefs, or even the beliefs of everyone within their buildings. Nor can they rewrite the history books, expunging the legacies of Kant, Jefferson, Emerson, and all who subscribed to the Color of Mind. Nor can they control how black lives are dealt with in police encounters, which make many people think that black lives do not matter, or certainly do not matter as much as white lives do. Clearly, there are many things beyond the authority and control of school leaders, and it is unreasonable to hold them accountable here. However, systemic everyday school practices can either aggravate or ameliorate the sense of dehumanization or affront to equal dignity that black children may experience behind school doors, and this, in turn, can impact their academic achievement.

Whatever the reasons for in-school sorting practices, and there may even be good ones, they nonetheless send a powerful and pernicious message: *when blacks are underrepresented in high-status classes, overrepresented in the group receiving punitive school discipline, or assigned to special education for "mild retardation" or lack of self-control, the message is that these kids are not persons with equal dignity.* Rather, they are problems to be separated, sternly managed, and prevented from interfering with the "real" mission of educating the other kids—the smart ones, the ones who want to learn, the well-behaved ones, and the ones with disabilities that do not prevent them from learning. In short, such school practices sustain the Color of Mind.

Researchers today argue that most of the racial achievement gap exists within schools, not between them, even if socioeconomic factors remain important.[36] The educators that our kids deserve should be held responsible for fixing this within-school problem. And this, as we will argue, is not only a matter of what dignitary justice requires—it is a vital part of what it will take to mitigate the black-white achievement gap, as each of these sorting practices bears on why some black students are academically less successful. In chapter 4, after showing how voices of dissent including most notably Frances Ellen Watkins Harper historically linked the struggle for black education with human dignity, and took this to be imperative of dignitary justice, we put dignity back to work in chapter 9 to assess the injustice of systemic sorting practices taking place within our schools today, and to call for their undoing insofar as they sustain the Color of Mind.

For kids in our K–12 schools who hope that education is a genuine pathway to success and opportunity in America, and who desire to be treated as human beings with equal dignity, continued racial progress is needed. This will require taking on schools' systemic sorting practices conveying the message that blacks aren't intelligent, are poorly behaved, and can't concentrate long enough to learn. The stakes of repudiating this message in K–12 schools are considerable, given the economic and social benefits associated with education in our schooled society. The next chapter examines how the Color of Mind was constructed.

TWO

The Color of Mind: Constructing Racial Differences in Intellect, Character, and Conduct

It was once commonplace to claim that blacks are inferior to whites in intelligence and in other ways. This was often stated more grotesquely than former Harvard president Lawrence Summers's speculation that gender differences in aptitude, particularly in math and science, explain why women are underrepresented in science, technology, engineering, and mathematics (STEM) fields.[1] For example, Harvard alumnus Ralph Waldo Emerson, for whom the university's philosophy building is named, professed the intellectual inferiority of blacks. Influenced by then prevailing theories of race, Emerson, writing in his journal in 1822, remarked, "The Monkey resembles Man, and the African degenerates to a likeness of the beast. And here likewise I apprehend we shall find as much difference between the head of Plato & the head of the lowest African, as between this last and the highest species of Ape."[2]

Although it is tempting to think that assertions of black inferiority are antediluvian history, we still find them today, even among highly educated persons. For example, Dr. James Watson, a Nobel Prize–winning geneticist, made news in 2007 when he claimed that "black people are less intelligent than white people," and that "our wanting to reserve equal powers of reason as some universal heritage of humanity will not be enough to make it so," although he later recanted such statements as lacking scientific justification.[3] The denigration of black intellect, character, and conduct, and the general presumption of black inferiority and white superiority—which are affronts to black dignity and obstacles to whites and blacks relating to one another as equal persons—have a long and infamous history. Our examination of how the Color of Mind was constructed in the United States begins with a nineteenth-century schoolbook.

Mrs. Moore's Unhidden Curriculum

Antebellum Southern authors argued that racial differences in intelligence, character, and conduct made the idea of slaves gaining freedom as citizens unacceptable. During the Civil War, these ideas found their way into a schoolbook, *The Geographical Reader for the Dixie Children*, written by Mrs. M. B. Moore. Published in 1863 and reflecting pro-slavery arguments, it featured a lesson on the "races of men," informing readers that "Caucasians" were "civilized and far above all the others." On the other hand, Moore declared the "African or negro race" to be "slothful and vicious, but possess little cunning." Those who became slaves, she wrote, were "better fed, better clothed, and better instructed than in their native country."[4]

Such works held that blacks were highly dependent as a group and in need of cultured authority to function appropriately and productively. And Southern apologists like George Fitzhugh suggested that a slave society ruled by an enlightened and privileged white elite was preferable to the uncertainties and incessant tumult of democracies.[5] What is most striking about Mrs. Moore's unhidden curriculum was her appeal to the Color of Mind, on which her justification of black subordination and white superiority was predicated.

We would expect antebellum Southerners to subscribe to such views, and most certainly did. Some made explicit mention of philosophers to defend the racial order. For example, George Fitzhugh declared, "The true vindication of slavery must be founded on (Aristotle's) theory of man's social nature, as opposed to Locke's theory of the social contract, on which latter Free Society rests for support." His appeal to Aristotle is instructive. Fitzhugh's point, which echoes the qualified egalitarianism expressed by Emerson, Jefferson, and many other past defenders of black subordination to whites, is that a society based on qualified egalitarianism was preferable to one premised on universal egalitarianism, such as supposedly found in Northern states. Well aware that many people viewed this as "merely repulsive," Fitzhugh nevertheless assured readers that Aristotle's view had "two thousand years of human approval and concurrence in its favor."[6] If it was derived from Aristotle, Fitzhugh surmised, it must be reasonable.

It is not difficult to imagine why Fitzhugh and other pro-slavery writers would be drawn to Aristotle. Arguably, the ancient Greek philosopher was an egalitarian, but only in a sense. He lived much of his life in putatively democratic Athens and believed that there should be equality between equals, and that treating equals unequally was unjust. Yet there was a rub: being a man, or being human for that matter, was not enough to count as an equal during his time. Non-Greeks generally were not equal to Greeks; women were not equal to men; children were not equal to adults; and slaves typically were not equal to their masters. Hence there would have been little injustice in Plato, Aristotle, and other Greek men of wisdom ruling over "barbarians," slaves, women, and brutes. In the case of slaves in particular, and others deemed devoid or deficient in deliberative rational intellect, it was their lack of this particular capacity that Aristotle used to distinguish those fit to rule from those destined to serve. Aristotle thus espoused a form of qualified egalitarianism, a doctrine calling for equality among equals and inequality among unequals, long before antebellum Americans such as Emerson and Fitzhugh embraced this perspective. Many other Americans employed it to resolve the apparent contradiction between proclaiming "all men are created equal" while simultaneously denying equality to slaves and free blacks.[7]

Although he did not have *racial* slavery in mind, in his great work the *Politics* Aristotle declares and defends the inferiority of those he describes as "natural" slaves.[8] This was hardly a minor issue in ancient Athens and other cities, where a majority of residents could be slaves. Some were captured in war, and thus were subjugated by circumstance. But Aristotle took others to be devoid of reason, and he cited this to explain why they found themselves enslaved:

> Therefore those people who are as different from others as body is from soul or beast from human, and people whose task, that is to say, the best thing to come from them, is to use their bodies are . . . natural slaves. And it is better for them to be subject to this rule. . . . For he who can belong to someone else (and that is why he actually does belong to someone else), and he who shares in reason to the extent of understanding it, but does not have it himself (for the other animals obey not reason but feelings), is a natural slave.[9]

The status of these natural slaves supported Aristotle's more general philosophy of nature. He held that everything naturally has its place, and that it is best in an organic or functional sense for some individuals to rule others. Among the latter were the "lowborn," slaves by nature, who represented a large portion of the population in ancient societies. Thus, in addition to establishing a natural hierarchy among human beings, and grounding social subordination and social inequality in it, Aristotle bequeathed a legacy of using reason or intellect to distinguish those persons for whom slavery was appropriate. This view clearly accords with what many Americans later came to think about blacks, namely that inferior reasoning ability or intellect justified their low status and servile roles in society.

When he turned to Aristotle to vindicate slavery, Fitzhugh no doubt had this in mind, believing blacks to be natural slaves who should be ruled by "superior" whites. Yet he and other white supremacists had to approach Aristotle with caution, since some whites, or persons antebellum Americans would classify as such, could also be considered to be natural slaves in the ancient world.[10] Consequently, for many antebellum pro-slavery thinkers, the basis of equality was not deliberative rational intellect but pure-white ancestry. Unlike Emerson, Fitzhugh did not take it for granted that all whites were necessarily more intelligent than blacks, so intellect could not be the only measure of who should be subordinate. However intelligent they might be, even gifted blacks could not be white, and so it was race that provided the basis for his and others' qualified egalitarianism in the nineteenth century.[11] This doctrine has had enduring consequences for thinking about justice.

Distributive justice is concerned with how societies should allocate divisible material and nonmaterial goods among persons. It addresses questions of how rights and liberties, money, property, power, prestige, and educational opportunities should be distributed. Aristotle, an important source of classical philosophical wisdom about this, maintained that a sure path to human conflict, and the epitome of injustice, is when equals are allotted unequal shares, opportunity, or treatment and when unequals receive unequal ones. To apply this abstract egalitarian formula, we must first identify the properties of persons that will serve to distinguish equals from unequals for a given purpose. Historically, traits such as noble birth, wealth, citizenship, religion, virtue, and various definitions of merit have served such purposes. Presumed natural endowments such as intellect, race, or gender did so as well.

These properties of persons, or categories of difference, have figured prominently in philosophical understandings of distributive justice throughout history. While it may indeed be "self-evident, that all men are created equal," as proclaimed in the American Declaration of Independence, the question of whether manhood, humanity, or some other category of difference constituted a basis for distinguishing equals from unequals has long been a matter of contention. For ancient, early modern, and contemporary egalitarians alike, the basis for placing people into natural or artificial hierarchies has often entailed deliberate and conscious contrivance. The generic egalitarian imperative to treat people differently has always been qualified and tethered to an understanding of status. Qualified egalitarianism thus is a useful conceptual framework for making sense of the long-standing socially and legally constructed racial patterns of unequal treatment and opportunity in America. Among other things, this doctrine helps explain how antebellum and postbellum American egalitarians could justify educating blacks for servile labor while reserving higher or more "advanced" forms of education for whites.

English philosopher John Locke is generally regarded as representing a more universal and unqualified egalitarian outlook. He conceived of political society as a product of a social contract entered into by free and equal persons to secure their lives, liberties, and estates, or their natural rights, by accepting the authority of representative government. In principle, this did not rule out blacks from being members of the polity, which is why Fitzhugh was hostile to this way of thinking and refused to use Locke as a source of inspiration for his white supremacist vision of the American polity. Had Fitzhugh anticipated the work of philosopher Charles Mills, who argues that Locke's social contract tradition is also racially qualified, he might have thought a bit differently.[12]

It would be wrong to assume, however, that prejudicial attitudes regarding racial differences were limited to the South. Regardless of the Lockean principles embedded in Northern state constitutions and political culture (which Fitzhugh correctly surmised), white antipathy to black equality was pervasive there as well. This became especially clear during the 1830s and beyond, following the advent of common school campaigns and the escalation of abolitionist efforts to promote the idea of racial equality. The result was a number of incidents of popular white rejection of black residents and schools in Northern communities, sometimes marked by violence, and furious debates about racial equality.[13] Later, white mobs attacked black institutions in Philadelphia and New York, burning a church in the former and an orphan asylum in the latter. African Americans suffered discrimination in housing and employment throughout the North.[14] Hence when it came to race, a practice—if not always a doctrine—of racially qualified equality was widely observed there as well.

Popular attitudes about the status of blacks inevitably affected public support for their schooling. This became clear as common school systems were established in the antebellum era. Most Northern states and municipalities with substantial numbers of blacks provided separate institutions for them, where any were available at all. Proposals to permit blacks to attend school with whites were routinely rejected, as blacks were considered, in the words of one Iowa parent, "not by nature equal to whites."[15] In some cases, local leaders worried that integrated schools would offend potential white settlers and attract blacks, which could lower property values—a familiar complaint even today.[16]

One extreme case of white resistance took place in Canaan, New Hampshire, where in 1835 local men used nearly a hundred oxen to drag the edifice of Noyes Academy off its foundation, to prevent fourteen black students from studying with twenty-eight whites. An even more telling incident occurred in Canterbury, Connecticut, when Prudence Crandall admitted a black girl to her female boarding school. After most of the white students withdrew, Crandall opened a school for African Americans, leading the state legislature to forbid institutions to admit blacks from outside Connecticut.[17] To be sure, racist ideology in the North rarely reached the heights of chauvinism evident in the South, at least in published form; but few whites in the North believed that blacks were any more their equals. Mrs. Moore's unhidden curriculum was hardly provincial.

Antebellum Americans did not invent the Color of Mind, though they readily incorporated it into everyday legal and social practices and institutions. Carving up the world into "races of mankind," and asserting that races had different cognitive, moral, and behavioral characteristics, was a European inheritance central to their creation of alien "Others," which in turn advanced the aims of conquest, exploitation, and migration. Philosophers played a vital role in this enterprise.[18] Indeed, they account for why the emancipatory ideals of freedom and equality were not the only ideological exports from Europe to America. Cultural anthropology, as understood by Immanuel Kant and others, afforded European migrants to America a template for distinguishing themselves from indigenous peoples who were there long before Columbus, and from the blacks they would later transport, enslave, and subordinate for generations.

Developing a Philosophy of Race

The racist ideology featured in Mrs. Moore's schoolbook, and on display in popular white resistance to black education and racially integrated schooling, was not an aberration. More than a century earlier, European philosophers and naturalists had given systematic thought to the race idea and contributed much to its development. Moreover, as Thomas McCarthy argues, "hierarchical race theory" was a driving force behind Western imperialism, colonialism, and nationalism.[19] During the Age of Reason, or the Age of Enlightenment, as it is also known, philosophers, scientists, and other thinkers divided humankind into races. Human beings were classified and distinguished by perceived physical, behavioral, moral, and cognitive characteristics. While some thinkers believed that these characteristics were innate and immutable, others like Kant and his student Johann Gottfried Herder argued that variations in the races of humankind were due to environmental factors such as climate, habitat, and diet. This distinction between innate and environmental bases of racial differences would be a subject of dispute later, and eventually resolved in favor of the latter.

In 1735, in his *Systema Naturae*, biological taxonomist Carolus Linnaeus grouped human beings into four races: white, black, yellow, and red.[20] With his classification of human beings by their physical traits and behavioral dispositions, which he believed to be fixed by nature, he sought to adapt Aristotle's notions of genus and species, and to situate the varieties of humankind within the animal kingdom. Within this order, he presumed that each race was identified by different characteristics, not merely physical but also dispositional: Europeans were "white" and "governed by law"; Native Americans were "tanned" and "governed by custom"; Asians were "yellow" and "governed by opinion"; and Africans were "crafty, lazy, careless, black," and "governed by the arbitrary will of the master."[21]

Later, Johann Friedrich Blumenbach, who Ivan Hannaford calls the father of modern "skin and bones" anthropology, extended and further developed this classificatory scheme by recognizing five races instead of four—a count that would become authoritative. However, he refrained from postulating a racial hierarchy, or agreeing with Linnaeus that the varieties of humankind and their racial characteristics were fixed or immutable.[22] During the Enlightenment, some of the most influential philosophers of modern Europe, including Hume, Kant, and their successors, sought empirical proof for what they presumed to be the obvious truth of black intellectual inferiority, despite strong normative misgivings about slavery (which historically was also associated with Slavic people in Europe). Their views on the physical, ethical, emotional, and aesthetic attributes of races were informed by European travel reports and the emerging natural sciences. The same was true for the subsequent emergence of racial ideology in nineteenth-century America. Hume, Kant, and other influential eighteenth-century thinkers made substantial contributions to the formation of the black image in the early modern white mind.

In his 1754 essay "Of National Characters," Scottish philosopher David Hume, despite believing that domestic slavery debased both slaves and their masters, remarked, "I am apt to suspect the Negroes to be naturally inferior to the whites. There scarcely ever was a civilized nation of that complexion, nor even any individual eminent either in action or speculation. . . . Not to mention our colonies, there are NEGROE slaves dispersed all over EUROPE, of whom none ever discovered any symptoms of ingenuity; though low people, without education, will start up amongst us, and distinguish themselves in every profession."[23]

For his part, Kant expanded substantially on Hume's viewpoint, and is widely regarded as having made the most comprehensive and systematic philosophical contribution to racial ideology before it ultimately made its way to the New World colonies,[24] as reflected in the following:

> The Negroes of Africa have by nature no feeling that rises above the trifling. Mr. Hume challenges anyone to cite a single example in which a Negro has shown talents, and asserts that among the hundreds of thousands of blacks who are transported elsewhere from their countries, although many of them have even been set free, still not a single one was ever found who presented anything great in art or science or any other praiseworthy quality, even though among the whites some continually rise aloft from the lowest rabble, and through superior gifts earn respect in the world. So fundamental is the difference between these two races of man, and it appears to be as great in regard to mental capacities as in color.[25]

Apart from dividing the "races" of humankind and the nations of the world, philosophers speculated about why these purported racial differences exist. Many thinkers have cited such distinctions to explain and justify the social and political subordination of blacks and Africans. Colonialism, slavery, and the theft of land and resources of indigenous peoples were often justified on the grounds that whites were purportedly superior (in ways that mattered most) to colored peoples of the world. Hannaford recounts one such argument, made in Spain in 1547, justifying wars against American Indians on the grounds that "as *people* they were inferior by nature: they were as children to adults, women to men, cruel to mild, monkeys to men. They were without laws, property, and civilization; they were Aristotle's *barbaros* by nature and might, on the same grounds as the Jews and the Moors, be forcibly converted or extirpated from the face of the earth."[26] Like Africans, they were considered inferior, and subject to rule, because of purported qualities of mind.

Regarding speculation about the source of the intellectual differences between blacks and whites, Kant and Hume did not suggest that these distinctions were biologically inherent. Such concepts were not yet fully developed. In Kant's posthumously published lectures on physical geography, he argues that climate was associated with such differences: "In hot countries the human being matures in all aspects earlier, but does not, however, reach the perfection of those in temperate zones. Humanity is at its greatest perfection in the race of the whites. The yellow Indians do have a meagre talent. The Negroes are far below them and at the lowest point are a part of the

American peoples."[27] And he adds that these differences account for why the races of humankind in temperate climates have been able to dominate the races of people in warmer countries:

> The inhabitant of the temperate parts of the world, above all the central part [meaning modern-day Europe] has a more beautiful body, works harder, is more jocular, more controlled in his passions, more intelligent than any other race of people in the world. That is why at all points in time these peoples have educated the others and controlled them with weapons.[28]

While Hume agreed with Kant's proposition that people who lived in the more extreme climates on earth, beyond the polar circles or in the tropics, were "inferior to the rest of the species and are incapable of higher attainment of the human mind,"[29] he did not believe this to be primarily due to climate. Rather, he emphasized patterns of association and custom over long periods, and the development of a legitimate polity organized for the common good.[30]

Prevailing images of black inferiority thus were far from the racist expressions of isolated extremists in Confederate states. They began with influential intellectuals and grew widely in popular thought, eventually becoming deeply rooted in the European and American consciousness. Their status as mainstream ideas is also evident when considering this entry in the first American edition of the *Encyclopaedia Britannica* (1798):

> The negro [sic] women have the loins greatly depressed, and very large buttocks, which give the back the shape of a saddle. Vices the most notorious seem to be the portion of this unhappy race: idleness, treachery, revenge, cruelty, impudence, stealing, lying, profanity, debauchery, nastiness and intemperance, are said to have extinguished the principles of natural law, and to have silenced the reproofs of conscience. They are strangers to every sentiment of compassion, and are an awful example of the corruption of man when left to himself.

Mrs. Moore's unconcealed curriculum also found support in Thomas Jefferson, a statesman and an author of the Declaration of Independence. This revered national document proclaims that "all men are created equal, that they are endowed by their Creator with certain unalienable rights, that among these are Life, Liberty and the pursuit of happiness." But Jefferson was also a slaveholder whose slaves were not recognized as having these rights.[31] While there is no denying his commitment to America's founding ideals, it is also true that he unabashedly embraced the view that Africans were naturally inferior to whites in intellect, emotion, and spirit. Such ideas about black inferiority were used to justify black chattel slavery in a nation avowedly committed to upholding the ideals of the American Revolution.

Jefferson did not lack morals, compassion, or a vigorous sense of honor. He thought that slaveholders should be mindful of how they treated slaves, especially in the presence of white children, lest they abuse the smaller slaves. He also feared that a just God might one day render justice to America for black enslavement, and expressed the hope that white masters would willingly consent to eventual emancipation. Of course, it ultimately required a prolonged and violent war to emancipate African Americans, and Jefferson freed only two of his many slaves during his lifetime. Like many of his contemporaries, he thought that there were numerous natural differences between blacks and whites, and he made this quite clear in his only published book, *Notes on the State of Virginia* (1787).

In this work, Jefferson devoted considerable attention to the question of race, beginning with allegedly physical distinctions. "Besides those of color, figure, and hair," he notes, "there are other physical distinctions proving a difference of race. [Blacks] have less hair on the face and body. They secrete less by the kidneys [*sic*], and more by the glands of the skin, which gives them a very strong and disagreeable odor." To this he adds, "They seem to require less sleep. A black, after hard labor through the day, will be induced by the slightest amusements to sit up till midnight, or later, though knowing he must be out with the first dawn of the morning." And when noting something potentially positive about blacks, he believed that it revealed yet another deficiency: "[Blacks] are at least as brave, and more adventuresome. But this may perhaps proceed from a want of forethought, which prevents their seeing a danger till it be present." Moreover, Jefferson, who fathered children with his slave Sally Hemings, expresses misgivings about black love: "[Black men] are more ardent after their female; but love seems with them to be more an eager desire, than a tender delicate mixture of sentiment and sensation."[32]

But purportedly physical, behavioral, character, and emotional differences did not get to the crux of the matter, which was the view that blacks were taken to be *intellectually* inferior. On this point Jefferson wrote, "Comparing [blacks] by their faculties of memory, reason, and imagination, it appears to me, that in memory they are equal to the whites; in reason much inferior, as I think one could scarcely be found capable of tracing and comprehending the investigations of Euclid; and that in imagination they are dull, tasteless, and anomalous."[33]

As a former leader of the republic, Jefferson's views carried considerable weight, especially in the South. But similar views were commonly expressed by other leading figures as well, lending them even greater legitimacy. This was especially true in the years leading up to the Civil War, when pro-slavery writers such as George Fitzhugh argued that human bondage was a natural and predictable social practice, especially well-suited to blacks.[34] Eventually, these views gained the sanction of the nation's highest court. In the infamous 1857 *Dred Scott* decision, Chief Justice Roger Taney of the US Supreme Court affirmed the assumption of blacks' inferiority and ruled that the egalitarian ideals articulated in the Declaration of Independence were clearly not meant to apply to them, thereby acknowledging the racially qualified nature of America's egalitarianism. The court held:

> [Negroes] had . . . been regarded as beings of an inferior order, and altogether unfit to associate with the white race, either in social or political relations; and so far inferior, that they had no rights which the white man was bound to respect. . . . This opinion was at that time fixed and universal in the civilized portion of the white race. It was regarded as an axiom in morals as well as in politics, which no one thought of disputing.[35]

This ruling summarized an entrenched body of belief that blacks were inferior to whites and not their equals in any meaningful manner. It also added that Dred Scott and other blacks could not be regarded as American citizens protected by the rights asserted in the Declaration of Independence and codified in the Constitution. Thus affirming the principles expressed in Mrs. Moore's textbook, and issued seven decades after Jefferson's *Notes*, the court's decision was an unmistakable legal articulation of the principle of racially qualified egalitarianism: inequality among unequals simply on the basis of race.

Scientific Racism

As Frederick Douglass observed, men often find a rationale for subordinating others in allegations of inferiority. Nineteenth-century slaveholders asserted that blacks and whites were different species of men, with immutable differences in character, conduct, and intelligence. These and similar ideas, which also influenced the likes of Northerners such as Emerson, were widely taken to justify white supremacy in civil, social, and political relations. An elaborate literature on skull size, facial structure, and other presumably distinctive anatomical features of various races appeared in the early to mid-

nineteenth century. Popularly called "niggerology," it defended chattel slavery based on a changing conceptualization of race. Central to this approach
was the claim that the "white" race was intellectually and culturally superior
to all others, and that the African race was the lowest.

Despite the asserted influence of environmental factors on learning and
intellectual development, many nineteenth-century theorists clung to innate explanations of human differences in intelligence and character. Such
ideas had a long lineage, dating from works of Carolus Linnaeus, Georges
Cuvier, Christoph Meiners, Charles White, Samuel Morton, and others. They
laid an intellectual and pseudoscientific foundation for believing that blacks
were naturally inferior to whites in intelligence and moral sensibility. As Stephen J. Gould demonstrates in his historical work, *The Mismeasure of Man*,
this line of inquiry clearly reflected the biases and beliefs of its authors.[36]
Skull measurements eventually fell out of favor, but researchers continued
to measure and weigh brains well into the twentieth century, before creating
aptitude tests to "measure" intelligence.

Even though they still could not directly link variation on these counts
to actual biological endowments, proponents of the Color of Mind continued to presume that whites were inherently smarter than blacks. And this
conjecture was used to support state and local policies that separated whites
and blacks in schools, along with inferior provision of resources for black
education, during the nineteenth century and long afterward. In the antebellum South, of course, education for African Americans was systematically
suppressed altogether, especially after the bloody rebellion of 1831 led by
the slave preacher Nat Turner. Free blacks were widely viewed as troublesome, and struggled to gain any sort of schooling or social advancement.

Although these champions of the Color of Mind claimed to be scientists,
it is important to note that their ideas had little basis in the actual science of
human genetics, still in its infancy during the nineteenth and early twentieth
centuries. Today, of course, after decades of research on variability in human
intelligence, there is no credible scientific evidence that racial differences on
this score have a genetic foundation. Researchers have explored hereditary
links with technology stemming from the Human Genome Project, and determined that no identifiable genetic factors can account for black-white
differences on IQ or achievement tests. As bioethicist Pilar Ossario recently
observed, "Cognitive abilities are complex and will likely be influenced by
a myriad of environmental factors *and* genes." But racial differences in these
abilities are not rooted in genetic factors: "It is statistically implausible that
variants of the numerous genes relating to intelligence would be distributed among racial groups in a manner that systematically confers cognitive

advantage on one group or disadvantage on another. Furthermore, there is no evidence that current racial differences in mean IQ scores are caused by racially distinctive differences in genetic variation." In short, "the evidence suggests that (such) differences in IQ scores are the result of social inequality rather than the cause."[37]

Scientific racism, as it came to be called, is no longer a widely acceptable view, even if its influence continues to be evident. More sophisticated research eventually demonstrated the importance of environmental influences on variability in human skills and abilities. Gradually, environmentalist views of racial differences came to dominate public discourse, especially following World War II. However, as we argue in chapter 5, the older ideas—used as a basis for subordination based on racial characteristics—were eventually replaced by cultural explanations of racial differences. And these ideas eventually began to look very similar to earlier notions of innate distinction.[38]

Contesting the Color of Mind

Even though its influence was widespread, the Color of Mind proved difficult to square with the presence of blacks in antebellum America who gave the lie to it in both deed and word. James McCune Smith and Frederick Douglass were leaders among this illustrious group. Smith was born a slave in New York in 1813. Remarkably, he became the nation's first university-trained black physician and a leading intellectual of his time. Educated at the New York African Free School and the University of Glasgow, he returned to the United States in 1838 with three degrees and training as an intern in Paris. Despite being denied admission to the American Medical Association and local medical societies because of his race, he became a successful physician and pharmacist treating both black and white patients. He also wrote essays attacking the prevailing theories of racial inferiority. As an accomplished medical practitioner and passionate intellectual, Smith tirelessly sought equality for blacks in the United States.[39]

Like other nineteenth-century black leaders, including his friend Frederick Douglass, Smith was keenly aware that a presumption of black intellectual inferiority was a basis for inequality of educational opportunity. While he hoped that an exemplary record of academic and professional accomplishment would help refute the idea that blacks were incapable of intellectual achievement, he eventually would learn that black educational achievement and attainment could not extinguish racist beliefs, even in the North. Nevertheless, like other prominent blacks, he was committed to advancing educational opportunity for black children. Describing schools as the "great caste abolisher," Smith dedicated himself to educating black students so "they may be better and more thoroughly taught than their parents are."[40]

Smith understood the power of education from his own experience. He and other free blacks outside the South worked persistently to combat the Color of Mind. Expanding educational opportunities for black children was a critical part of the task. They sometimes encountered violent opposition, which was a telling reflection of the challenge they faced. Their struggles did result in isolated victories, which created opportunities for a limited number of educated blacks to assume leadership positions in their communities.[41] William Cooper Nell, for instance, graduated from the segregated Smith School in Boston and became a well-known journalist and abolitionist leader, agitating for equal education among other causes. Henry Highland Garnet was a classmate of Smith's at the New York African Free School and graduated from the Oneida Theological Institute, which admitted both blacks and whites, before becoming a celebrated minister and abolitionist writer and speaker. Sarah Parker Redmond was educated in the schools of Salem, Massachusetts, and Bedford College for Women in London, and became a physician and anti-slavery activist.[42] These individuals and others like them were object lessons demonstrating the potential in black education. Yet few white Americans were prepared to acknowledge such accomplishments—and when they did, these cases often were dismissed as exceptions to the general rule. Such was the immense power of the Color of Mind regarding the "educability" of African Americans.

Accomplished blacks posed a direct challenge to the black inferiority thesis, not only in deed and action but also in word and theory. Few were more influential in the latter regard than the great abolitionist Frederick Douglass. If opponents of slavery and black subordination were to challenge and contest these practices, they would have to find ways to expand the meaning and implications of the American creed that all men are created equal and have natural rights to life, liberty, and the pursuit of happiness. But this was not simply a matter of pointing to blacks like Smith who achieved great heights intellectually. It would also require a philosophical assault, making the case that the founding ideals provided a normative basis for challenging slavery and black subordination.

This was the strategy taken by Douglass, one of the most remarkable philosophical minds of his time. He saw the universalism of the founding ideals as the saving grace for African Americans. In his speech "The Constitution of the United States: Is It Pro-slavery or Antislavery?" delivered in Glasgow, Douglass explained why he came to view these principles as universal rather than as racially inflected doctrines: "My position now is one of reform, not of revolution. I would act for the abolition of slavery through the Government—not over its ruins. . . . If the South has made the Constitution bend to the purposes of slavery, let the North now make that instrument bend to the cause of freedom and justice."[43]

In his famous speech, "The Meaning of July Fourth for the Negro," delivered in 1852, Douglass characterized the ideas featured in the Declaration of Independence as "saving principles." Disagreeing with abolitionists who saw the Constitution as pro-slavery, Douglass argued that these principles could be wielded on behalf of black emancipation. One of his key philosophical strategies was to expose the inconsistency between America's acceptance of these ideas and the practice of slavery. From this vantage point he asked, "Are the great principles of political freedom and of natural justice, embodied in that Declaration of Independence, extended to us?"[44]

Douglass realized, however, that there were serious obstacles to utilizing such ideas for emancipatory purposes, most notably the widespread belief in black inferiority. He contested this forcefully in an 1854 address entitled "The Claims of the Negro Ethnologically Considered."[45] If the saving principles were to provide a comprehensive normative platform for black emancipation, it had to be argued that they were "colorblind" and "raceless"; moreover, it had to be argued that blacks were part of the human family and descended from a common ancestry. For as Douglass keenly observed, "The whole argument in defense of slavery, becomes utterly worthless the moment the African is proved to be equally a man with the Anglo-Saxon. The temptation therefore, to read the Negro out of the human family is exceedingly strong."[46] From 1851 until shortly before his death in 1895, Douglass sought to overcome these grim obstacles to utilizing the saving principles on behalf of black emancipation. As he put it, "Human rights stand upon a common basis, and by all the reason that they are supported, maintained, and defended, for one variety of the human family, they are supported, maintained, and defended for *all* the human family; because all mankind have the same wants, arising out of a common nature."[47] Once such premises were accepted, it naturally followed that African Americans must be accorded equal rights.

There were yet other outspoken opponents of the Color of Mind, both white and black. The growing abolitionist movement helped to mobilize opposition to slavery and racism in the years leading up to the Civil War. The crowning achievement of this crusade was the passage of the Thirteenth, Fourteenth, and Fifteenth Amendments to the US Constitution following the South's defeat. These measures nullified the principles of qualified equality expressed in *Dred Scott*, establishing the citizenship of blacks and by extension their humanity before the law. It was a monumental accomplishment, achieved after a bloody war against slavery and in the face of widespread racism, and it continues to echo today.[48]

The Color of Mind and Its Consequences

The historical record of philosophical and pseudoscientific writing on the question of race clearly demonstrates that the presumption of black inferiority in intellect, character, and conduct was constructed during the eighteenth and nineteenth centuries. Fully articulated by Americans as a defense and justification of black chattel slavery, although it had deeper roots in the European Enlightenment, the Color of Mind reached its pinnacle in the decades following the abolition of slavery. In later years, IQ testers and new forms of scientific racism sustained the Color of Mind. And, as we will also demonstrate, its pernicious effects endure.

This presumption has long been used to justify and support the treatment of African Americans as a stigmatized and degraded caste in American life. Among its most odious influences has been its impact on education. More than a century ago, the Color of Mind served to justify racial inequalities in the distribution of school resources in the post-Reconstruction South, where the vast majority of African Americans lived. Substantial differences between black and white schooling existed elsewhere in the country as well. Although scientific racism was a catalyst for and a consequence of these circumstances, the ideas informing it survived slavery and have endured, albeit in a somewhat different form.[49] Older versions of anti-black sentiment, which had been cloaked in the language of innate or biological mental inferiority, have been replaced in recent decades by contemporary denigrations of black choices, culture, and character.[50] These cultural explanations of the achievement gap constitute a persistent obstacle to appreciating and addressing the opportunity gaps that continue to shape the racial achievement gap.[51]

The Color of Mind's legacy is consequential. Education (or its lack) plays a profound role in a child's future life prospects in the schooled society. David F. Labaree calls the school system "the greatest institutional success in American history."[52] How the Color of Mind has contributed to constructing the racial achievement gap within this system is the next part of our story.

THREE

The Color of Schooling: Constructing the Racial Achievement Gap

In 1845, a group of black Bostonians petitioned to enroll their children in a local school. They argued that skin color was an arbitrary and thus unjust reason to require their children's attendance at the only segregated black school in the city, which had long been a point of contention with the local African American community.[1] Like Oliver Brown in Topeka, Kansas, more than one hundred years later, these parents wanted the same right as whites to send their children to neighborhood schools. The school committee's representatives, however, rejected the suggestion that skin color was the important distinction in segregating schooling. "It is one of *races*," they wrote (emphasis in original), "not of colors, merely," adding that dissimilarities were "found deep in the physical, mental and moral natures of the two races." While the committeemen would not say which group was superior, they added that "a promiscuous intermingling in the public schools" would be damaging to both.[2]

With this conceptual leap from color to race, segregated schooling became linked to a particular notion of human difference, hinging on cognitive ability and other qualities of mind. Accordingly, the schoolmen also argued that blacks required "an educational treatment different in some respects from that of white children," emphasizing "study and instruction in which progress depends on memory or on the imitative faculties, chiefly." White children, on the other hand, were judged superior in "the faculties of invention, comparison and reasoning."[3] In other words, black children were held to be intellectually inferior, even if members of Boston's school committee were unwilling to state it plainly. Thus, insofar as blacks and whites were not considered to be equals, and they certainly were not, it was primarily because of presumed differences in their mental faculties. This is an early example of how the Color of Mind resulted in limited educational opportunities for blacks. Policy decisions such as this, including others we discuss throughout the book, represented critical steps in constructing the racial achievement gap.

The appeal to race rather than just color embodied the basic elements of an emerging American racial ideology of white advantage, holding that whites were superior and that their elevated social, political, and economic status hinged on moral sensibility and capacity for reasoning. These ideas and the suggestion that such differences necessitated educating the two races differently were widespread, and came to have a profound practical impact in the United States. Eventually the Color of Mind permeated the nation's education system, institutionalizing the racial achievement gap.

Justifying Jim Crow

The Boston report was a prelude to a famous 1849 case challenging school segregation, *Roberts v. City of Boston*, which was argued by Charles Sumner and ultimately failed in the Massachusetts Supreme Court. Boston schools eventually integrated following state legislation requiring it, but most schools elsewhere in the North remained segregated until after the Civil War. Ideas like those expressed in 1845 continued to characterize the thinking of most whites. Reaction to Massachusetts's integration legislation was sharply negative, with one New York newspaper declaring that "the North is to be Africanized . . . God save the Commonwealth."[4]

As the Boston committeemen's response showed, the question of skin color had become subsumed in the far more problematic issue of race. A presumption of distinctions in mind made the very idea of equal education unacceptable to most whites, which had telling consequences, because schools for blacks had fewer resources. Indeed, even in New York and Philadelphia, among the most cosmopolitan places of the time, black students attended separate institutions with far less public support than their white counterparts. The limited number of such schools also meant that black children often walked great distances to attend, which discouraged attendance. In the words of historian Leon Litwack, these schools were "separate and unequal." This would remain a norm for decades, allowing whites to focus public resources on their own children and leaving blacks to make do the best way they could.[5]

A tension existed between racially separate and unequal schooling and the American creed of equality among men, and black legislators and their allies sought to resolve it. Formal segregation of schools by race eventually ended in many Northern cities, most by the end of the century, thanks to their campaigning against it. As black Ohio legislator Jere A. Brown declared in 1886, "Separate schools engender a spirit of inferiority in the mind of the colored race, while it cultivates and fosters a spirit of superiority in the bosom of the more favored one." Along with Benjamin Arnett, the nation's first African American legislator to be elected from a predominantly white district, Brown succeeded in ending mandatory racial segregation in his state's public schools.[6] With these changes, African American children attended school at rates comparable to whites in some communities.[7] These were important success stories, even if most blacks still suffered the effects of racial segregation.

More than 90 percent of African Americans lived in the South, however, and blacks were a tiny fraction of the North's population. This meant that reforms such as those in Boston, Ohio, and elsewhere were quite limited in impact. Segregated schooling was a norm throughout the South, and black schooling came under sharp attack following Reconstruction. Deprivation of black education also predominated below the Mason-Dixon Line, and became especially virulent following the institution of "Jim Crow" laws that sharply restricted black political power in the 1890s. By century's end, most black children received only a modicum of schooling, leaving them little alternative to a lifetime of work in the region's cotton fields.

Just how this occurred is a historical puzzle, particularly after passage in 1868 of the Fourteenth Amendment, which was intended to guarantee newly freed African Americans equal protection under the law. But Southern segregationists found a way around it with the doctrine of "separate but equal," designed to prevent African Americans from gaining access to facilities and institutions deemed white-only. The infamous 1896 *Plessy v. Ferguson* ruling by the US Supreme Court effectively sanctioned the unequal treatment of blacks in everyday life, arguing that separate institutions could be considered equal. This decision helped establish a post-Reconstruction "racial contract" among whites, a term coined by philosopher Charles Mills, which opened the door to systematic attacks on the rights of blacks as citizens.[8]

But more than this, *Plessy* firmly entrenched the principle of racially qualified egalitarianism on the eve of the new century, guaranteeing an unjust distribution of societal benefits and burdens as well as a continuing affront to black dignity. With respect to education, it made racial distinctions key to the formal segregation of schooling in a nation that espoused equality before the law. As the Boston school committeemen's reply to the African American parents' petition made very clear, whites and blacks were not viewed as equals in 1845; nor were they in the 1890s. In his famous dissent in *Plessy*, Associate Justice John Marshall Harlan observed, "The white race deems itself to be the dominant race in this country. And so it is, in prestige, in achievements, in education, in wealth, and in power. So, I doubt not, it will continue to be for all time, if it remains true to its great heritage, and holds fast to the principles of constitutional liberty."[9] Even a proponent of legal equality such as Harlan, who was unwilling to affirm a subordinate class of *citizens*, readily affirmed the allegedly superior position of the white race. His views paralleled those of most Americans at the time, reflecting the legitimacy that the Color of Mind had attained.

So the question of whether schools should be racially integrated was a matter of debate long before the Supreme Court's *Brown v. Board of Education* decision in 1954. Earlier segregationists used the Color of Mind to defend the racial status quo, which permitted whites to hoard educational opportunities. Of course, this was not lost on critics of racial segregation, and some even succeeded at challenging the Color of Mind and reaffirming black dignity, a story we consider in greater detail in chapter 4. But with superior schools and resources for whites, along with curricula designed to ensure white advantage, it was predictable that a black-white achievement gap would emerge.

How "Negroes" Should Be Educated

Perceived differences in cognitive abilities informed nineteenth-century perspectives on how blacks, whether enslaved or free, should be educated. Many believed that schools should prepare them for manual labor, which allegedly suited their supposedly inferior mental endowments. And some saw great economic benefits from this as well. "The potential economic value of the Negro population properly educated is infinite and incalculable," declared Northern philanthropist William Baldwin in 1899. "Time has proven that he is best fitted to perform the heavy labor in the Southern states." Like many Southerners, Baldwin believed that this arrangement would make it possible for whites "to perform the more expert labor," which generally required greater education. They could thus "leave the fields, mines and simpler trades for the Negro."[10]

Baldwin and those who agreed with him could have referenced Immanuel Kant to elaborate this point. In doing so, they would have distinguished between "educating" and "training" blacks, and following Kant, they could claim that blacks should be prepared only for servile labor by being trained. Antebellum Southerners such as Fitzhugh likely would have agreed with this and, perhaps also following Kant, could suggest that "Negro" training required a heavy hand. Kant recommended the use of a split bamboo cane, "so that the Negro will suffer a great deal of pain."[11] Such sentiments pointed to a division of labor with deep roots in slavery, when blacks performed a host of menial tasks under duress that most whites could not or would not contemplate. Their arduous physical labor made the expansion of cotton trade possible, and as historian Edward Baptist has shown, their rapidly rising productivity was driven by the overseer's lash. This too was a form of training, so to speak, with brutality in line with Kant's recommendation.

But life under slavery was not all work for blacks; they had families, music, stories, and a rich spiritual tradition to help them endure life within the "peculiar institution." Even if formal instruction for them was generally banned, it was impossible to prevent learning from occurring altogether.[12] Considerable evidence suggests that many—perhaps most—slave children received an important informal education within their immediate slave communities, where lessons about their circumstances, proper behavior, and a range of additional matters were conveyed by parents and other elders.[13] Some masters took pains to teach these children Christian principles and doctrine, although this was often a pretext for making their slaves more compliant and less unruly.

Slaveholders' desire for docility was evident in the work of philosopher Edmund Burke.[14] In 1780, he wrote *Sketch of the Negro Code*, which laid out a plan for the eventual abolition of slavery in the British West Indies. His plan, which placed great emphasis on moving gradually, specified the importance of slaves having "a disposition to receive [freedom] without danger to themselves or to us."[15] According to Burke's vision, this would involve compelling them to attend church services every Sunday, and tolerating neither laziness nor shiftlessness. In short, Christian masters had to provide their black slaves with a Christian education to overcome their purported tendency to misbehave and spurn responsibility, so that they could behave properly as able-bodied persons.

Still, in practice, most slaves were forbidden from pursuing even the most basic forms of literacy. This meant that children received little instruction beyond that deemed necessary for daily tasks, their adult roles as manual laborers, or Christian education aimed to teach them that their subordination to whites was the will of God. The inability to read, of course, constrained their knowledge and intellectual development, and contributed to white impressions of inferior black intellect.[16] Many slave children also suffered from malnutrition, and this too undoubtedly impaired their attentiveness and growth.[17] Furthermore, they learned from experience to treat whites with great deference and care, veiling evidence of knowledge and understanding lest it arouse doubts about their servility and trustworthiness. Given such legally and socially imposed limitations in their immediate environment, it is little wonder that most slaves appeared quite ignorant, buttressing white presumptions of black intellectual dependency.

The antebellum North had more formal schooling opportunities for blacks, mainly in the larger cities, but these were generally limited to the elementary level. With few exceptions, more advanced schools were not open to African Americans until after the Civil War. This would gradually change, but for decades it meant that ambitious black students had few options for continuing their studies. Such restrictions contributed to perceptions that blacks could not benefit from advanced schooling, since so few had been allowed access to it.[18]

In the elementary grades, African Americans attended school in relatively large numbers, especially later in the nineteenth century when urban school systems in the North became more extensive and compulsory school laws went into effect. Because most black families were quite poor, they often took their children out of school to work and contribute to household income when possible. The numbers who did so, however, tended to be lower than for immigrants, largely due to discrimination in the labor market. In addition, African American children advanced from elementary or grammar schools into public high schools at rates considerably lower than whites, and fewer graduated. Those that did succeed often found that additional education did little to help them find commensurate employment. The adult job market was also rife with discrimination, and blacks competed with the Irish and other European immigrants, who were quick to press their racial advantage with employers. As a consequence, some African Americans became disillusioned with education, even if overall attendance rates among them remained relatively high, at least at the elementary level.[19]

Opportunities for black students continued to be highly constrained in colleges and universities. John Russworm, among the first black college graduates, completed his studies at Maine's Bowdoin College in 1826 and helped establish the nation's first African American newspaper in New York a year later. Other blacks, like James McCune Smith and Alexander Crummell, attended universities abroad. But even with such exceptional leaders, the tiny number of highly educated blacks could hardly offset popular impressions of black intellectual deficiency, or displace the view that they should be educated only for servile labor and social subordination. Just before and immediately following the Civil War, a number of higher-education institutions were established exclusively for African American students, creating greater opportunity for enterprising young men and women. But these institutions generally were quite small, and only a slight fraction of the nation's black youth could even contemplate attending them.[20]

Most blacks lived in the South, of course, and opportunities for education developed somewhat unevenly there through the latter years of the nineteenth century into the twentieth. The period immediately following the Civil War witnessed dramatic improvements in African American schooling throughout the region. This began during Reconstruction, a federally supervised time of recovery in the South. Spearheaded by the federal Freedmen's Bureau and created to aid former slaves in their transition to freedom, thousands of schools were established. Northern religious groups and missionary societies and local black communities contributed as well, and by 1870 more than a quarter million black children were in school. In subsequent years, their numbers went up dramatically to more than a million by the mid-1880s, exhibiting a higher rate of attendance in many instances than white children. Schooling was enabled further by new constitutions required of Southern states for readmission to the Union and by reform-minded legislatures, which generally funded African American education equitably. These measures reflected the political power wielded by blacks during Reconstruction and immediately afterward. Between 1860 and 1900, the national rate of black illiteracy was cut in half, from more than 90 percent to less than 45 percent, testimony to educational advances across the South.[21] These developments gave the lie to those who claimed that blacks placed little value in education, or that they could not benefit from it. In fact, the historical evidence indicates that they prized it very highly and learned quickly.[22]

Jim Crow Goes to School

Unfortunately, this period of expansion and accomplishment in African American education was short-lived. As Reconstruction ended, indeed almost immediately, the Ku Klux Klan and other violent white vigilante organizations attacked black schools.[23] The end of federally enforced Reconstruction policies in 1877 paved the way for a new era of Jim Crow schooling. School funds were formally separated along racial lines, and funding disparities eventually reached dramatic proportions, particularly after 1890 and the advent of Jim Crow policies of segregation throughout the South. Black efforts to resist such changes proved largely futile, especially after most were effectively disenfranchised by discriminatory voter registration laws that were abetted by poll taxes and the use of literacy or civics tests to limit voter eligibility. By 1900, expenditures on African American schooling were about a third that of white schooling across much of the region, and white enrollment rates increased substantially.[24]

In many respects, the situation grew even worse after that. Black teachers had been paid at levels similar to their white counterparts during and immediately after Reconstruction, but after 1890 their compensation declined significantly in comparative terms. The length of sessions in black schools, formerly equivalent to those for whites, did not change, while the length of the school year expanded for white schools. A recent study found that black and white school terms were roughly equivalent as late as 1897 in predominantly black counties, but by 1915 the black average was more than ten weeks less than white schools, and teacher pay was less than half.[25] Facilities, such as existed, were threadbare. As a consequence, both the *quality* and *quantity* of black schooling was inferior. When asked about this in testimony to a federal commission in 1901, a white farmer declared, "The money does the most good in the white school."[26] Policies informed by the view that blacks had little need for education remained in place for decades.

After the Civil War, motivated by a commitment to national unity and socioeconomic development, Northern philanthropists provided limited financial support for Southern black education. Wealthy benefactors such as George Peabody, John F. Slater, and Caroline Phelps Stokes gave thousands annually for both black and white schooling, which contributed modestly to better schools and improved instruction. After 1901, the Southern Education Board, a private entity dedicated to the region's development, coordinated these efforts, but the overall impact was slight. The South was an immense region, and many blacks were scattered across the countryside. Much of the aid went to higher-education institutions, aiding a relatively small segment of the population. Consequently, most black communities hardly benefited from such philanthropy.[27]

Northern white patrons also had specific ideas about the kind of education most appropriate for black students, and it was in this regard that their influence probably was most widely felt. They typically chose to support vocational or "industrial" training rather than classical or other scholarly curricula. Perhaps the best-known example was the Tuskegee Institute in Alabama, led by Booker T. Washington. Influenced heavily by Virginia's Hampton Institute, where he was educated, Washington became a celebrated spokesperson for manual training and vocationalism. Among whites, this seemed an appropriate form of education for blacks, better suited to their presumed proclivities, limited mental ability, and moral shortcomings. Even though he recognized the value of a classical education for some, Washington preached an educational doctrine of accommodation, and Tuskegee students spread it widely as they became leaders across the region. A number of other institutions received support of this kind as well.[28]

Washington and other supporters of industrial education may have appeared conservative, but they clearly opposed Jim Crow schooling. Washington pointed out that spending on black schools was far less than on white institutions, and diplomatically declared that "opportunities for education are woefully inadequate for both races." Like other black leaders, he argued that black education was a good investment in lower crime rates and higher employment and income, addressing concerns that many whites harbored. While opposing the oppression of African Americans, he appealed to the traditional impulses of leaders in both the South and the North, offering assurances that blacks were not as potentially threatening as widely feared.[29]

Washington was criticized by a number of black intellectuals in his time, most notably Anna Julia Cooper and W. E. B. Du Bois, both of whom called for improved academic preparation of black students and additional support for collegiate education. These critics certainly appreciated the value of vocational training, however. Cooper argued, "If [a child's] hand is far more cunning and clever than his brain, see what he can best do, and give him a chance according to his fitness; try him at a trade."[30] But she also stressed the importance of education that goes beyond this: "The old education made him a 'hand,' solely and simply. It deliberately sought to suppress or ignore the soul. We must, whatever else we do, insist on those studies which by the consensus of educators are calculated to train our people to think, which will give them the power of appreciation and make them righteous."[31] And while Du Bois also was not wholly opposed to manual education, he declared that there was nothing more valuable to blacks than "a well-equipped college and university," especially for providing highly competent teachers.[32]

But black institutions at the end of the nineteenth century were often dependent on white patronage, and philanthropists favored manual education. Moreover, the Morrill Land Grant Act of 1890 provided federal funds for agricultural and mechanical colleges, including a number of institutions for African Americans, which helped to augment tendencies that Washington and his followers advocated.[33] The Washington-Du Bois debate reflected philosophical differences, including over how to properly realize the dignity of black folks. While both sides agreed that offering them no education was an affront to black dignity, one side thought self-esteem could be achieved primarily with industrial, vocational, or domestic training so that blacks could take advantage of the limited opportunities open to them. The other view called for a broader academic education in the arts and sciences so that blacks could aspire to the same heights as whites and become social equals.[34]

Despite the growth of Tuskegee and similar institutions, by the end of the nineteenth century black education had reached a low point. Jim Crow legislation and voting restrictions had greatly reduced black political power, creating a regime of highly unequal educational expenditures across the South. Poorly funded by state and local authorities, African American school- ing was sustained by philanthropic and black community resources that permitted only the barest modicum of education for most students. His- torian Horace Mann Bond estimated that by the early twentieth century, African Americans represented about 40 percent of Alabama's population, but received just 11 percent of the state's public school fund. In 1915, the average black school in the heavily populated middle of the state was in ses- sion for eighty-nine days, as opposed to 143 for white institutions. Similar conditions prevailed across most of the South. Hundreds of new secondary schools were built for white students and a much smaller number for blacks, principally in the larger cities. The result was a new level of educational inequality between the races, greater than at any time since the end of the Civil War.[35]

This was also a time of extreme racial violence against African Americans. More than three thousand lynchings occurred across the South between 1880 and 1940, most between 1880 and 1900. As Ida B. Wells and others observed, these ritualized outbursts of inhuman viciousness were precipi- tated by allegations of misconduct, frequently baseless and often including charges of sexual impropriety. Calling it "the same old racket," Wells cou- rageously exposed this pretext for white-on-black violence. "To palliate this record (which grows worse as the Afro-American becomes intelligent) and excuses some of the most heinous crimes that ever stained the history of a country," Wells observed, "the South is shielding itself behind . . . defending the honor of its women."[36] Southern authorities did little to restrain these eruptions of hatred and assaults on black dignity, as they helped sustain black fear, ensure white domination, and guarantee quiescence in the black workforce. Symbolically, the mob's noose became Kant's split bamboo cane, which many whites thought was necessary to "train" blacks to accept their subordinate status. Lynching thus served as a powerful form of informal education for blacks and whites alike, demonstrating that resistance to white supremacy would be met with deadly force.[37]

Racial disparities in formal education and extralegal violence both served the interests of white planters. Lynching maintained white hegemony, and unequal schooling limited the prospects for African Americans elsewhere. In the words of John W. Abercrombie, Alabama Superintendent of Schools in 1900, black schools were intended to "keep the masses of the colored people in the rural districts," where white landowners could rely on their labor.[38] Where they existed, African American secondary schools and colleges were also poorly funded, and focused mainly on manual training and industrial education. This did little to dispel popular myths about blacks' cognitive abilities, or their suitability for higher levels of scholarly accomplishment. Even though public schools for whites had become widely available, with greater resources, the education of Southern blacks had advanced little—if at all—in the years since Reconstruction.[39]

Let Them Eat Meal and Bacon

The historical record shows that state authorities played a major role in prescribing patterns of racially inferior and unequal schooling, premised on the Color of Mind. This would have a far-reaching impact, but everyday discrimination and racial violence was perhaps even more important in the nineteenth century. Northern European immigrant groups were anxious about gaining status as whites and enjoying the advantages it bestowed. Like Southern whites, they fought to maintain the presumption, clearly and succinctly expressed by Thomas Jefferson, that blacks were "inferior to whites in the endowments both of body and mind."[40] Most white Americans did not believe that formal education could change this, particularly those who held that black inferiority was innate, a natural or divinely created condition that could never be overcome. Consequently, most deemed futile or pointless any efforts to provide advanced education to African Americans.

Opposition to educating blacks for anything more than servility was stout, even violent at times, and was hardly limited to the South. It was a telling moment when working-class whites—many of them Irish immigrants— burned the Colored Orphan Asylum to the ground during the 1863 Draft Riots in New York City. Many of the city's residents viewed the asylum as a symbol of hope for black children, providing them with an education and aiding their transition to responsible adulthood. But to white rioters it was an abomination, assisting members of an allegedly inferior, despised group and perhaps encouraging them to aspire to higher status. They believed that blacks were supposed to be poorly educated, and to perform only those forms of menial labor that others judged too unseemly to even consider.[41] Fear of black demands for civil and social equality animated the most diehard opposition to racially equitable education among Northerners.[42]

This position was expressed clearly by pro-slavery author John H. Van Evrie, who helped instigate the New York riots through his white supremacist newspaper the *Weekly Daybook*. In an 1868 book, *White Supremacy and Negro Subordination*, Van Evrie exclaimed that "God has made the negro an inferior being, not in most cases, but in all cases. . . . There never could be a negro equaling the standard Caucasian in natural ability."[43] In other words, even the least-educated whites were judged superior to any black person. Such ideas undoubtedly appealed directly to poor immigrants, who competed with blacks for status and work in New York and elsewhere. For poor native-born whites, especially in the South, these propositions were comforting as well.

Regarding black education, Van Evrie wrote that it "must be oral and verbal, or, in other words, that negro should be placed in the best position possible for the development of his imitative powers—to call into action that peculiar capacity for copying the habits, mental and moral, of the superior Caucasian."[44] This, of course, was a view strikingly similar to that proposed by members of the Boston School Committee two decades earlier. But Van Evrie went considerably further. In his view, a black person was perpetually a child, and an ""educated' negro [sic], like a 'free negro,' is a social monstrosity, even more unnatural and repulsive than the latter."[45] In short, only the barest rudiments of education were appropriate for blacks.

Many Southern whites agreed with this perspective, but political questions often animated their discussions of black education. With the advent of Jim Crow policies, there was growing concern that any formal education of blacks posed a problem. This view was rooted in the idea that teaching even basic literacy skills would make them unfit for manual labor and thus a threat to regional security and stability. A Southern judge asked, "What does the laboring class want of knowledge? Give them meal and bacon to make more muscles and we will direct the muscles."[46] Such sentiments were consistent with a view that held blacks to be an inferior species, useful only for hard manual labor. Racial denunciations filled Southern white newspapers, reflecting anxiety about these questions.[47]

Part of this concern, according to historian Leon Litwack, was recognition of the power of literacy: "Knowledge encouraged independence and free thought. Knowledge opened up new vistas . . . [and] permitted workers to calculate their earnings and expenditures. These were sufficient incentives for whites to maintain black illiteracy—or to place certain limits on how much knowledge blacks should acquire."[48] This recognition echoed a desire for a servile labor force, of course, but also reflected a worry that educated blacks posed a threat. In 1903, South Carolina congressman Ben "Pitchfork" Tillman declared that "every man who can look beyond his nose can see that, with Negroes constantly going to school, the increasing number of people who can read and write among the colored race will in time encroach upon and reach and over-balance our white men." In short, black education threatened white hegemony. As many whites saw it, not only did this demand a violent response, which Wells condemned in her anti-lynching campaign, it also required an ideological one.[49]

Other white intellectuals took a somewhat different position. Influenced by Darwinian ideas about evolution, they argued that black intellectual deficiencies also had environmental roots. According to Professor Kelly Miller of Hampton Institute, blacks and whites were "separated by many centuries of development," which could not be bridged by schools alone. "Education may assist," he declared, "but it cannot supplant evolution." Such commentators felt that education could help African Americans, but only over many generations. "The progress of the race," Miller wrote, "must be provokingly slow as compared with that of the individual."[50] The implications for education were clear: "The education of a people should be conditioned upon their capacity, social environment, and the probable life which they are to lead in the immediate future."[51] Racial equality in education was hardly imminent.

Emancipation did little to alter prevailing beliefs regarding black intellect, but attention did turn to other aspects of African American schooling. While many whites opposed any black education, some felt that basic elementary instruction could help African Americans better adapt to the duties of citizenship. A smaller number advocated higher schools of one sort or another for future leaders. All thought that blacks most needed moral and behavioral guidance to become worthy citizens. For them, the Color of Mind was a matter of "character" and "temperament" more than intellectual ability. They too believed in industrial education, but not simply because they felt blacks were incapable of demanding academic work.

General Samuel Armstrong, founder of Hampton Institute and an influential educator, fell into this category. He sought to teach blacks to accept their place in the social order, and believed manual labor to be the appropriate purpose of their schooling. Armstrong and his peers also advocated black political exclusion, mainly on moral grounds. In his view, blacks were not only intellectually deficient but also "morally feeble." This constellation of ideas reflected the evolution of the Color of Mind. According to Armstrong, the most important problem with the black race was "not one of brains, but of right instincts, of morals and hard work."[52] While purported distinctions in intelligence remained central to the dominant racial narrative, in keeping with Mrs. Moore's public curriculum, differences in character and conduct also were seen as part of the problem after emancipation. The academically inferior schooling that these ideas justified also contributed to the systematic subordination of African Americans.

This emphasis on morals and hard work, or on culture as it would come to be described, was a view that became more influential with time. Writing in 1891, and anticipating later arguments about black inferiority, J. L. M. Curry of the Slater Fund identified the chief obstacle facing African Americans in largely cultural terms: a "lack of self-restraint, of obedience to moral law, of chastity, of a sense of the difference between emotional religion and living rightly, [that] is too notorious to require the adduction [sic] of proof." Curry was a leading Southern educational reformer, and in his mind the principal value of industrial education thus lay not in the applied skills it provided but rather in the values it represented. "Manual training as fostered by the Fund," he declared, "should not be, primarily, to make engineers, architects, carpenters, brick masons, of pupils. The object should rather be to modify traditional methods so as to make more useful members of society." The goal was principally moral rather than practical, developing "the consciousness of inventive and constructive faculty, the cultivation of the perceptive powers, the appreciation of the dignity and value of intelligent work, the widening of wants, [to] lift the negro [sic] out of degrading environments into the responsibilities and aspirations of manhood." Such were the chief perceived "deficiencies" associated with blacks, "whether they be racial or the result of environments," and industrial training was deemed "the most important factor in the proper education" apart from religion.[53]

Such views were hardly at odds with the egalitarian ideals of American society, provided that egalitarianism was understood to be racially qualified. As Curry pointed out, in the end it mattered little whether these shortcomings were the result of innate or environmental factors affecting African Americans. A particular form of education was deemed best for them, one quite different from that provided for whites. Given this, distributive justice, or matters of fairness in the distribution of societal benefits and burdens, was taken to demand equality only for equals. Thus, what remained distinctive about the brand of qualified egalitarianism that developed in nineteenth-century America was that it was deeply racialized. This had profound implications for racial distinctions in everyday schooling, and resulting group differences in education and attainment.

Identifying the Racial Achievement Gap

Given the extensive inequities in education between blacks and whites in the United States during the nineteenth century, and resulting opportunity gaps, it would be surprising indeed if there were not a sizable racial gap in academic achievement at the period's end. The Color of Mind was utilized to justify unequal education for African Americans, where any was offered.

And it justified the denial of education to many, especially in the South. Systematic evidence on academic achievement during this time is quite limited, but where it does exist, racial gaps in both attainment (levels of education) and achievement (measureable knowledge and skill) are clearly apparent. This evidence, of course, was simply a prelude to the considerably more methodical examination of such disparities in decades to come.

Perhaps the earliest systematic evidence of racial differences in educational outcomes is offered in Joel Perlmann's study of Providence, Rhode Island, during the period between 1880 and 1935. As indicated earlier, Perlmann found that African American school enrollment rates were quite high in the nineteenth century, but that attainment levels—the grade levels black students reached—were lower than for other groups of children, including immigrants. At age fifteen in 1911, the mean attainment of black students was the middle of the seventh grade, while for immigrant children it was the beginning of ninth grade. Racial differences on this measure were similar in other Northern cities as well. Related to this, grade-point averages (GPAs) for black students in Providence also were consistently lower than for other groups of students. Some of these differences undoubtedly reflected the lower socioeconomic circumstances of black families: African Americans were twice as likely to be employed in the lowest strata of jobs as any other group, and their wages were typically lower than for whites in such positions. But black GPAs were lower even within this occupational category, suggesting that discrimination also may have been a factor. Despite their high rates of attendance, black students did not fare as well as their white peers in the public schools of Providence and other Northern cities.[54]

These patterns were also evident in the numbers of black students who advanced to public high schools, which required good grades and passing a competitive examination in the nineteenth century. In 1880, fewer than 4 percent of Providence's African American students accomplished this, a rate similar to foreign-born immigrant children, who had much lower overall enrollment rates. By 1900, the black rate of high school enrollment was about 12 percent, and by 1925 it had increased to 30 percent, but in both cases it was still below the levels of immigrants and native-born whites, more than half of whom attended secondary school by the latter date. Moreover, African American students were overrepresented in so-called technical high school subjects such as industrial education and home economics. In this respect, their circumstances were similar to racial peers in the South, who were directed away from academic classes in favor of subjects deemed suitable for their presumed abilities and interests. Black education may not have been formally separate in Providence, but it was still quite unequal.[55]

While black students in Providence clearly had greater access to education than their peers in the South (and many Southern whites as well), they continued to lag behind proximate white attainment rates throughout the late nineteenth and early twentieth centuries. They also were tracked into classes that would do little to advance their academic ability. This was telling evidence of racial differences in academic accomplishment, indicative of achievement levels. But this is an *indirect* assessment of a racial distinction in achievement. To directly consider racial gaps in knowledge and skills, or what we now call the racial achievement gap, it is necessary to examine yet a different form of historical evidence.

The Color of Mind Goes to War

As the United States entered World War I in 1917, the Army decided to utilize an early IQ test to help determine which of more than a million draftees would be eligible for officer training. Harvard psychologist Robert Yerkes persuaded military leaders to consider this, and the result was the now famous Army Alpha and Beta tests, the first mass deployment of standardized assessments in American history. Although the Army made limited use of the tests' results in identifying officer candidates, it did help to legitimize such testing as a measurement of human abilities, establishing it as an important branch of psychological and educational research. The Army testing program thus was deemed a success by Yerkes and his colleagues, and became the foundation on which other such instruments were built. The tests also confirmed long-standing conceptions of ethnic and racial differences in intelligence, offering seemingly scientific evidence of native white superiority over African Americans and other ethnic and racial groups.

In subsequent reports, psychologists who assessed the Army IQ test results left little doubt about such racial differences. They noted that native-born white men scored the highest on the tests as a group, followed by immigrants and blacks. Overall, black scores on the Alpha exam, designed for literate recruits, were little more than half the value of white scores. Yerkes and his colleagues classified 89 percent of African Americans who took the test as "moronic." Despite the fact that he reported a high (.75) correlation between the education level of recruits and scores on the Alpha exam, Yerkes insisted that the "examinations were originally intended, and are now definitely known, to measure native intellectual ability."[56] With black recruits scoring so low, this seemed to solidly confirm the Color of Mind, and blacks were declared inferior to whites in intelligence. Eugenicists cited these results to protect white "racial purity," and politicians called on them to defend restricting large-scale immigration from certain parts of the world.[57]

The results of the 1917 Army IQ test eventually became a source of academic controversy, especially after Harvard anthropologist Ashley Montague pointed out in 1945 that blacks from most Northern states had scored higher on the Alpha test than whites from the South. Consequently, Montague suggested that "socioeconomic conditions" and not inherent differences in intelligence were responsible for variation in test results. This eventually led other scholars to examine the data even more carefully, using more sophisticated methods of econometric inquiry to identify factors associated with differences in the scores. In a more recent statistical analysis, Fred J. Galloway determined that educational differences across the states, particularly both the quantity and the quality of schooling, measured by the length of terms and amount of expenditures, along with enrollment levels, were the most important determinants of test score variation. As such, his study confirmed Montague's analysis, conducted nearly fifty years earlier, in that "differences in socioeconomic history, rather than differences in innate ability, were to blame for the observed Army Alpha score differentials."[58]

Although not exactly an achievement test, the Army Alpha was largely an examination of verbal comprehension, numerical skill, and "knowledge of information," much of which was taught in schools. It was administered to more than half a million American men and thus was generally representative of the population, or at least the male half of it. Galloway's analysis, and those of other scholars, drawing on a sample of more than thirty-two thousand, clearly demonstrated that inferior educational experiences afforded African Americans in the South—rationalized by the Color of Mind—accounted for the largest portion of black-white test score differences. This was the earliest comprehensive assessment of a racial achievement gap in history. While the test did not assess knowledge in specific subjects, it did offer a global indication of essential academic skills. And the results were clearly linked to schooling. When racially unequal conditions across the states were statistically controlled, most of the gap in test scores disappeared. In other words, African Americans who received equivalent levels of formal education, including comparable school terms and expenditures, performed about the same on the test as whites.[59]

This is compelling evidence of the impact of unequal education on African American academic performance and perceptions linked to the Color of Mind. As Galloway stated, "The results leave little doubt that the institutionalized racism that pervaded the educational system in this country at the turn of the century was, to a large extent, responsible for the Black-White score differential on the 1917 Army Alpha."[60] This indicates that the racial achievement gap then revealed was principally the product of inferior and unequal education, or racial opportunity gaps, which were a consequence of policies premised on the Color of Mind, a belief in the mental inferiority of African Americans. These test results, of course, only served to further legitimize the Color of Mind at the time, leading to restricted educational resources for future generations of black students. The racial opportunity gaps were thus sustained, and the "educational debt" of African Americans continued to accumulate.

Echoes of David Walker's Appeal

Thomas Jefferson, his contemporaries, and subsequent generations of antebellum and Reconstruction-era Americans debated whether purported cognitive, character, and conduct differences between blacks and whites were a product of nature or the environment, whether blacks were educable and, if so, how and what they should be taught. But few, if any, thought that blacks could ever be equal to whites in intelligence or cognitive achievement, that black minds could ever be equal to white minds. Indeed, many concluded that educating blacks for anything other than servile labor or vocational training was a waste of time and resources.

In addition to being brutally enforced at times, the Color of Mind pervaded the institution of public education in ways that made the racial attainment and achievement gap a foregone conclusion. Although the original interpretation of Army Alpha test results was lamentable, it was hardly surprising. And the irony of all this was certainly not lost on critics of the Color of Mind, who recognized that the racial achievement gap was largely a *product* of inferior and unequal education. As David Walker, Boston's black printer and agitator, passionately observed in 1829, "They beat us inhumanely, sometimes almost to death, for attempting to inform ourselves, by reading the *Word* of our Maker, and at the same time tell us that we are beings *void of intellect!!!*" (emphasis in original).[61] In the next chapter, we hear from more such critics, who like James McCune Smith, Frederick Douglass, and Sarah Parker Redmond challenged the Color of Mind, not only in deed but by affirming the equal dignity of black humanity and advocating for improved black education.

FOUR

Voices of Dissent: Dispelling an Inglorious Fallacy

In 1923, Princeton psychology professor Carl Brigham published *A Study of American Intelligence*, a book about the Army IQ testing that documented alleged differences in intelligence between native-born whites and various immigrant groups. It also observed that blacks underperformed whites, which invited the question: Did this racial achievement gap stem from "innate" racial differences in intelligence, or was it due to unequal opportunities to learn? In other words, was it caused by the Color of Mind, or was the color of schooling to blame?

Brigham offered conflicting answers. On the one hand, he claimed, "it is absurd to attribute all differences found between northern and southern negroes [*sic*] to superior educational opportunities." However, at the same time he argued that social position itself was evidence of "superior intelligence," and that "educational institutions are themselves a part of our own racial heritage."[1] So, while Brigham conceded that better-educated blacks were "smarter" than their group average, suggesting that test score gaps could be influenced by racial differences in education, he also claimed that schooling could not be their principal cause. This left the door open to innate racial differences in explaining test results.

Although Brigham would later resolve this dilemma by unequivocally linking standardized test score differences to unequal schooling, the popular impression that racial differences in intelligence were innate proved slow to change. Indeed, as the twentieth century unfolded, this "scientific" vindication of the Color of Mind provided a ready source of support to white supremacist segregationists. This group eventually included opponents of the *Brown v. Board of Education* decision by the US Supreme Court in the 1950s, who sought to reverse its ruling and halt the expansion of African American educational opportunity that occurred in its wake.

Despite his changing views on testing, Professor Brigham never did re-
nounce racism, lamenting that the "importation" of blacks was "the most
sinister development in the history of this country."[2] Many people before
and after him agreed. And they cited the alleged innate intellectual inferiority of African Americans to defend denying or constraining black educational opportunities. These proponents of the Color of Mind gave voices of
dissent seeking to affirm black dignity much to take issue with. Generations
of white and black intellectuals, from W. E. B. Du Bois to Langston Hughes,
Ralph Ellison, and James Baldwin, challenged the myth of African American
inferiority. As Du Bois himself observed: "I was a part of the movement that
sought to set the accomplishments of Negro ability before the world."[3] In
doing so, he and his compatriots paved the way for a revolution in educational thinking, culminating in the historic *Brown* decision of 1954.

An Inglorious Fallacy

Upon its publication, *A Study of American Intelligence* was hailed as scientific
proof of why immigration restriction was crucial for national racial purity.
Brigham readily acknowledged an intellectual debt to Madison Grant, an
influential New York attorney who argued strenuously against mixing the
country's racial and ethnic groups. In Brigham's words, "It is a foregone
conclusion that this future blended American will be less intelligent than
the present native born American."[4] However, unlike Grant, Brigham was
able to utilize his academic credentials to provide the Color of Mind with
an authoritative endorsement. After his intelligence study was published, he
served as chair of the College Board and played a leading role in the development of its Scholastic Aptitude Test (SAT). Brigham's career thus linked the
infamous Army Alpha IQ test, which applied a scientific veneer to the idea of
heritable racial differences in intelligence, to the subsequent development of
standardized testing as a major component of American education.

   In the second decade of the twentieth century, the attention of racially
minded observers shifted to differences between various European groups,
particularly those who had arrived during the preceding decades, such as
the Italians, Poles, and Russian Jews. The perceived mental abilities of these
groups were contrasted with so-called Anglo-Saxons or Nordic people, who
were deemed superior.[5] After World War I, the results of the Army IQ test
were invoked to support arguments about the intelligence levels of immigrant groups. Polish recruits, for instance, performed at the bottom of whites
on the Alpha test, only slightly better than African Americans, and Italians
scored only a little higher. Of course, these were groups that migrated from

countries or regions with comparatively few schools, and their children dropped out earlier than those from other groups. But these facts were ignored, and Brigham and other commentators remained worried that these foreign "races" posed a danger of diminishing the intellectual capacity of the nation.[6] Such reasoning, of course, was employed before these groups "became white."[7]

In 1916, Madison Grant, an amateur anthropologist, sounded an alarm about the looming racial contamination of "pure" Nordic intelligence. In his book, *The Passing of the Great Race*, Grant argued that the immigrants from northern Europe represented the pinnacle of human development, and that other groups trailed them, especially those from eastern and southern Europe. He warned that social intermingling in American society threatened to "dilute" the nation's stock of intelligence and ingenuity. Grant was a major proponent of eugenics, a movement to promote human betterment through selective breeding. Its followers believed in racial purity and favored segregation of groups deemed inferior, along with systematic sterilization of those deemed "defective." Although it never attained a mass following, eugenics nevertheless exerted considerable influence. In addition, until his death in 1937, Grant served as vice president of the Immigration Restriction League, which lobbied for limiting immigration from parts of the world judged to have inferior races. His influence was evident in the Immigration Act of 1924, which sharply restricted immigrants from southern and eastern Europe, while permitting larger numbers from England, Germany, and other northern European countries considered more advanced.

Although Brigham was indebted to Grant, he eventually realized the limits of standardized testing. Indeed, he later repudiated the idea that standardized tests such as the Army Alpha or the SAT could be used to measure innate intelligence differences. In 1934, he wrote that the testing movement had been "accompanied by one of the most glorious fallacies in the history of science, namely, that tests measured native intelligence purely and simply without regard to training and schooling. I hope nobody believes that now." Unfortunately, Brigham's recantation of his earlier insistence that tests measured heritable differences in intelligence was not widely publicized, and it came too late to impact prevailing ideas on the topic.[8] Those seeking to preserve the Jim Crow status quo in schooling utilized his earlier work, and the Color of Mind continued to shape popular thinking.

The glorious, or better yet, inglorious fallacy gained significant attention with the arrival of thousands of Southern blacks in Northern cities during the war years and immediately afterward. In 1920, Lothrop Stoddard published *The Rising Tide of Color: The Threat against White World-Supremacy*, a call for eugenic segregation to forestall racial amalgamation and the loss of white hegemony around the globe. Stoddard also was a protégé of Grant's, though his ideas more closely matched those articulated by Mrs. Moore in 1863. Of the nation's many racial and ethnic groups, it was African Americans that Stoddard judged the most debased. He asserted that until Europeans arrived in Africa, "the black man vegetated in savage obscurity, his habitat being well named the 'Dark Continent.'"[9] Stoddard believed that the black presence in America continued to threaten the purity of unadulterated whiteness.

Altogether, during these early decades of the 1900s, Grant, Stoddard, Brigham, and like-minded thinkers ushered the Color of Mind into the new century. It was developed, extended, and given "scientific" creditability, thereby ensuring that it would continue to exert influence on schooling and other facets of everyday life. Race thus remained a fundamental dividing line for differences in educational opportunity. Despite this, African American education continued to develop, due in part to the tireless efforts of black educators, including growing numbers of women, and other voices of dissent who shared a moral vision for racial uplift through education.

Reverence for Black Dignity

An especially powerful voice utilized a familiar ethical ideal to ground her advocacy of racial justice in education. Frances Ellen Watkins Harper anchored her argument against the Color of Mind in the ideal of reverence for black dignity. Harper called for blacks to be respected for their equal status as human beings created in the image of God. She also believed that blacks should be educated in ways that affirmed this status and, just as important, empowered them to secure it for themselves and others. Born in 1825 to a free black family of some means, Harper was a prominent literary figure — poet, essayist, and novelist — of the time, and much of her writing provided perspective on the plight of blacks. She was an influential participant in egalitarian movements for abolition and suffrage, and lectured around the country advocating for these causes. Harper completed formal schooling around the age of thirteen, but continued an informal process of education on her own. She received high praise from her contemporaries. In the words of one such admirer, "Frances E. W. Harper is one of the colored women of whom white women may be proud, and to whom the abolitionists can point and declare that a race which could show such women never ought to have been held in bondage."[10]

Some of Harper's most significant work was devoted to the cause of black uplift through education. In one of her many poems, "Learning to Read," she penned these verses:

> Very soon the Yankee teachers
> Came down and set up school;
> But, oh! how the Rebs did hate it, —
> It was agin' their rule.
>
> Our masters always tried to hide
> Book learning from our eyes;
> Knowledge didn't agree with slavery—
> 'Twould make us all too wise.[11]

Yet for Harper, education was not merely a matter of making blacks wise; it was also about the development of their character, or, as she put it, "a higher cultivation of all our spiritual faculties."[12] In her view, development of character would help blacks foster a spirit of self-sacrifice and integrity, resulting in the emergence of true manhood and womanhood vital to overcoming "the cause of crushed humanity" and realizing "the glorious idea of human brotherhood."[13]

In this way, Harper expressed Immanuel Kant's ethical concern with respect for the dignity of humanity, which she took to be a preeminent goal of black education. She argued that African Americans should be educated to develop the character they would need to be champions for black dignity. This was a core value of her philosophy of education. While Kant presented his moral vision in entirely secular terms, Harper articulated one in accordance with her Christian upbringing and training. Yet both thinkers were deeply concerned with reverence for humanity, with Harper believing that this moral imperative should direct, and be used to assess, America's treatment of blacks. As she put it, "The nation that has no reverence for man is also lacking in reverence for God and needs to be instructed."[14]

Harper did not stop here, however. She linked a vision of respecting the personhood or dignity of blacks explicitly to the demands of justice, thereby bridging her moral and political philosophies. Although never recognized as such, Harper may well have been the first American thinker to suggest that condemning dignitary harm was not only a moral imperative but an imperative of justice as well. Her pivotal connection between reverence for humanity and justice is expressed in the following passage:

But two things are wanting in American civilization—a keener and deeper, broader and tenderer sense of justice—a sense of humanity, which shall crystallize into the life of a nation the sentiment that justice, simple justice, is the right, not simply of the strong and powerful, but of the weakest and feeblest of all God's children; a deeper and broader humanity, which will teach men to look upon their feeble breth[r]en not as vermin to be crushed out, or beasts of burden to be bridled and bitted, but as the children of the living God.[15]

Harper's groundbreaking philosophical insight implores us to see all human beings—from the strongest to the feeblest—as possessing an inner worth and thus being equal in dignity. She took this to be an imperative of justice that could inform normative assessment of education practices. Later, in chapter 9, our argument that tracking, school discipline policies, and racial disproportionality in special education are unjust will likewise be informed by such a normative perspective, particularly on how these contemporary sorting practices sustain the perception that blacks do not have equal status as persons. In this regard, they constitute a dignitary injustice.

A Rising Tide of Black Education

Throughout the antebellum period, committed black educators and activists such as Frances Ellen Watkins Harper—propelled by a moral vision of reverence for black dignity—pushed for better schools while working to get the most out of educational institutions that served black children. There were successes and failures, of course, but not for lack of effort. In 1830, they successfully petitioned the Connecticut legislature for black schools in Hartford, though black activists in antebellum Baltimore did so without success, despite repeated efforts. In the 1840s, as noted earlier, black parents in Boston petitioned to end segregated schools, a controversy that culminated in the famous *Roberts v. City of Boston* case. There were many other such struggles seeking to expand educational opportunity, to affirm the dignity of African Americans, and to vindicate their claim to be treated as equals.[16] These efforts picked up considerably around the turn of the twentieth century, thanks to black women educators from the South and other important voices. Perhaps none was more influential during this time than Anna Julia Cooper, whose 1892 book, *A Voice from the South*, was a ringing endorsement for improved educational opportunities for black women. A teacher and principal at the famous M Street High School in Washington, DC, she was an eloquent and outspoken advocate for racial equality and freedom, and the significance of education for black dignity.[17]

Other pioneering black leaders such as Mary McLeod Bethune and Nannie Helen Burroughs devoted their lives to black education and expanding opportunities. They focused especially on the training of black girls and women, believing that it was essential not only for their well-being but also for the uplift of the race and society. Unlike Cooper, who joined Du Bois in advocating for black education in the liberal arts and sciences, Bethune and Burroughs followed Booker T. Washington's example at Tuskegee. While there was continued debate among them over what kind of education blacks should receive, for most black educators it was largely a question of how best to achieve greater black dignity, and to improve the lives of African Americans more generally. It was a dialogue about means more than ends in education, and all agreed that social, spiritual, and material uplift was the ultimate goal.[18]

As was the case in the nineteenth century, concerned white philanthropists also contributed to funding the expansion of black educational opportunity in the twentieth. For instance, black schools and educators in the South received support from Northern philanthropies such as the Julius Rosenwald Fund and the Anna T. Jeannes Foundation. In a period of less than twenty years, the former helped build nearly five thousand new schools, enhancing elementary education for about a third of the region's black population. The resources utilized to erect these institutions were drawn from foundation funds, local black donations, and limited public funding. African Americans raised more than $4 million to support these schools. While many parts of the South still lacked satisfactory facilities for black education in 1930, the Rosenwald schools helped a great deal. The Jeannes Foundation provided support for supervisory teachers who traveled the countryside to aid African American teachers, assisting with lesson planning, curriculum development, and school organization. This too was a valuable service, even if it also affected a minority of black schools.[19] These contributions were starts, but much work remained to be done.

Although the Washington model held sway over many whites too, larger systemic problems as well as continuing problems of access entrenched racial inequality in education. One of the most troublesome was the different pay scale for black and white teachers. Beginning in the latter half of the 1930s, it became the object of litigation conducted by the National Association for the Advancement of Colored People, or NAACP, marking the start of a strategy of carefully planned legal actions that eventually led to the *Brown* decision.[20] And these actions were successful, forcing school districts to compensate black teachers equally. Progress was slow, however, as change occurred incrementally, and conditions endured by millions of

African American children throughout the South continued to be deplorable, especially in rural communities. Black schools were small and poorly equipped, and their terms remained relatively short, while ever-greater numbers of white students attended larger consolidated institutions with substantial libraries, modern science equipment, and other amenities. Whites had longer school terms on average, and were transported in buses, while most black students still walked to school.[21]

Perhaps most significantly, growing numbers of white students attended public high schools, while only a small minority of African Americans had similar opportunities. Because the region's black population was still largely rural, relatively few could take advantage of the substantial black high schools located in cities. Migration to the cities and the growth of African American neighborhoods there put enormous pressure on these schools in any case, and many became overcrowded and somewhat poorly maintained as a consequence. Students used textbooks discarded by white institutions, and the libraries and lab facilities were rarely kept up to date. Still, some black high schools became outstanding institutions, such as the M Street High School (renamed Dunbar in 1906) in Washington, DC, where Mary Church Terrell and Anna Julia Cooper worked. Exceptional schools eventually developed in smaller communities too, such as in Caswell County, North Carolina, as described by historian Vanessa Siddle Walker.[22] Dedicated black teachers in these institutions provided a sound education to students able to attend, and the number of African Americans graduating from high school grew steadily. These accomplishments were sources of great pride, but it would be decades before black graduation rates began to approximate those of whites.[23]

African American educators and communities across the South strived against great odds to improve the educational opportunities available for their children. High schools established in the cities often featured an industrial or manual vocational education curriculum, to prepare students for "Negro" jobs, at least until the 1930s. This, of course, echoed nineteenth-century proposals for black schooling, which emphasized morality and vocational training rather than academic courses of study.[24] Such a curriculum also was consistent with prevailing views regarding the intellectual inferiority of African Americans, and popular doubts about providing advanced education of any sort for them. When proposals came for building new secondary schools for blacks in smaller cities and towns, white-controlled school boards often ignored them.[25] If such opportunities were to be made available, local African American communities had to use their own resources to make it happen.

Such initiatives could take a variety of forms, but usually entailed adding rooms and new classes to an existing institution. Sometimes it was a matter of enhancing the curriculum of country training schools, basic teacher-preparation institutions established in many areas of the South after 1911. More commonly, it meant building an addition to an existing elementary school, providing rooms for teaching secondary subjects. Lacking resources, most such "high schools" offered just two years of instruction, and the possibility of eventually earning a diploma at a city school. This was a big step, however, and typically meant that the students would be staying with relatives or friends in that city during the school year. But some managed to do it, and secondary enrollments began to increase slowly into the 1940s.[26] This grassroots expansion of African American schooling defied claims that blacks had little interest in education and were incapable of learning the "higher branches" of knowledge.

As limited as their secondary schooling was, significant numbers of those African Americans who did graduate were determined to continue their education. According to the census of 1940, black high school graduates were just as likely to enroll in college as whites, at a rate of about 25 percent for both groups.[27] Of course, given the scarcity of secondary schools for African Americans, the proportion actually attending college lagged far behind the corresponding number for whites. But the equal probability of college enrollment for high school graduates of both races was compelling evidence of the significance that African Americans attached to higher education.

Black institutions of higher learning eventually moved decisively away from the Tuskegee-Hampton model of industrial education that Washington and others had advocated. This was especially evident following 1920. Despite the efforts of white educators and foundations to retain a focus on vocational or industrial education, there was a decided drift toward the liberal arts. Reflecting the viewpoint of Du Bois and other critics of the "Tuskegee Machine," segregated black colleges in the South focused on preparing future leaders. These institutions enrolled the vast majority of African American collegians, and their graduates became educators and ministers, the largest categories of black professionals, along with lawyers, doctors, and other white-collar workers.[28] By the middle of the century, a small but growing educated black middle class existed in most large cities, anchoring their communities and providing ambitious students to attend local schools.

African Americans outside the South faced somewhat different circumstances, but they too struggled to realize greater opportunities for their children. In some places this meant supporting segregated institutions, much like in the South. This situation was especially prevalent in so-called border states,[29] where many Southern whites had settled and local customs reflected their preferences. Elsewhere, African American students had considerably greater access to secondary education, often in schools that were predominantly white.[30] Since the majority of blacks outside the South lived in large cities, these were urban institutions, and racial conflict at school was a common experience. If African American youth wanted a high school diploma in these settings, they often had to literally fight for it.[31]

Between 1910 and 1940, nearly 14 percent of the South's black population left the region for jobs or better living conditions. This marked the beginning stages of the Great Migration, which brought more than six million blacks to states in the North and West by 1970.[32] As urban black communities grew, some high schools became racially segregated due to housing discrimination. School district leaders saw integrated schools as troublesome and manipulated attendance boundaries to abet and maintain segregation. Predominantly black schools typically received less attention from the districts, and often became overcrowded as the black population grew. They consequently became known as inferior educational institutions. It was a process that eventually became quite commonplace in cities across the country.[33] Black education came to be widely viewed as substandard, because of the schools' relatively meager resources and also the Color of Mind presumption that African American students could not perform high-quality work.

Despite these challenges, black schooling advanced incrementally through the first half of the twentieth century. While the vast majority of black children did not attend high school, a growing number did, and the number of secondary graduates increased slowly but steadily. By 1940, they represented about 15 percent of African American youth. Black colleges and universities trained teachers and other professionals to serve the growing African American communities in the South and elsewhere.[34] This middle-class segment of the nation's black population, although much smaller than its white counterpart, provided critical leadership in establishing institutions that became a foundation on which further progress would be made.

In short, the ideological assault on black dignity that the Color of Mind represented did not go uncontested. In the nineteenth century, African Americans challenged it with a record of advances, as well as philosophical arguments. In the twentieth century, they did so by promulgating a moral vision for promoting black dignity and equality in education, and by continued personal and collective accomplishments that gave the lie to the Color of Mind. The authoritative voices of Frances Ellen Watkins Harper, Anna Julia Cooper, Mary Church Terrell, Mary McLeod Bethune, and Nannie Helen

Burroughs joined a chorus of others, including Booker T. Washington's and W. E. B. Du Bois's, to cultivate black educational accomplishment.

These and other African American leaders continually highlighted the importance of education, recognizing that the lack of schooling only helped perpetuate the myth of mental inferiority. The result was a recurrent campaign to establish more educational opportunities for blacks beyond the basic elementary level, even if most whites believed advanced education for blacks to be pointless, if not an abomination. The voices of dissent clearly understood the black predicament, which Frederick Douglass poignantly captured in 1849: "Our ignorance is pleaded as a reason for withholding our rights, while knowledge itself has been locked up from us."[35] It would take constant vigilance to fight this predicament, especially given the lasting influence of Carl Brigham's inglorious fallacy. However, other important developments would aid these efforts to dispel the Color of Mind and undo the color of schooling.

The Color of Mind in Retreat

The theory of inherent racial inequality gained new momentum thanks to Brigham, among others, who continued to proclaim black inferiority and to muster seemingly scientific support for it. However, as the twentieth century continued to unfold, resistance to the Color of Mind gained new momentum as well, owing to developments in a number of realms: chiefly the emerging academic discipline of anthropology, the fresh new black literature associated with the Harlem Renaissance, and the rise of brutally racist Nazi Germany.

With time, an interpretive framework took shape that competed with scientific racism for explaining differences in achievements and other aspects of life. Since before the abolitionist movement, critics of hereditarianism concerning race and mental traits had objected to that view on humanitarian, religious, and philosophical grounds.[36] Their critiques continued to appear in the twentieth century, but a new source of reproof came from the new scientific field of anthropology, with its cultural interpretation of human behavior and development. The leading figure in this process was Franz Boas, a German scholar trained in geography and physics who became a professor of anthropology at Columbia University.

Boas was educated in the German empiricist tradition of searching for facts and examining phenomena on their own terms rather than interpreting them from within a larger theoretical or ideological tradition. His fieldwork with indigenous peoples in the Canadian Northwest fueled his conviction

that culture and environment are predominant factors in social development, rather than race or inherited traits such as a fixed conception of intelligence. He refuted craniology studies by demonstrating that nutrition
and other environmental conditions affect variation in head and brain size.
He also rejected contemporary theories about the superiority of Western
civilization or modern American society, along with social Darwinist ideas
regarding the supposedly natural advantages of the wealthy.

By and large, Boas represented a view holding that people of all races possess equivalent endowments of natural ability, and that observable group
differences are products of history, especially the environmental and cultural conditions they experienced.[37] Regarding African Americans, he wrote
in 1911, "without doubt the great bulk of the individuals composing the
race are equal in mental aptitude to the bulk of our own people," and "it is
very improbable that the majority of individuals composing the white race
should possess greater ability than the Negro race." These were radically
egalitarian ideas at the time, and Boas never wavered from them.[38]

After Columbia University established the nation's first anthropology
department in 1896, Boas served as its chair and intellectual leader. Over
the next four decades, his students became influential leaders in the field,
and advanced the ideas of essential human equality and the importance of
cultural diversity in comprehending behavior and beliefs. Among them were
Alfred Kroeber, Ruth Benedict, and Margaret Mead, all well-known spokes-
persons for the Boasian perspective on the significance of environment in
shaping social injustice.[39] In particular, Benedict became quite active in promoting the view that the various racial groups of the world are the same in all
significant respects, and that tolerance of differences in physical appearance
and cultural heritage is essential to social progress. During World War II, she
coauthored *The Races of Mankind*, a pamphlet distributed widely to schools
and communities, which presented the scientific argument against inherent
racial differences in plain language and pictures. Both Mead and Benedict
were active in efforts to promote intercultural understanding though formal
curricula in public schools, especially during and after the war. This work did
much to advance the idea that observable differences in academic performance between various racial and ethnic groups in American society are the
product of environmental factors, including prejudice and discrimination.[40]

Scholarly writing rarely affects popular attitudes, but other developments
helped to undermine long-standing racially oppressive ideas. The experience of the Great Depression and World War II caused many Americans to
question prevailing theories of social superiority, especially those based on
race and social class. During the 1930s millions lost their jobs, shattering

illusions about the stability of social status and the promise of economic security. Socialists and communists gained credibility and helped foster new ideas about equality and social justice. More important, the rapid growth of industrial trade unions, particularly the Congress of Industrial Organizations (CIO), promoted ideals of brotherhood, unity, and fairness, and militated against exclusionary practices and divisiveness. Civil rights for African Americans began to emerge as an important national issue.[41] It was the start of an important shift in popular thinking about a range of social issues, including race.

At about the same time, black writers, artists, and other intellectuals started gaining national and international fame for their many accomplishments. Growing out of a 1920s movement known as the Harlem Renaissance, and rooted in the growing African American communities in Northern cities, black literature, music, and other artistic works received wide critical acclaim and a diverse popular following. "New Negro" authors such as Langston Hughes, Zora Neale Hurston, Claude McKay, and later Richard Wright and Ralph Ellison helped to redefine American letters, while musician Duke Ellington, actor Paul Robeson, and dancer Josephine Baker were celebrated in the performing arts. There were many others, marking a dramatic flowering of black literary and artistic achievement.[42] The many accolades received by these figures challenged the idea that African Americans were incapable of intellectual and creative accomplishment.

At the same time, black scholars were making important contributions to a number of academic fields, including educational research. They included historians such as Carter Woodson, Horace Mann Bond, and Rayford Logan; sociologists such as E. Franklin Frazier, St. Clair Drake, and Charles Johnson; and later other social scientists including Ralph Bunche and Alison Davis. A number of these figures contributed to a special issue of the prestigious *Annals of the American Academy of Social and Political Science* in 1928, focusing on problems in and prospects for the nation's black population. As a whole, their work challenged the presumption of innate mental differences distinguishing the races. Noting "Negroes, and increasing numbers of them, who are equal to, and above the average of the white nation," W. E. B. Du Bois argued that there was "no reason to believe that the possibility of improvement among blacks is not just as great as among whites."[43] Other contributors to the issue agreed, including editor Donald Young, a white sociologist who observed "the successful Negro in the professions is now a commonplace," and concluded that "the changes of the past fifteen years are of such a magnitude that a new accounting requires that old theories and attitudes be held up to the light of our newer knowledge."[44] By the end of the 1920s, black and white academics had clearly demonstrated many problems with the Color of Mind as an explanation of social and educational inequality.[45]

In a similar vein, social scientists began studying racism, particularly beliefs about black inferiority, as a social and psychological problem of whites, especially in the South. Referring to "white caste consciousness," sociologist Lewis Copeland documented the ideas of white women about African Americans, noting that many had become "emotive" in nature. Fisk University's Charles S. Johnson catalogued theories of racial differences from various periods, noting that several "museum pieces" from the past—such as the purported significance of skull sizes and shapes—still exerted influence. Johnson also wrote about the rise of Nazi ideas regarding Nordic superiority, expressing concern about their influence in Europe. For his part, Du Bois noted the pervasive effects of racial prejudice in predominantly white schools, the theme of his 1935 essay quoted earlier, wondering if most black students would be better off in schools of their own. In each of these instances, the hostility of whites toward other racial groups was treated as irrational and unreasonable.[46]

If the Great Depression raised questions about race and social status, World War II was yet another difficult period that brought about positive change. It arrived suddenly for Americans with the bombing of Pearl Harbor, but its greatest impact came with the US mobilization for a global conflict. The very fact of millions of men and women leaving the country to fight abroad, and the deployment of millions more to work in war industries, highlighted the need to fully utilize the nation's human resources. Consequently, discrimination against racial and ethnic minorities and women had a cost, raising critical questions about fair practices in the civilian workforce and the armed services.[47] African American union leader A. Philip Randolph organized a national March on Washington movement to protest discrimination in the military, resulting in an executive order from President Roosevelt in 1941 outlawing such practices in the government and companies with federal contracts. Touting the "four freedoms" that Roosevelt had declared in defining goals worth entering the conflict for, African American leaders pushed for change throughout the war years. Strikes and housing "riots" in Detroit and other industrial centers highlighted racial tensions that had to be addressed if the war effort was to proceed smoothly.[48]

Discord did occur, but it mainly underscored the need for unity. Discrimination against "enemy" groups such as Japanese Americans was rampant, and minority youth were violently attacked in Los Angeles and other cities as racial tensions escalated.[49] But the war also did much to diminish intolerance among many Americans. It was widely considered to be a good fight, intended to save democracy and turn back the forces of avarice and hatred. The opponents were contemptible, especially the Nazi regime in Germany. Consequently, the conflict helped Americans celebrate the nation's egalitarian traditions. Many thought of it as a struggle of democracy against totalitarianism, giving credence to pleas for equality and social justice.[50]

In many instances, the war effort itself contributed to greater interracial understanding. Increased integration in war industries provided new opportunities for black and white workers to interact and learn about one another. Collaboration in these settings often led to mutual respect and amity, resulting in friendships that would have been highly unlikely in earlier times. Similar dynamics existed in the armed forces, despite policies for formal segregation that existed throughout the war. While many black military men and women served in support roles, others were engaged in combat. On the battlefield, segregation often broke down, and white soldiers came to admire the bravery and skill of their black compatriots. Cases such as these helped to establish a new level of respect for African Americans. And this caused some whites to reconsider racist stereotypes they had grown up with.[51]

The struggle against Nazi Germany added another racial dimension to the war. Americans found themselves confronted by an explicit ideology of Aryan racial superiority that was used to justify military aggression. This was more than a little ironic, given the long history of racial oppression in the United States and its brutal legacy of violence against blacks. Indeed, Madison Grant and other eugenicists had influenced xenophobic Nazi ideas. Yet the battle against Nazism helped to turn many people against outright theories of racial predominance, perhaps for the first time in American history. It was the dawn of a new era in thinking about such questions.[52]

In engaging in a global war effort, the United States had to work with new allies, some of whom questioned its history of racial prejudice and exploitation. It also had to worry about the Russians citing segregation of blacks in Dixie to expose American hypocrisy.[53] These themes and worries extended into the postwar period as the nation entered into a protracted ideological and political confrontation with the communist Soviet Union. Labeled the Cold War, this conflict contributed to feelings of vulnerability in the United States, but also gave credence to the idea that Americans should set a democratic example for the world to follow. This was especially important as the nation attempted to form alliances with newly established nations in Africa and Asia. Its racism and discrimination were problems that the Soviets and their allies were quick to point to. Suddenly, the colonizing legacy of slavery and racism had become a strategic liability. Given this turn of events,

American leaders became quite interested in demonstrating that racial bigotry in the United States was a thing of the past.[54]

These developments were abetted by advances in the thinking of leading social scientists and other prominent public intellectuals, building on the work of Boas and other scholars, black and white, who had confronted racist ideology. Swedish economist Gunnar Myrdal published his classic work on American race relations, *An American Dilemma*, in 1944, suggesting that racism was an anachronistic holdover from the nineteenth century, an ugly remnant of slavery. Myrdal noted that practices of discrimination stood in stark contrast to American ideals of liberty and equality and accounted for the debased condition of most blacks. He rejected innate theories of racial difference, arguing that "white prejudice and discrimination keep the Negro low in standards of living, health, education, manners and morals. This, in its turn, gives support to white prejudice. White prejudice and Negro standards thus mutually 'cause' each other." Myrdal was optimistic that this could eventually be changed for the better with liberal reform of social conditions, including equal opportunities for education. He may have promulgated a rather naive view of racial discrimination rooted in Southern individual prejudice and ignorance, but it firmly rejected the idea of essential black inferiority.[55] Roosevelt's executive order banning discrimination at workplaces with federal war contracts was in step with this way of thinking, opening a wide field of wartime employment to African Americans. The demand for workers during this period helped launch a new migration of African Americans from the South into the industrial cities of the North and West, where they came to enjoy new freedoms and higher income along with greater educational opportunity. As Myrdal predicted, this too represented progress in race relations.[56]

These developments helped set the stage for a measured shift in American public opinion about race and discrimination. The Truman administration's decision to desegregate the armed forces soon after the war reflected this, as did new federal civil rights measures in the areas of housing and employment. Jackie Robinson's 1947 move from the Negro League's Kansas City Monarchs to the Brooklyn Dodgers, which broke the color barrier in major league sports, marked another transition, and this coming just over a decade after track star Jesse Owens won four gold medals in Hitler's Germany during the 1936 Summer Olympics. Black actors began finding more positive roles in Hollywood films, including *The Negro Soldier* in 1949. A United Nations panel of scientists issued a report in 1950 stating "that there was no scientific justification for race discrimination." This was the culmination of decades of work by Boas and other antiracist scholars, and national newspaper coverage gave it wide circulation. Old theories of inherent or genetic distinctions that underlay the Color of Mind were giving way to environmental or cultural explanations.[57]

Meanwhile, the NAACP, which had emerged as the nation's chief advocate for minority rights, undertook a series of legal challenges to segregation in education, most of them at the university level. Its legal team, led by Thurgood Marshall, argued that discrimination was inherently inconsistent with the basic principles of American life, including the legal system. An important precedent was set in 1947, when Mexican Americans successfully challenged Southern California's segregated school policies in *Mendez v. Westminster*, decided by a federal district court. At about the same time, NAACP lawyers began attacking similar policies requiring black children to attend separate schools, still widespread in the South and certain other parts of the country. It was a difficult legal strategy, requiring an expensive and time-consuming process of confronting individual districts in the hope that the federal courts would establish clear precedents extending beyond a particular school system or state. Within these constraints, the judicial challenges pushed forward.[58]

Saving Hearts and Minds

To separate [children] from others of similar age and qualifications solely because of their race generates a feeling of inferiority as to their status in the community that may affect their hearts and minds in a way unlikely ever to be undone.[59]

—*Brown v Board of Education*, 1954

A well-organized campaign of litigation gave rise to the monumental *Brown* decision by the US Supreme Court in 1954, an event that shook the very foundations of systematic racial inequality in education.[60] This ruling was a landmark in civil rights and educational history, but it also marked a triumph for the environmentalist interpretation of racial differences in ability and character. The court's finding that segregation is unavoidably discriminatory, damaging to the hearts and minds of black children, implicitly endorsed the view that blacks are just as capable of benefiting from education as whites, and that to deny them educational equality is tantamount to shortchanging their futures. In noting advances made since earlier times of severe inequities, Chief Justice Earl Warren observed, "Today, in contrast, many Negroes have achieved outstanding success in the arts and sciences as well as in the business and professional world."[61] With this statement, the presumption of black intellectual and academic inferiority was swept aside.

In support of its decision, in a now famous footnote, the court cited Kenneth and Mamie Clark's doll study showing that black children judged white dolls to be better than black ones, even though they recognized that the black dolls looked most like themselves. The court took this to be empirical proof of the adverse psychological effects of racial segregation on black students' motivation to learn and to benefit from education. Such an appeal to social science would not go unnoticed by staunch supporters of the racial status quo, including Carleton Putnam, a Northern airline executive who agreed with Alabama governor George Wallace and other white supremacists that racial segregation should remain in place.

In many respects, *Brown* and the decades of school desegregation battles that followed represented a high point for the environmentalist view regarding the causes of racial differences in achievement, graduation rates, and other indicators of academic success. Research on school integration has indicated that it has historically helped to boost black achievement substantially while having little adverse effect on the success of white students.[62] For the generation of black students who fought to see schools desegregated, the promise of an equal education was seen as a pathway out of poverty and discrimination. And for many it was. The problem, however, was that the apogee of the environmentalist moment was fleeting, and soon a new, somewhat modified form of the Color of Mind emerged to challenge it. Ironically, while this reaction began in the South, it was the nation's liberal supporters of desegregation and racial equality that helped to hasten its development. How and why this happened is described in the next chapter.

FIVE

"A Tangle of Pathology": The Color of Mind Takes a Cultural Turn

Sociologist Daniel Patrick Moynihan's federal memorandum, *The Negro Family: The Case for National Action* (also known as the Moynihan Report), caused quite a stir in 1965. It noted a high rate of single-parent households in black communities, leading to a greater probability of black children dropping out of school and engaging in deviant behaviors. Moynihan, at the time assistant secretary of labor in the Johnson administration, attributed this situation to historical factors dating to slavery and persistent black unemployment, resulting in a "matriarchal" community structure that "seriously retards the progress of the group as a whole." Describing black poverty and family structure as "a tangle of pathology," this document was widely interpreted as reflecting long-standing stereotypes about African American social behavior and values. Consequently, use of the term *cultural deprivation*, commonplace by the 1960s, became especially problematic, particularly in describing the condition of black children.[1]

Referring to children from impoverished backgrounds as "culturally deprived" began in the latter half of the 1950s and became widespread in the following decade. With respect to African Americans, it was typically seen as an improvement over hereditarian or strictly racial explanations of low achievement, as it suggested that social and economic factors were most significant. In the wake of the Moynihan Report, however, the term came under attack as being insensitive and misleading, and possibly an excuse for educators to disregard the education of black children. In the ensuing debate, some commentators suggested that it was actually white children who were culturally deprived, as they were denied access to the rich traditions of African Americans and other ethnic and racial minority groups. It was widely observed that the school represented a dominant white culture that many black children were required to acquire, whether they wanted to or not.[2]

The controversy came to a head in 1971, when Kenneth Clark, the re-nowned black psychologist, issued a sharp rebuke concerning the use of the term and similar expressions. He declared that students needed "to be free of this type of label; to be free of fashionable categorizing and educational stereotyping which subordinates their individuality to this catchall phrase, 'the disadvantaged.'" Clark did not dispute the idea that children from poor urban backgrounds often lagged behind their middle-class suburban peers academically. But he rejected the proposition that disadvantages such as these made children "uneducable," a term then gaining favor among some educators. Clark suggested that this usage reflected a subtle form of racism, wherein educators shift expectations for "darker skinned" students from poor backgrounds, after providing opportunities for "generations of poor urban whites in the past."[3]

Clark's insight was an important one, but it came at a point when popular attitudes about education and family background had already begun to shift toward cultural frames such as Moynihan's. Use of the terms *culturally deprived* and *disadvantaged* led to far-reaching perceptions that differences in achievement were a result of a home life that failed to impart the proper values, stimulation, and socialization experiences needed for school. While this may have represented a liberal shift in attitudes, observers such as Michael Harrington, Frank Riessman, and Moynihan, among others, made the case that culture explained differences in attitudes and performance in schools. Middle-class values were painted as advantageous qualities that low-income families simply did not have, consequently leaving them "deprived" and "deficient."[4] This development came to represent a cultural turn for the Color of Mind as popular conceptions of racial differences shifted away from matters of intellect to questions of behavior and values.

Despite the appearance of new explanations for racial achievement differences, hereditarian arguments occasionally resurfaced that invoked racial differences in cognition. This became clearly evident in a 1969 paper published in the *Harvard Educational Review* by Arthur Jensen, who claimed that educational programs were unlikely to improve the achievement of African Americans because of genetic factors. Jensen later recanted somewhat, suggesting that "there exists no scientifically satisfactory explanations" for racial IQ differences, but doggedly maintained that a "biological component" was probably involved. His paper ignited a firestorm of debate and a flurry of research focusing on the sources of variation in IQ and related measures, much of which shed little light on racial differences in achievement. In the end, Jensen's argument regarding a genetic basis for between-group variation in IQ was strictly correlational, not causal, as he utilized little or no genetic information to make such claims.[5] In this respect, his argument was similar to other proponents of the Color of Mind whose work relied principally on test score data.

Richard Herrnstein and Charles Murray made a similar argument twenty-five years later in *The Bell Curve: Intelligence and Class Structure in American Life*, a study based on analysis of data from the National Longitudinal Study of Youth. This book focused less on race than Jensen's work, arguing that IQ was a central factor in determining social status and success in many facets of life. Like other such studies, it was wholly correlational, and it failed to control for the effects of schooling in much of the analysis. Also like Jensen's work, genetic explanations of group differences were assumed rather than demonstrated causally. Subsequent studies demonstrated the many weaknesses of the book, which had been published without peer review.[6] Regardless of its critical reception, however, it spent fifteen weeks on the best seller list, selling more than half a million copies within a year of its publication. This was an astounding figure for a bulky, academic-style book, suggesting a high degree of public interest in its argument. Presuming that individuals predisposed to agree with Herrnstein and Murray were most likely to purchase it, the *public* response to *The Bell Curve* suggested that Americans still held a high degree of interest in arguments supporting innate or genetic explanations of differences in intelligence and social status.

The old hereditarian viewpoint may have fallen out of favor among scholars in the twentieth century, but it continued to exert considerable appeal for a sizable minority of Americans. Given the weight of scientific evidence against a clear link between phenotype and IQ or achievement, the appeal is difficult to explain apart from the persistence of ideas dating from the nineteenth century, if not earlier. The general decline of this viewpoint, however, did not mean that the Color of Mind had also diminished as an explanation of the achievement gap. The inherent differences argument, it seems, was replaced by one featuring dispositions and culture.

A New Era in Studying Disadvantage

During the postwar era, a shift in thinking occurred concerning racial distinctions in education and group behavioral traits. Genetic arguments lost ground and were replaced by cultural explanations to account for such differences. Researchers argued that minority and lower-class children, including poor whites, did not perform well in school because they had been "deprived" of opportunities to learn requisite social and linguistic skills. Consequently, compensatory education was deemed necessary to provide positive stimulation to increase the cognitive abilities and moral sensibilities of "disadvantaged" children who did not succeed academically.[7]

The initial discussion of cultural deprivation focused on social class rather than race or ethnicity. With publication of Frank Riessman's *The Culturally Deprived Child* in 1962, the term gained a more concrete definition rooted in poverty, irrespective of race. Riessman, a psychologist, argued that the condition was largely a matter of motivation and familiarity with academic expectations, emphasizing that most poor children were white.[8] Before long, however, the idea of cultural deprivation became associated in the public mind with African Americans and other racial or ethnic minority groups, especially Mexican Americans. This became evident as black communities grew in bigger cities and urban public school systems became majority African American. By the mid-1960s, popular accounts used the term increasingly in reference to schools and classrooms that were predominantly black or Hispanic. Poverty became highly racialized in the nation's larger metropolitan areas, and cultural deprivation was widely linked to segregated "slum" communities. As the *New York Times* reported in 1963, "Social workers have noted that Negro children from culturally deprived homes often lack simple communication skills—the ability to talk and read at a level equal to their intelligence."[9]

An extension of this reasoning was evident in president Lyndon Johnson's celebrated speech at Howard University in June 1965, in which he argued that black poverty was unlike the disadvantages suffered by other Americans. He called for programs and opportunities targeted to help African Americans overcome the accumulation of obstacles that they faced; these initiatives found expression in the term *affirmative action*. Historian Gareth Davies has suggested that the event became a telling moment in the national shift to viewing poverty increasingly in racial terms.[10] From that point forward, antipoverty initiatives would be linked in many people's minds with African Americans, especially in urban settings.

At first, the shift to cultural explanations for differences in academic achievement and behavior appeared to represent a positive change, a move away from genetic arguments, but it ultimately became clear that these distinct ideas, though from different periods, had been cut from similar ideological cloth. To be sure, linking the racial achievement gap to lack of learning opportunities, discrimination, and segregation did not seem to presume essential differences in intelligence or behavior. But the question of culture was different. Black crime rates, attitudes toward work, school dropout rates, and taste for certain types of music were invoked as evidence of cultural dispositions and preferences that undermined academic achievement.[11] While not exactly a genetic explanation of behavior, such factors still served to identify characteristics seemingly distinctive about African Americans that accounted for racial disadvantages. As such, these explanations helped to obscure just how the racial achievement gap was created, and the injustice in school practices that historically perpetuated it.

Litigating the Racial Achievement Gap

Somewhat ironically, cultural explanations of black underachievement occurred when African American education was improving rather dramatically. Black attainment surged forward in the postwar era, extending into the 1970s. The initial impetus for this was litigation launched by the National Association for the Advancement of Colored People (NAACP); it was challenging the unequal provision of public schooling on grounds of the "separate but equal" provision of the 1896 *Plessy v. Ferguson* case decided by the US Supreme Court. By this point, the federal courts were far more amenable to seeing education as a fundamental civic activity that fell within the purview of the Constitution's Fourteenth Amendment. While some Southern whites called for improved education for blacks, believing it essential to regional development, most remained indifferent or hostile to racial justice in education. Consequently, there was little doubt that utilizing the courts was essential to realizing change. When the NAACP shifted its focus from equitable funding to achieving integration, it began to win important cases challenging segregation at Southern universities in the years following World War II.[12]

Sensing their vulnerability to this litigation, Southern states began investing greater resources to "equalizing" black schools, spending more on education for blacks than whites in some instances. Most of this came into play between 1948 and 1953. Millions of dollars were spent to build modern, expanded elementary schools and new black high schools across the region. Enrollments surged upward throughout the 1950s. Funding increased for white education as well, which helped make these expenditures palatable to white voters. Most believed that improvements to black schools were necessary to forestall eventual desegregation. While this policy shift did not avert court-ordered school desegregation as planned, it did produce a significant infusion of new resources into black institutions and a dramatic improvement in attainment levels, particularly high school attendance and graduation.[13]

This equalization campaign built on the grassroots efforts of Southern black communities to expand and improve the meager educational facilities they had acquired under decades of Jim Crow segregation. Local activists had often built or expanded their schools with donated time and resources, but state funds provided by equalization measures accelerated these endeavors. Black children had been taught for generations in rundown single-room schools, many of which were now consolidated into new multiple-classroom facilities, with buses to bring students to school. New high schools significantly expanded opportunities for the generation of black students born after 1940. By 1960, a majority of African American youth were attending secondary schools for the first time in history, most of them in the South. It was a virtual revolution in educational attainment, in mostly still-segregated schools.[14]

The Supreme Court's *Brown v. Board of Education* decision in May 1954 ruled segregation in public schooling unlawful, dramatically reversing *Plessy* and signaling that the court considered equality of educational opportunity to be a critical facet of modern life. The court declared, moreover, that segregation itself represented discrimination and injustice. The ruling immediately affected thousands of children who lived in states and localities that responded positively to the decision. For those in most of the South, however, it had little immediate impact. State authorities across the region declared opposition to the very idea of racially integrated schooling, vowing to close the public schools in many instances rather than see black and white students attend them together.[15] Southern politicians rushed to oppose school desegregation. A hundred members of the US Congress signed a Southern Manifesto, labeling *Brown* a "clear abuse of judicial power" and vowing to use "all lawful means to bring about a reversal of this decision."[16]

In border states, which historically required segregated schooling, desegregation occurred much sooner. Missouri, Maryland, Kentucky, and West Virginia declared an end to separate schools within a year of *Brown*, although some localities took longer to change long-standing policies. The national media trumpeted the announcement of desegregated schools in Louisville, Baltimore, St. Louis, and Kansas City, although the actual success of desegregation varied a great deal. Even in the most dramatic cases of changed policy, the practice of desegregation was slow to take root.[17]

Where it did occur, school integration raised the issue of achievement differences between white children and impoverished blacks who had been educated in under-resourced schools. This is when terms such as *culturally deprived* started coming into widespread use. Many white families felt that integration threatened the quality of local schools, and long-standing perceptions about race and education resurfaced, regardless of the explanation. Whites quickly abandoned institutions where African Americans began to appear in substantial numbers.[18] Lasting desegregation was elusive from the start.

"Massive resistance" to desegregation from Southern whites, encouraged by political leaders, dominated the decade following *Brown*, especially in the former Confederate states. It resulted in flashpoints of violent confrontation, such as Clinton, Tennessee, in 1956 and Little Rock, Arkansas, the following year. Televised to a national audience, the latter instance resulted in President Eisenhower sending federal troops to enforce a court order permitting black students to attend the city's Central High School.[19] These events and others like them helped engender sympathy for blacks struggling to desegregate schools. Images of hysterical white protestors broadcast on television made Southern resistance to young black students appear irrational and hateful. And to make matters worse for the persistence of Jim Crow education, in 1963 Alabama governor George C. Wallace declared "segregation today, segregation tomorrow, segregation forever," playing to Southern white fears but sounding abhorrent to many others.[20]

Consequently, despite its symbolic power, the *Brown* decision did not immediately result in extensive change to racially unequal schooling. While growing numbers of white Americans were ready to entertain the idea that African Americans were entitled to equal rights, fewer were prepared to allow black children to attend school with their own sons and daughters. Even if they may have supported desegregation in theory, they often opposed it in practice. In everyday settings, it mattered little whether African American academic performance was explained in hereditarian or cultural terms. De facto Jim Crow segregation continued to be enforced throughout most of the South, and when it was formally ended, many whites fled neighborhoods and institutions where school desegregation was attempted.[21] The ideology of black inferiority remained a potent force in American life, even if its terms eventually shifted somewhat. Continued segregation, whether formal or de facto, contributed to widespread perceptions of inadequacy in African American schooling, which still fueled myths about racial differences in academic ability.

Segregationists Fight Back

Brown provoked a dramatic response from Southern conservatives vowing to preserve segregation at all costs. One aspect of this was a revival of traditional racist thought, holding blacks to be innately inferior to whites and thus unfit to attend schools with them. Like Carl Brigham and other adherents of the inherent differences argument decades earlier, proponents of this view used test score results to buttress their position that desegre-gated schooling would not help black children attain educational equal-ity. They also argued that desegregation would lower standards for white children, thus debasing their education. *Brown* also raised the specter of interracial sexuality, given the growth of white and black secondary enroll-ments and an increasingly permissive national youth culture that flour-ished in coeducational settings.[22] The mere possibility of this was enough to raise Southern white resistance to a fever pitch, readily apparent in Little Rock and other places where court-ordered school desegregation met fierce opposition.

A familiar defense of the Color of Mind surfaced soon after the *Brown* decision, and was featured in the September 21, 1956, edition of the conser-vative newsweekly *U.S. News and World Report*. Psychologist Frank McGurk argued that standardized test results indicated that black aptitudes were an impediment to desegregated schooling. "The vast improvements in the social and economic status of the Negro," he declared, "have not changed his relationship to the whites regarding capacity for education." The im-plication was that racial differences were innate and thus not amenable to change through education or improved social conditions. Consequently, McGurk suggested that schools remain segregated, so that children of each race could receive instruction best suited to their abilities.[23] He was quickly rebuffed by civil rights organizations, but it was a sign of things to come.

The Pioneer Fund, a foundation established by eugenics supporter and millionaire Wickliffe Preston Draper in 1937, financed opponents of *Brown* who focused on "scientific" arguments against desegregation. A 1913 Har-vard graduate born to an old New England family, Draper was resolutely opposed to racial integration of any kind. He provided generous funding to academics and other figures committed to making the argument against desegregation on seemingly scientific grounds. After being spurned by a number of distinguished geneticists, the Pioneer Fund began supporting a relatively small band of determined "scientific" segregationists.[24]

A seemingly unusual source produced an energetic defense of the original segregationist argument for separate and different. Carleton Putnam, like Draper, was a scion of an established New England family, a 1924 Princeton graduate who was also sympathetic to a eugenicist point of view. He had experienced success in business and served as president of Delta Airlines during the 1950s. Then in 1961, with support from Draper's Pioneer Fund, he published *Race and Reality, A Yankee View*, which vilified racial integra-tion and its supporters, whom Putnam viewed as "equalitarian" commu-nistic conspirators. For authority, the book cited, among others, the work of psychologist Henry Garrett of Columbia University and William Shockley, a Nobel Prize–winning physicist who became a professor at Stanford University and a eugenics supporter. Putnam revived arguments based on presumed genetic differences between the races. "When the Negro has bred out his limitations over hundreds, or thousands, of years," he wrote, "it will be time enough to consider absorbing him in any such massive doses as would be involved in the South today."[25] But in the meantime, Putnam was determined to see segregation maintained as essential to the preservation of white supremacy.

Coming from such a seemingly unlikely source, Putnam's work was enthusiastically received in the South, where white opponents to desegregation introduced him in packed public forums. *Race and Reality* sold more the 150,000 copies, many of them in Mississippi and Louisiana, where it was distributed to schools and white community groups. Putnam became a popular spokesman for the segregationist cause, and helped to bolster white-supremacist resolve to oppose school integration at all costs. He also helped to marshal support for a group of academic opponents of desegregation, mostly funded by the Pioneer Fund. These individuals also bolstered opposition to *Brown* as they prepared to challenge the decision based on presumably scientific evidence against integration in education.[26]

The so-called scientific segregationists attempted to use their arguments and evidence, mainly in the form of expert witnesses, to challenge desegregation in the federal courts. The most important of these cases were *Stell v. Savannah-Chatham County Board of Education* and *Evers v. Jackson Municipal Separate School District*, both argued in 1963. In each case, the strategy was to maintain that African Americans were not capable of success in white schools and would cause irreparable harm to students if desegregation were to be imposed. In *Stell*, a friendly district court judge indulged this testimony while the NAACP offered little counterargument, and the court ruled against the order to desegregate. This decision was summarily overturned by the Fifth Circuit Court of Appeals, which also reprimanded the judge for improperly using discretion in the ruling.[27] The court ruled alleged differences in intelligence or other attributes to be irrelevant to the rights of children for an equal education, just as the NAACP had maintained.

Putnam and the other segregationists had imagined *Stell* becoming a celebrated challenge to *Brown*, and were exhilarated by the initial judgment. But the allegedly scientific evidence that had been marshaled in the case did not have the planned effect. Instead, it revealed the limited legal impact of their outdated ideas about race and social inequality, and their isolation within the larger academic and scientific community. Given the circuit court decision in *Stell*, the judge in *Evers* decided in favor of desegregation, even though he agreed with the segregationist arguments. Although there were other cases, the failure in these instances "took the wind out" of the scientific segregationists' plan to overturn *Brown*.[28] Their defeat did not end the effort to argue that racial differences in achievement or other school outcomes were inherent or genetically based. But such studies lacked credibility as the body of scientific and social-science research shifted decidedly in favor of environmentalist views in the 1960s and beyond.

Mandating School Desegregation

These ideas were debated in the context of a rapidly changing policy landscape, especially after the latter half of the 1960s, when school desegregation became a compelling political issue for most Americans. Notwithstanding greater public receptiveness to the idea of school integration, resistance to desegregation proved largely effective until federal judges finally lost patience with Southern authorities, which took more than a decade. Many school districts and municipalities in that region adopted so-called voluntary desegregation plans, requiring black students to apply individually for transfers to white schools. This placed enormous pressure on families deciding to take this step, often involving threats of job loss and physical violence. Consequently, the pace of change was very slow and required continual pressure from the NAACP and other African American civil rights organizations.[29] It was not until a series of decisive Supreme Court decisions, particularly *Green v. New Kent County* in 1968, that Southern resistance finally was overcome. After that, change occurred quickly. By the early 1970s, desegregation had proceeded further in the South than in any other region.

Despite pockets of intransigence and the exodus of many white students to private segregated academies, especially in the former Confederate states, most public schools across the South were racially desegregated within five years. By 1973, a majority of the region's black high school students attended integrated institutions, nearly two decades after the *Brown* decision.[30] At about the same time, African American secondary attainment began to reach levels comparable to whites, the result of a long struggle to expand educational opportunities across the country. Following these developments, the black-white achievement gap, measured systematically by the National Assessment of Educational Progress (NAEP), began to shrink appreciably. Altogether, differences in the test scores of black and white students diminished by nearly half between 1970 and the latter 1980s, almost entirely due to improvements in African American performance.

Elsewhere, however, the struggle against segregated schooling was not so successful, and ideas about cultural deprivation connected to race began to take root. Almost half of all African Americans lived outside the South in 1970, and most were concentrated in large cities. This was a result of the Great Migration, when more than four million African Americans left the region following World War II. Most settled in rapidly growing ghetto communities in the North and West, where they encountered crowded, deteriorating schools and neighborhood crime and disorder.[31] It was these conditions, of course, that became associated with concepts of deficiency and disadvantage. Even so, the graduation rate of black students in these circumstances exceeded that of their counterparts in the South.[32] In this respect, the promise of migration as a search for opportunity was fulfilled, but there were problems too.

Before long, levels of school segregation in the North and West came to exceed those in the South, even though it was not legally required. This was "de facto" segregation, caused by dual housing markets that prevented African Americans from living outside certain neighborhoods. These housing trends were created and enforced by the real estate industry, with help from zoning requirements, restrictive covenants (until the 1950s), and government and bank mortgage policies. Since school districts were locally controlled and often conformed to community boundaries, housing segregation contributed directly to racially segregated schooling. Larger districts, typically in big cities, often abetted these tendencies by drawing school catchment areas to conform to racially defined neighborhoods. The result was a high degree of segregation by the latter half of the 1960s, along with the concentrated poverty that contributed directly to the cultural deprivation thesis.[33]

Given this situation, civil rights groups challenged the legality of school assignments based on such de facto patterns of racial segregation, ushering in a new phase of the civil rights battle for racial justice in education. The principal remedy that emerged from this litigation was busing students from one part of a school district to another, to create racially integrated classes at schools that were formerly segregated. A turning point outside the South came in the 1973 Supreme Court case *Keyes v. School District No. 1, Denver, Colorado*, when a majority of the justices agreed that the district "intentionally created and maintained the segregated character of the core city schools."[34] The result was a busing plan that established acceptable levels of both races at schools throughout the city. It was a solution to de facto segregation that was viable so long as there were enough children of both races to make districtwide integration feasible.[35]

By the mid-1970s, busing had emerged as a widespread response to segregated schooling, meeting a great deal of resistance from whites opposed to blacks enrolling in their schools. Changing conceptions of the Color of Mind did little to temper such reactions, as opponents of desegregation used the language of "cultural differences" to resist busing. In Kansas City, for instance, white parents complained that "children of a different (and supposedly lower) cultural level" would threaten the academic success of their own children.[36] Perhaps the most vehement and violent opposition, however, appeared in larger Northern cities such as Boston and Chicago, where black students were greeted with hostility and aggression. Scenes reminiscent of Little Rock nearly twenty years earlier appeared again on television. Old racist ideas were revived, and George Wallace ran a presidential campaign that drew surprising support from white working-class voters in the North. As black neighborhoods expanded, white families abandoned the cities, moving to largely middle-class suburbs in a process popularly known as "white flight."[37] As a consequence, urban school districts were transformed from predominantly white student bodies to a majority black population. This, of course, made it much harder to realize meaningful desegregation, as there were many fewer white students to help constitute integrated schools.[38]

These were changes that had already been under way in many larger cities; busing did not cause "white flight," but certainly accelerated it. Detroit's public schools turned majority black in 1963, Chicago's in 1966, and Kansas City's in 1970. As a consequence, black students were more likely to attend a segregated school in the Midwest and North in 1975 than in other regions. The promise of social justice and affirmation of black dignity that initially seemed so bright in the struggle against segregated schooling had dimmed appreciably.[39] The *Milliken v. Bradley* Supreme Court decision in 1974 ruled against a plan to bus students across district lines in metro Detroit, which would have sent African American students to the suburbs and white suburban kids to city schools. The court asserted that unless suburban districts had intentionally contributed to segregation within the city, they could not be compelled to participate in busing. *Milliken* thus effectively precluded cross-district busing for integration in most Northern metropolitan areas.[40]

In the South, on the other hand, busing turned out to be considerably more successful, although it was growing ever more unpopular everywhere, especially among whites. Southern school districts were commonly organized on a county basis. This reflected the region's agricultural roots, but meant that many school districts eventually spanned both urban core and suburban communities. The *Milliken* ruling, consequently, did not apply in these cases, and students from both city and suburban schools could be bused, so long as they were in the same district. As a result, the most successful desegregation plans occurred in the South. These included the Charlotte-Mecklenburg schools in North Carolina, the first general busing plan approved by the Supreme Court in 1971, and widely judged to be among the most comprehensive and effective. Busing in Southern districts contributed to the region's overall advantage in desegregating public schools.[41]

Struggles over desegregation and justice prompted debate about observable racial differences in academic success. It also occasioned concern about a "crisis" of urban education linked to the perceived decline in schools that transitioned from majority white to African American. These circumstances contributed to the cultural turn in the Color of Mind. When racial transition in the schools became associated with higher dropout rates and lower test scores, many whites assumed it was due to a lack of commitment to education in black communities. It was in this context that the terms *disadvantaged* and *culturally deprived* became most widely used, particularly with regard to poor African Americans and other minority group members, especially Hispanics.[42] This was hardly a recipe for enhancing the dignity of these students.

All this added controversy to urban education, but relatively few observers took note of what actually was occurring in the schools. Amid the talk about failing institutions and higher dropout rates, African American high school graduation rates continued to improve through the 1960s and into the seventies, even in the larger cities. Although dropout rates and other problems were higher than when schools were white, they represented a significant improvement for most black students.[43] Many problems still existed, of course, but African American educational performance showed substantial progress by the 1970s.

Accountability and Achievement

The election in 1980 of conservative Republican Ronald Reagan to the presidency represented a watershed in prevailing attitudes regarding the fundamental purposes of public education. The federal focus on social justice and desegregation, which had been constrained somewhat since Richard Nixon's election in 1968, gave way to a new emphasis on academic achievement and accountability. This was highlighted in the 1983 "A Nation at Risk" report by the presidentially appointed "National Commission on Excellence in Education," which aimed to improve the quality of American schools.[44] Although some desegregation cases continued to go forward, public opinion regarding their efficacy turned decidedly negative. Disenchanted by busing, many Americans concluded that desegregation did not seem practicable and had failed to live up to expectations. Even though there was abundant evidence of success in desegregated schools, popular outcry pilloried policies that appeared threatening to whites. The Color of Mind was revived under changing conditions. With this, a new era in the continuing saga regarding race and education began, one that eventually drew greater public attention to the matter of racial differences in educational achievement.[45]

The years following 1980 witnessed an "educational excellence" movement, which created interest in standardized measures of educational achievement framed in terms of educational "accountability." This movement was abetted by the development of curriculum standards to ensure higher achievement, accompanied by a proliferation of standardized assessments. In step with such efforts at "systemic reform," a series of national commissions set ambitious goals for improving the performance of American students, especially in light of global studies that showed them lagging behind their international peers. Initiatives such as these helped set the stage for racial achievement gaps to become a growing national concern.[46]

In certain respects, the 1980s brought good news regarding academic achievement differences. As noted earlier, African American students exhibited steadily rising scores on the NAEP, closing the gap with whites by more than half by 1988. Research showed that it was the children of educated, middle-class black parents who exhibited the biggest gains in achievement, and desegregated schooling may have contributed too. This was symptomatic of the growing black middle class, typically college educated, moving out of traditionally impoverished neighborhoods and seeking better opportunities for their children. The rapid gains in black educational attainment during the sixties and seventies, evident in rising secondary and postsecondary graduation rates, bore fruit in the next generation.[47] At the same time, however, the seeds of new problems were sowed that would eventually prove to be critical obstacles to further progress.

While some successful African Americans were able to leave their historic urban ghetto communities by the latter half of the 1970s, millions remained, constrained by a lack of options in segregated housing markets. At the same time, the low-skill jobs that had drawn their families out of the rural South began to disappear, moving elsewhere or being eliminated by technology. The result was rising levels of unemployment and a host of related social problems. As documented by William Julius Wilson and other social scientists, growing joblessness contributed to greater instability in black families, higher levels of poverty, and increased crime and drug use.[48] Heightened law enforcement, "zero-tolerance" discipline policies in the schools, and stricter sentencing guidelines in the latter years of the decade contributed to a rising number of incarcerated young black males, issues discussed in greater depth in the next chapter.[49] Dropout rates in inner-city high schools increased, and achievement scores stagnated. Changes in federal financial aid initiated by the Reagan administration contributed to a drop in black college enrollment. These developments marked an end to the progress that had been exhibited in NAEP scores through much of the decade, giving rise to a growing public awareness of racial differences in academic achievement.[50]

As the standards and accountability movement in education gained national momentum in the 1990s, standardized test scores became a growing concern. President Clinton's 1996 condemnation of "social promotion" during a State of the Union address signaled heightened popular support for clear measures of academic performance.[51] Growing numbers of students attended racially separate schools due to gradual resegregation in many districts, and racial differences in test scores became increasingly evident. The publication in 1998 of "The Black-White Test Score Gap," a compendium of research edited by Christopher Jencks and Meredith Phillips, called attention to the issue. Unlike previous treatments of racial test score disparity, Jencks, Phillips, and their collaborators did not suggest that it was caused by cultural differences or heritable IQ distinctions. Because these tests were linked to improved curricular standards, they were widely considered to be a reflection of schools as well as student performance. As Jencks argued, the "gap" reflected substantial differences in skills, linked to readiness for various types of employment, especially in the economy's rapidly growing service sector. This in turn linked the "achievement gap" to the crisis in employment faced by many urban black communities.[52] After decades of progress, it appeared that African American education had reached a critical impasse.

Events in the ensuing years have done little to change this perception, and recently it has grown more widespread. The major educational reform thrust of the early twenty-first century was No Child Left Behind, a major federal program of incentives to improve schools based on standardized assessments. President George W. Bush initiated the program with support from congressional Democrats and civil rights groups interested in improving education for blacks and other minority groups. The heightened attention to the testing results certainly raised national awareness of the achievement gap, but progress was slow. While the legislation required schools and districts to focus attention on closing racial achievement gaps, the results were uneven and did not begin to match the gains of the 1970s and 1980s. Without significant additional resources for the schools and attention given to segregation and issues of concentrated poverty and the disparities they occasioned, assessment alone proved insufficient to substantially improve black educational performance.[53] After a time of great advances, improvement had largely stalled.[54]

An Unintended yet Pernicious Consequence

The cultural turn in racial discourse, the limited but notable success of desegregation, and the rise of a substantial black middle class led many Americans, most of them white, to imagine that the country had moved beyond its brutal and oppressive racist past. A utopian post–civil rights understanding of America as a "colorblind" or "postracial" society, where all persons regardless of skin color are able to climb the ladder of opportunity, is consistent with philosopher John Rawls's ideal vision of a well-ordered society where race does not determine life's prospects.[55] But unfortunately, the United States at the end of the twentieth century was far from being so well ordered.[56] At most, postracialism was a vision of a possible future. However, the belief that it had been largely realized was a popular perspective that made the continuing pursuit of dignitary justice in education especially challenging.

Social and behavioral scientists, on the other hand, have quite clearly documented continuing racial disparities in education and social status. They show that progress on desegregation and the racial achievement gap stalled in the 1990s. And they have led the way in challenging new forms of the Color of Mind, especially cultural explanations of racial achievement differences, by supplying considerable evidence against them.[57] For instance, social psychological research was particularly useful in demonstrating the inadequacy of one-dimensional, individual-choice explanations of racial disparities in achievement. It also highlighted the relevance of contextual circumstances that shaped individual choices, both consciously and subconsciously. Psychologist Claude Steele's pioneering studies of stereotype threat provided an especially illuminating empirical account of racial test score differences, highlighting the problem's complexity by considering perceptions of inferiority and their effects on performance.[58] At the same time, however, cultural explanations of the achievement gap advanced by white and black conservatives as well as increasing numbers of liberal thinkers continued to resonate with both academic and lay audiences.[59]

The appearance of a new discourse in the 1990s concerning racial "gaps" in achievement was reminiscent of earlier academic and popular debates over intelligence and scholastic ability that had occurred in the latter half of the 1960s and the early seventies. The difference at the end of the century, however, was that Jencks and Phillips did not inspire the sort of response that Jensen and other IQ theorists had evoked nearly thirty years earlier. By the 1990s, the focal point of achievement gap scholarship was the improvement of school outcomes, not the classification of students according to allegedly fixed measurements of "intelligence." Publication of the *Bell Curve*, despite its popular reception, did little to change this. New forms of remedial programming or targeted "comprehensive" school reform measures were developed to address newly identified achievement gaps. Organizational changes were made to districts and schools to improve instruction and consequently achievement. The effects were modest, to say the least, but equality of educational opportunity remained a focal point of public discourse.

In addition, and most significantly, sorting practices were taking place within racially integrated schools feeling the pressure to raise test scores and close achievement gaps, despite mandates to increase achievement for all groups. This had the rather pernicious yet unintended consequence of sustaining the view that blacks were inferior to whites in intellect, character, and conduct. Chapter 7 describes how the Color of Mind thrives in today's schools due to sorting practices such as tracking, discipline, and special education, which contribute to the current racial achievement gap. But first we must consider the recent revival of integration as a prospective solution to the achievement gap, as well as some of the bigger and more complex social and structural problems that are beyond the capacity of schools to remedy, and for which school leaders cannot be held accountable.

SIX

What Schools Cannot Fix: Poverty, Inequality, and Segregation

Brown v. Board of Education, which ushered in an era of racial integration, rested on a premise that would soon reveal its limits. The Supreme Court was convinced that to save the hearts and minds of black children, formal barriers to attending schools with whites had to be abolished. But ruling that racially enforced segregation was unconstitutional did little to undo the legacy of the Color of Mind, which sustained beliefs about racial differentiation and racial hierarchy. In fact, somewhat naively, the court implied that eradicating this legacy could be accomplished simply through integration. A more literal interpretation of *Brown's* impact is that it merely proscribed state-sanctioned racial school segregation, providing black families an opportunity to send their kids to schools previously closed to them. *Brown* did not require whites to remain in newly integrated schools. It did not compel them to accept blacks as equals. And it did not foreclose the evolution of policy options—such as tracking—to maintain the Color of Mind within racially mixed schools.

To be sure, without court-ordered school desegregation, important problems tackled in this book—involving dignitary injustice within schools—would not have become critical issues. But most African American children remained in segregated schools for decades following *Brown*, despite the period's many desegregation plans and the use of busing to achieve racially integrated institutions. This was especially true in larger cities, where highly segregated black ghetto communities became sites of concentrated poverty and related problems of crime and family instability. Educational achievement faltered under these conditions, contributing to the achievement gap and perceptions of racial differences in ability. In fact, it was these circumstances that prompted Arthur Jensen's attempt to resurrect theories of racial differences in cognitive ability. All this led to perceptions of a much-discussed "crisis" in urban education, accelerated "white flight" to suburban school districts, and a revival of the Color of Mind in its new cultural guise.[1] These developments posed a host of challenges to urban educators, many of which continue to be problems today.

Growing out of this period and continuing to the present, researchers suggest that *residential* desegregation is necessary to address many of the challenges facing children in these inner-city communities today. They also argue that *school* desegregation has had a positive impact on the achievement of African American students, along with other positive outcomes. This was due both to the additional resources that newly integrated schools provided, and the positive influence of high-performing peers.[2] On the other hand, school desegregation, while a necessary and highly productive step, was far from a comprehensive solution to the nation's legacy of racism. And this certainly remains true today. Indeed, the move from racial segregation of schools to their full integration required much more than court-ordered desegregation, as the history outlined in the previous chapter has demonstrated. Resistance to racial justice in education has proved to be quite resilient, despite decades of struggle to achieve it.

But even if educators adopt a robust understanding of what full or genuine integration entails, they must take care not to assume that this will lead readily to change. Formal social integration of schools, say, by putting more black students in predominantly white schools and classes, is insufficient for addressing the Color of Mind and its effects on academic achievement. The problem is much more complicated than simple integration, and correspondingly difficult to resolve, as racial sorting can and does occur within schools, contributing to the achievement gap. In addition, we must resist holding schools and their leaders accountable for complex societal problems outside their purview, such as poverty, inequality, and residential segregation, even though all these problems surely affect the racial achievement gap.

Fish Too Big for Schools to Fry

As mentioned in the previous chapter, progress in closing the racial achievement gap ceased after 1990, when most African American students who began their education in the 1970s had completed it. Those that came afterward encountered a different social and political scene. Their formative years occurred during the era of Ronald Reagan's presidency, with cuts in federal and state education funding and the rise of the accountability movement. It also was a time of accelerating change in the nation's largest cities, with widening economic inequality and, for urban black communities in particular, a crack cocaine epidemic, drug-related street violence, deepening poverty, and political wars on poverty and drugs causing chaos. These were events and circumstances that schools could not control, but which held profound implications for their students.

Researchers have identified a number of other changes that affected schools during this time, including resegregation of institutions, rising unemployment, especially for African American men, attendant changes in black families, and increasing imprisonment of black youth.[3] Many of these events unfolded most visibly in the cities, where the "crisis" conditions of past decades reappeared in even more conspicuous form in the 1980s and beyond.[4] These too were developments that lay beyond the schools but that affected them significantly, especially as larger numbers of students from extremely disadvantaged backgrounds appeared in their classrooms. Critics who suggest that such developments are immaterial to the performance of schools are either naive or disingenuous. Decades of research have confirmed the findings of the 1966 Coleman Report that highlighted the key roles of family background and social circumstances in determining variation in achievement levels.[5]

As an institution, the school builds on a foundation established by the child's household and its immediate community, and the ability to take advantage of educational opportunities such as school choice is measurably impacted by factors such as poverty and community instability.[6] Research by economists Greg Duncan and Richard Murnane indicates that poor families have become increasingly segregated in certain neighborhoods, especially in larger cities, where schools struggle to serve them effectively. As a consequence, "between 1978 and 2008, the gap between the average mathematics and reading test scores of children from high- and low-income families grew by a third," and "the rate of affluent children who completed college increased by 21 percentage points, while the graduation rate of children from low-income families increased by only 4."[7] History has demonstrated that schools lack the power to wholly change these conditions, although they certainly can help to ameliorate their impact.

Since the 1970s and perhaps earlier, the United States has experienced a process of widening socioeconomic inequality that has continued up to the present. Families in the lower half of the national income distribution, headed generally by adults without collegiate education, have experienced stagnant or declining income and greater unemployment and residential instability than their more affluent counterparts. At the same time, as suggested above, they have become increasingly segregated geographically, living in separate communities and served by different schools.[8] This has contributed to a widening achievement gap along social and economic lines. African Americans, however, represent the very poorest of the poor as a group, and still experience the highest levels of segregation in the nation. If inequality is growing, they are getting the worst of it.[9]

This is clearly evident in the nation's largest metropolitan areas, where most African Americans live today. According to data from the 2000 census, Chicago and Detroit were among the most racially segregated urban regions in America, and they continue to be so today. Over 80 percent of white residents would have to move to a different census tract to achieve integration in either metropolitan area. The poverty rate for black households is more than double that of whites in metropolitan Chicago, and in Detroit it is more than triple. Blacks in both cities are twice as likely as whites to be unemployed, and their income is about half that of whites. And in both cities their economic status has declined in the wake of inner-city job losses and a shifting metropolitan labor market that favors white-collar workers. Similar trends have affected metro areas in other parts of the country as well.[10]

Such trends are manifest in a range of problems. Poor families have fewer resources to devote to school success, are more likely to be headed by a single parent, and often change residences quite frequently, disrupting school attendance.[11] They also have less reliable access to health care. Richard Rothstein has decried the disproportionate number of poor children who suffer from undiagnosed vision problems, which affect their ability to read, take tests, and perform other functions essential to success in school. Hearing problems and a lack of regular dental care affect academic performance as well. Moreover, poor children are more likely to miss school due to illness, and to suffer from asthma and other debilitating conditions that affect their ability to focus on learning. Such problems tend to be especially pronounced in areas of concentrated poverty, particularly poor inner-city communities.[12]

Schools may be able to help address such problems if they could offer health care services for children needing them, but this would require additional resources that institutions serving impoverished areas rarely possess. One program that attempts to do this on a relatively large scale, the Harlem Children's Zone (HCZ), has succeeded in closing achievement gaps in math and reading. But it is limited in purview, accepting applicants from the area's population in an annual lottery. It is also quite costly and has not been replicated elsewhere.[13] While promising, it is thus hardly apparent that programs like HCZ have the capacity to dramatically change the lives of most inner-city children.

Another problem is a dramatically increased likelihood of incarceration for African American males, dating from the 1980s. As scholars such as Michelle Alexander and Becky Pettit have made clear, "get tough" and "zero tolerance" policies introduced then, especially in the war on drugs, escalated rates of arrest and imprisonment. In the ensuing years, the likelihood of black incarceration by age seventeen increased sixfold, from 4 percent to 24 percent. The corresponding change for whites was not nearly as dramatic in absolute numbers, from .04 percent to 2.9 percent, even if the growth rate was greater. By 2010, nearly one in four African American adults had spent time in jail, the vast majority young males. This was partly the result of a "school-to-prison pipeline," discussed in the next chapter, but the incarceration rate among black high school dropouts was much higher, nearly two out of three—reflecting the impoverished state of many black communities, but also the well-documented predisposition of police to target young black males for arrest. By 2005, more than a million African American children, about 10 percent, had a parent in jail.[14] This harmed black households by depriving these kids of at least one parent, thus reducing their likelihood of success in school.

A third issue, related to the growing prison population and touched on above, is the number of African American children living in single-parent households, headed mostly by women. In 1970, the number was about 32 percent, but by 1990 it had increased to 55 percent, about where it stands today. Another 8 percent of black kids currently live with no parent, a bit low by historical standards. The big shift to single–parent households occurred during the seventies and eighties, when industrial jobs left the cities in large numbers, raising black unemployment, especially for men. As sociologist William Julius Wilson has suggested, this placed enormous strain on marriages, adding substantially to the number of female-headed households. At the same time, white families underwent these changes too, but the proportions were more modest. White children living with single parents increased from about 9 percent to nearly 20 percent, about where it stands today. These shifts were especially notable among working-class families, subject to many of the same stresses as African Americans, though not always to a similar degree.[15]

Increased rates of black incarceration following 1980 added to these developments, as any kind of arrest record made it difficult for black men to find employment. As Michelle Alexander has pointed out, felony convictions also barred many from voting, diminishing black political power. The result was deepening poverty and associated problems of crime and community instability, all of which undercut the effectiveness of schools. And however hard single parents worked to prepare their children for school, one parental figure was rarely as effective as two. Research has demonstrated that living in these circumstances is typically an impediment to academic success.[16] When all the above conditions existed in a single neighborhood or district, the goal of realizing national achievement norms became a nearly insurmountable challenge. These problems, which schools could not resolve, made the task of formal education that much more difficult in the affected communities.

This was hardly an isolated issue; its extent is evident in contemporary school statistics. Today, some 42 percent of African American students are educated in high-poverty schools, compared with about 6 percent of white students (percentages for other minority groups range between these figures). Most of these black students live in central-city neighborhoods characterized by higher rates of poverty than most other American communities. It is in these settings of concentrated poverty that crime, unemployment, and family instability are greatest, and where students attend predominantly black schools. Nationally, 46 percent of African American students attend a majority black school, with about 39 percent attending institutions that are more than 90 percent black. Most students in these schools share the debilitating characteristics of their neighborhoods. Many change school frequently, as their families move to find better homes or avoid conflicts, among other reasons. It is little wonder, then, that achievement levels are generally quite low in these settings, among the worst in the nation.[17] And due to the importance of such out-of-school factors as parental education, income, family structure, and personal safety in determining school success, it would indeed be shocking if achievement levels were not low in these circumstances.

Predominantly black secondary schools located in high-poverty neighborhoods have been labeled dropout factories by some researchers, but it is hardly the schools that are primarily to blame for relatively low graduation rates in such circumstances.[18] While there certainly is more that schools can do to improve retention and graduation rates, it is factors outside the institution that produce most of the dropouts. Of course, innovative programs and highly dedicated educators can offset these factors to an extent, but sustained improvement in schools facing these conditions on a large scale has never been accomplished.[19] High-poverty schools have difficulty attracting and retaining highly effective teachers. In these settings across the country, more than half the math and science teachers do not hold certification in their teaching fields. Teachers in urban schools, moreover, are nearly four times more likely than their suburban counterparts to be dismissed or not have their contract renewed in any given year for poor performance in the classroom.[20] New curricula and inventive programs are hardly likely to succeed without capable personnel to carry them out. The challenge of improving high-poverty schools has captivated the imagination of generations of idealistic Americans, young and old alike, but the goal has proved to be a chimera. It has frustrated would-be reformers for many decades.

It is possible, of course, that additional resources could make a significant difference, if utilized properly. Research has suggested that smaller class sizes and more effective teachers can make a substantial contribution to improving urban, predominantly black schools, and responsive leadership and good coordination of resources can help too.[21] Urban teachers earn lower salaries, on average, than their suburban colleagues, and higher compensation could be a factor in attracting and retaining better candidates for the most imperiled institutions.[22] Researchers in Chicago and elsewhere, including those studying the HCZ and similar programs, have identified these and other effective measures that educators in urban schools can undertake to improve school success. Curricular changes can help if they raise expectations and are implemented with support to help students succeed. Chicago's public schools created academically demanding International Baccalaureate programs in high-poverty schools on the city's predominantly black South Side, and they have proved to be successful. Magnet schools have proved to be a pathway to academic success for thousands of poor Chicago public school students as well.[23] While the system as a whole still struggles to meet state and national benchmarks on standardized assessments, it provides promising options for students willing to work hard for goals they have set for themselves.

But even with excellent leadership, public schools in the most impoverished communities struggle to show sustained advancement. Chicago researchers found that institutions contending with the highest student mobility rates and related problems of irregular attendance and infrequent parental involvement made the least improvement in achievement.[24] It is hardly clear that offering additional options for academic success will help students in these circumstances. Advances in so-called improvement science, aimed at refining instruction and support services incrementally, may make a difference in such settings if sustained over a long period.[25] And smaller classes, better teachers, and health services would undoubtedly help as well. Changes such as these raise costs, however, and urban districts typically lack the resources required to undertake them on a large scale. And even if they did, the most efficacious reform measures probably would not raise the performance of many poor inner-city schools to the levels of their affluent suburban counterparts. Accomplishing this task would require an infusion of resources on a historically unprecedented scale, and even then the outcome would hardly be certain.[26]

Of course, the highly concentrated poverty of these urban settings, combined with the greater reported rates of crime and other problems, is largely a consequence of racial segregation and poses many hazards to the children who live there.[27] It also reflects the influence of the Color of Mind, with respect to lost opportunities for education in the past and as a source of discrimination in employment and other facets of life at present.[28] Insofar as the schools serving these children lack the resources to address their needs, questions of justice arise. This is especially true today, given the imperative of equal opportunity that informs most public education systems nationally. As recent research has indicated, the skills that well-functioning schools impart have never been more important to social and economic advancement.[29] Children in impoverished urban settings also need to be treated with dignity, and need a chance to realize their potential in today's putatively democratic social order. Regardless of whether remedies such as those touched on above are effective for all children in these circumstances, providing greater educational opportunity will undoubtedly improve the prospects for success of many, and offer encouragement and a greater sense of self-worth to those who might otherwise succumb to despair.[30] We suggest that this is reason enough to initiate such reforms, although abating residential segregation and the severe deprivation it engenders ultimately must be undertaken.

Yet some reform advocates argue that additional investment in urban public schools is unnecessary, or perhaps even a waste of valuable resources. They have proposed offering parents greater choice in selecting schools for their children, arguing that an enhanced educational marketplace would require schools to compete for students and lead to improvement. This has led to the creation of charter schools in most of the nation's cities, institutions free of many district and state requirements and typically open to students from wider catchment areas than other schools. In some places, vouchers have been introduced to permit broader access to private schools as well. These changes have generally occurred since 1990 and were intended to spur innovation and advancement in urban schools. By and large, these sorts of reforms have not been undertaken in affluent suburban communities, and urban families have rarely been offered the opportunity to choose schools in these settings for their children.[31]

Few states have embraced the logic of school choice as enthusiastically as Michigan, and Detroit has become the site of a massive experiment in reinventing urban schools through creating private and public options for students in a generally open education marketplace. Over a period of years, the enrollment of the city's public schools has dropped dramatically, from nearly 170,000 in the fall of 2000 to less than 48,000 in 2015. This occurred as the city lost population, but also as thousands of students and their families have sought alternatives for their education. Since 2012, charter school enrollment has exceeded that of the city's public schools, and charter institutions have proliferated with relatively little oversight from the state. In 2016, more than 50,000 Detroit children and youth attended these schools, many run by for-profit companies. The result has been considerable confusion and turmoil, as school capacity grew to exceed the city's student population, leading institutions to offer prizes and other incentives to families for enrollment. By and large, however, charters have not represented a substantial improvement over the traditional public schools in serving poor black students, the largest group in the city. Many perform at a lower level. In this respect, the charter experiment in Detroit can hardly be called a success.[32]

As a consequence of changes such as these, school choice has not had a systematically positive effect on urban school performance. While some outstanding choice institutions certainly exist, they often benefit from being able to select their students, and thus offer relatively few lessons for public schools, which are required to accommodate all who come. This adds a new dimension to the term *school choice*. On average nationally, charter schools and voucher-eligible private schools have not significantly outperformed conventional public institutions serving the same student populations, and they have not measurably changed the practice of educators in such schools. In this regard, the "choice" movement has not been an answer to the manifold problems facing urban schools.[33]

Students attending all-black, high-poverty schools, of course, are typically barred from moving to more affluent, predominantly white schools in nearby suburban districts. If such options existed, it could make choice a more meaningful and effective policy option. Unfortunately, few such opportunities have ever been afforded to black children, largely because of vehement suburban white resistance to the very idea of such a policy.[34] This, naturally, is reminiscent of the busing controversies of the 1970s, which undoubtedly helped to animate such opposition. In places like Detroit, where families in the city recently gained legal authority to enroll their children in suburban schools, the lack of public transportation has proved to be a daunting obstacle to poor parents wishing to take advantage of it. As a consequence, the long-standing urban/suburban divisions along racial lines remain largely intact there, as they do in much of the country, both reflecting and helping perpetuate the Color of Mind.[35]

If schools can't fix poverty, inequality, residential segregation, and other societal problems, which undoubtedly come to bear on the achievement gap, and school choice options have serious shortcomings, perhaps it is time to revisit racially integrated schooling. There is considerable evidence, after all, that it contributed to improved African American school performance in the past. A number of studies have documented the positive effect on that performance, including academic achievement, attributable to desegregation. As economists Eric Hanushek, John Kain, and Steven Rivkin argued in a 2009 study utilizing Texas data, "The elimination of all differences in the black enrollment share in Texas public schools for just grades 5–7 . . . would close over 10% of the seventh-grade black-white test score gap." Integration appears to have had a positive effect on graduation rates as well, along with the longer-term success of African American adults.[36] In a recent analysis of the educational problems of black males, Ronald Ferguson has suggested that greater school integration is a necessary step toward progress. But he notes, "While fighting that uphill battle, policymakers and community stakeholders must not wait to support educators, parents, and students to perform better and achieve more under still segregated conditions."[37] These findings suggest that many African Americans derived substantial benefits from attending school with students of other races and ethnic groups, along with measures to improve under-resourced, high-poverty institutions.

In view of this, it is understandable that some would-be reformers call for redoubling the push toward full racial integration. Today, a slight majority of black students attend integrated institutions, with a quarter attending predominantly white schools. Even larger numbers attend secondary schools with relatively high degrees of integration. While these numbers may be a bit lower than thirty years ago, at the height of the desegregation era, they still represent a major advance over the experience of most black students historically. Recent research suggests that school segregation has decreased in important respects in the past two decades or so.[38] This, of course, raises the question of why progress on black achievement has stalled in such circumstances.

An (Idealistic) Integrationist Revival

School desegregation became politically unpopular in the 1970s, especially following busing controversies, and eventually came to be viewed skeptically by the courts as more conservative judges were appointed to the federal bench. By the 1990s, a number of key decisions had brought litigation to combat segregation in education to a virtual halt. Even so, activists and scholars committed to racial justice continued to document the ill effects of racial segregation, in schools and in many other facets of American life. The Civil Rights Project, led by Gary Orfield at Harvard (and later UCLA), was a major contributor to these efforts, and legal scholars continued to examine the issue as well. Segregation remained an important issue in sociology, especially following publication of Douglas Massey and Nancy Denton's *American Apartheid* in 1993.[39]

This body of work made it impossible to argue that racial segregation had ceased to be a critically important facet of American life, despite the unwillingness of politicians and the courts to acknowledge its continuing significance. Most recently, educational researcher Sean Reardon has argued that segregation linked to concentrated poverty is a powerful driver of racial achievement gaps, concluding that "reducing school segregation—in particular, reducing racial disparities in exposure to poor classmates—may therefore be an effective means of improving the equality of students' access to high-quality educational opportunities."[40] Other researchers and policy analysts concur, and political momentum has returned to the idea of school integration as an answer to the achievement gap.[41]

The integrationist revival has recently found expression within social and political philosophy as well. Philosopher Elizabeth Anderson has contributed to this line of analysis by arguing that racial integration is an imperative of justice.[42] Like Massey and Denton, her writing has focused on residential segregation, though her arguments can be extended to schools as well. We pursue this topic in chapter 9, where we complete our case for why school sorting practices are unjust. As a prospective solution for the achievement gap, however, school integration has proved to be insufficient. Recent research, which we take up in the next chapter, suggests that a sizable portion of the racial achievement gap today occurs *within* schools, which complicates integrationist views about the positive effects of integration. A 2015 report from the National Center for Educational Statistics estimated that nearly 52 percent of the racial achievement gap nationally in mathematics was attributable to within-school differences in achievement. This suggests that integrated schools can function to preserve or even aggravate racial differences in academic outcomes, especially in secondary schools where tracking—the practice of placing students into separate groups with different curricula and instruction—is most likely to occur. Such findings are important, as these institutions are a focal point of transition to adulthood for young people. As mediators of social status, they help direct individuals to pathways that often shape their futures.[43]

The integrationist recommendation calls for the liberal egalitarian state to pursue racial integration, by endeavoring to bring students from different groups together. But is full integration, which involves formal social integration, in well-resourced schools enough to realize status equality between these racial groups? Is it enough to realize Du Bois's ideal of relations between students, and students and teachers, being based not on unequal social relations and beliefs about black inferiority but on perfect social equality? We doubt that it is, mainly because such integration could leave intact the systemic sorting practices that have sustained the Color of Mind in the past, and continue to do so in many institutions today. For this reason, we contend that many contemporary advocates of school integration can be characterized as *integration idealists*, who believe that simply mixing people of different races together within institutions and neighborhoods will be sufficient to overcome the stigmatizing effects of the Color of Mind.

The historical record, extending from the success of desegregation to the backlash against busing and stalled progress on the racial achievement gap, demonstrates that simply putting people together is insufficient to combat dignitary injustice. Indeed, as we document in the next chapter, a widespread effort to curtail tracking generally failed to end the practice of sorting students along racial lines in highly differentiated secondary schools. Creating racially integrated schools did not put an end to opportunity hoarding on the part of affluent white parents, who continued to demand the very best for their own children, typically at the expense of others. Inner-city schools facing the biggest challenges in educating their students got little sympathy from legislatures dominated by predominantly white suburbanites.[44] In each of these instances, the Color of Mind continued to function as a stigmatizing myth and pretext for racial sorting in American society, despite the historically high level of racial integration the nation has achieved.

To address these *intraschool* problems, we believe that it is necessary to articulate a more realistic conception of integration, one that is fully cognizant of the Color of Mind as an ideological bulwark against the possibility of change. For school integration to succeed in combating dignitary injustice, school leaders must expel the Color of Mind from their schools. History has shown that this will not occur spontaneously. It will require a highly focused and persistent campaign to expose the myths that underlay it and redirect the resources and professional attention necessary to overcome it.

Getting Our Schoolhouse in Order

Improving educational opportunities in communities ravaged by poverty, income inequality, and racial segregation is a political matter. These circumstances have been produced historically by innumerable acts of exclusion and discrimination, or white opportunity hoarding, contributing to an enduring system of racial inequality and black disadvantage. Not all African Americans prefer to live in such communities, though some might have good reasons for doing so. Others are certainly compelled to live in them because of white racism, systemic injustice, and apathy to their plight. At the same time, a prevailing ideology of personal responsibility and self-reliance has made it hard for most whites to accept the idea of devoting resources to ameliorate these conditions. Indeed, in keeping with ideas discussed in the previous chapter, some have continued to suggest that the problems of these communities are a function of a dysfunctional culture, values, and behaviors allegedly endemic among African Americans.[45] This is a widespread contemporary manifestation of the Color of Mind. The popularity of such views among many whites, and even some blacks, remains a major obstacle to addressing the complex problems of inner-city black neighborhoods, which schools cannot remedy.[46]

Serious societal problems are for all Americans to address in the political and legal arena, directed by grassroots activism. Such problems are clearly beyond the capacity and authority of schools and their leaders to wholly resolve, although there is much that they can do to ameliorate the problems existing outside the schools. To the extent that many such measures require additional resources, addressing the issues can prove quite challenging. However, school leaders can and should be held accountable for what goes on behind school doors, which includes how systemic sorting practices allow the Color of Mind to thrive in schools and affect the racial achievement gap.

SEVEN

Old Poison in New Bottles: How the Color of Mind Thrives in Schools and Affects Achievement

Elizabeth Anderson observes, "A school may be spatially but not socially integrated if students of different races attend different tracked classes."[1] Given the historical legacy of the Color of Mind, however, it is unlikely that simply mixing classes racially will suffice to contravene its influence. School leaders must do more than count heads in classrooms to fix the problem. They must self-consciously address the various manifestations of the Color of Mind in their schools. Achieving robust integration, or what Anderson calls "full integration," is not enough to expel the Color of Mind and address the affront to black dignity. The systemic sorting practices themselves must be undone, root and branch.

Decades of educational research, much of it focusing on secondary institutions, has demonstrated that schools contribute to dignitary injustice in many ways.[2] The issue that probably has received the most attention in this regard is tracking: segregating students into different groups for purposes of differentiating curricula and instruction. There is also a long-standing problem of black students being disciplined more harshly, or in a more punitive fashion, than their white peers. This practice results in a disproportionate number of these students being suspended or expelled from school, contributing to higher dropout rates and lower academic achievement. Similarly, there is a historical pattern of black students being referred in disparate numbers to certain classifications within special education. This process removes them from regular classrooms with their white peers and, as with the other sorting practices, adversely impacts their academic achievement. Added to this negative impact are yet other policies that have disproportionally affected African American students, such as exit exams or qualifying tests which contribute to higher failure and dropout rates. Like the unequal school policies of the past, these reflect the influence of the Color of Mind and contribute to its persistence as well. In this respect, such *intra*school sorting practices are little more than old poison in new bottles.

In what follows, we consider each of these sorting practices, and their impact on both educational attainment and achievement for black students. Addressing them can change the institutional atmosphere of schools so that they offer African American students and families a welcoming and nurturing environment. This could delimit the influence of the Color of Mind on future generations, and make educational success a more tangible reality. More to the point of our argument, addressing these practices, which sustain the Color of Mind and affect achievement, is imperative to deal with the continuing affront to black dignity behind school doors. And, as we argue in the next chapter, the rationale for these sorting practices is ultimately immaterial. In fact, it is possible to disagree, perhaps sharply, about why kids get sorted within schools the way they do and still recognize that undoing these racialized sorting practices is an imperative of dignitary justice. Consequently, this chapter and the two that follow work together: this chapter supplies a historical overview of these Color of Mind–sustaining sorting practices as well as their ripple effects, while the next one reviews explanatory arguments about why kids get sorted in schools, with chapter 9 addressing the injustice of these sorting practices and what to do about them.

Tracking

Historically, tracking is the practice of placing students judged to be better suited to one kind of academic experience or another into separate classes with markedly different curricula. It dates to the nineteenth century in this country, when large secondary institutions began to appear in American cities. Tracking became far more commonplace after the turn of the twentieth century, however, when standardized testing was utilized to identify student academic aptitude, widely associated with the concept of generalized intelligence (g) or IQ. As larger numbers of students from varied social and economic backgrounds entered the schools, these tests were deployed to sort them into different types of schools and classes. Many immigrant children were assigned to the lower tracks, often because of difficulty with English. But some of these groups eventually did quite well, such as the children of Russian Jews, who benefited from a religious tradition deeply committed to scholarship and learning. Not surprisingly, they also came to be deemed white.[3]

In its most highly developed form, tracking separated students from one another into large groups exposed to almost entirely different curricula. That is, students in a particular track typically took courses *only* with those from that track, and rarely were mingled with students from another track. Within most large high schools, standardized tests were widely used to assign students to these various curricular pathways by the mid-twentieth century. The most academically challenging courses in the college prep track were meant for those judged suitable for postsecondary study, while less academically rigorous courses were deemed appropriate for those thought less likely to succeed in college. Remedial work was reserved for students considered incapable of keeping pace with most of their peers. When the tracking system was fully developed, children were assigned to these sorts of curricula starting in elementary school, often constraining their options for academic accomplishment at a relatively young age.[4]

As seen in earlier chapters, through much of American history African Americans were typically restricted to classes in the so-called manual arts or vocational track for preparation as skilled workers or domestic servants. As the number of black high schools grew, however, more opportunities for studying the arts and sciences became available to them. This coincided with the equalization campaigns following World War II, a time when segregated secondary education flourished in much of the South and elsewhere. But with the advent of integration, tracking became a much bigger issue for African American students. Subjected to intelligence tests and other standardized assessments that historically represented an obstacle for them as a group, these students were overrepresented in remedial and lower-track classes, although they were typically no more likely than white students to be enrolled in vocational courses.[5] In Detroit during the latter half of the 1940s, some 45 percent of black students were assigned to the largely custodial "general track," as opposed to just 27 percent of white students. In Chicago, veteran teacher Mary Herrick counted as many as forty students in each remedial class at all-black DuSable High, making it virtually impossible to offer individual attention to those needing it most.[6] School policies and practices such as these, of course, conformed quite closely to long-held beliefs associated with the Color of Mind, and helped perpetuate popular ideas about racial inferiority.

The most academically advanced and challenging tracks were historically reserved for students judged able to excel in these classrooms, while those deemed inadequately prepared were relegated to less demanding curricula and often to less experienced teachers. This basic form of differentiation among students still generally operates in larger American high schools today, although it occurs in particular courses and may be more evident in English, math, or science. As many researchers have demonstrated, the typical result is that students in "higher" tracked courses learn much more than those in "lower" ones. Traditionally, teachers have favored this method of organizing schools, judging it easier to instruct students at a level thought "appropriate" to their abilities.[7] But this did not necessarily mean that the learning opportunities for all students were optimal.

From the standpoint of justice, of course, there is little conflict with sorting students for different curricula based on objective criteria, provided that the sorting does not present a potential harm to them in the present or future, and that all had an equal chance to satisfy the "objective" sorting criteria. The practice of tracking runs into trouble when systematic racial and ethnic discrepancies in assignment to favored "high" tracks come into play, and when learning opportunities for some students are foreshortened as a result. Historically, standardized tests often were used for assigning students to various curricula, along with the judgment of teachers and guidance counselors, an issue we return to in the next chapter. Consequently, many fewer black students were placed into college prep courses. In the past, African American students in Chicago and elsewhere, complained about outright discrimination by teachers in integrated schools. As noted above, most black students were typically assigned to the so-called general track in high schools in Detroit and other cities, rather than the more demanding academic courses. In 1968, black students at Detroit's Northern High School went on strike to demand more challenging math and science classes, including calculus and physics. This sort of response to the issue contributed to a national debate over tracking, leading many observers to call for an end to it in curriculum planning and practice.[8]

Tracking thus became a widely controversial issue in the 1960s and 1970s as civil rights groups and black students protested the overrepresentation of African Americans in lower-track classes. Concerns also were expressed over efforts to channel more black students into vocational programs offering little prospect of good jobs. Either way, protest focused on students being relegated to fixed curricula at relatively low levels of rigor or academic excellence. As a result, schools and districts across the country gradually moved away from designating formal curricular tracks based on test scores and other standardized criteria. Instead, students were recommended for individual classes based on relevant grades or teacher and counselor recommendations, and less emphasis was placed on testing. This was intended to allow individuals to follow their interests and academic strengths, without limiting them to the same expectations in all their coursework.

Yet, as Samuel Roundfield Lucas and other researchers have demonstrated, these changes did not completely eliminate curricular distinctions

within schools. Formal tracking of the sort practiced before the 1960s became less evident, but academic differences between courses and students
placed at different levels of "ability" in particular subjects remained quite
palpable. In fact, a large body of research indicates that a somewhat modified form of tracking persisted after this period of change, and in certain
respects it was nearly as pernicious as the form used in the past.[9] As Lucas
noted in 1998, "*de facto* tracking *does* exist," and it appears to have continued since then.[10] The growth of honors classes and so-called Advanced
Placement courses that carry college credit created yet another level of curricular differentiation in many schools. Placement in any particular course
ceased to be a function of assignment to a more general curricular track
or the results of a broad assessment of aptitude, but distinctions remained
salient nonetheless. And because new, seemingly individualized forms of
tracking came into existence, they contributed to the impression that student course choices reflected their interest and comfort level (or ability) in
particular subjects.[11]

One positive outcome associated with these changes was the widely reported finding that black students were just as likely as whites, if not more
so, to find their way into college preparatory classes, once individual differences in test scores and socioeconomic background were statistically controlled. However, this phenomenon was mainly due to larger numbers of
them taking such classes in predominantly black schools.[12] This level of
participation may have been true in the past too, especially with the development of larger African American high schools in urban districts during
the twentieth century. With the growth of middle-class black families during
and after the civil rights era, the numbers of such students enrolling in these
classes increased substantially.[13] Social class status, including parental education levels, became a critically important arbiter of the type of education
that students received in American high schools. This development, perhaps
more than any other single factor, appears to have contributed most to the
closing of the racial achievement gap between 1971 and the late 1980s.[14]

Nonetheless, the fact that disproportionally large numbers of African
American families remained in or near poverty status meant that their children were placed at a significant disadvantage in gaining access to the very
best classes that the schools had to offer. There is also the problem of African
American students systematically underperforming on standardized tests
of the sort traditionally used to make such class assignments.[15] Researchers
have been quite clear in suggesting that the less demanding classes where
these students generally land offer scant intellectual or academic growth,
doing little to prepare them for future study at the collegiate level or for

skilled employment.[16] The high representation of black students in such classes is probably the biggest curricular manifestation of the Color of Mind in contemporary high schools. Moreover, there is evidence that de facto segregated tracking of this sort is most prevalent in highly diverse institutions where African Americans do not predominate, contributing to the likelihood that black students are clustered nationally in this manner.[17] Like the separate and inferior schools of the past, this sort of racial sorting potentially reinforces stereotypes about unequal intellectual ability. As sociologist Karolyn Tyson has noted, "Racialized tracking fosters a growing sense of difference between black and white students and among blacks. To make matters worse, the difference also implies status."[18]

Despite the elimination of formal tracks in most American schools in the 1970s and 1980s, by the 1990s there was clear evidence of racial disparities in course taking. Table 1 presents data from a representative national sample of secondary students in different levels of mathematics instruction. Blacks and whites are separated out, along with totals that include other students. Altogether, whites were twice as likely to be represented in the two highest levels of math courses, and blacks were far more likely to be enrolled in the lowest levels. Some of this, of course, was related to the socioeconomic status backgrounds of students, but some was due to course placements too. The overall result was that African Americans received substantially less mathematics instruction than whites, a pattern of inequality that held important implications for their subsequent education and career prospects.[19]

These trends have persisted to the present. After decades of debate over the question, today the evidence is clear that many schools continue to practice one form or another of curricular differentiation that functions largely in the same fashion as tracking had in the past. In 2014, secretary of education Arne Duncan wrote to school districts across the country to express his concern about "disparities that persist in access to educational resources."

Table 1. High school mathematics course taking, 1990 National Education Longitudinal Study data (*n* = 13,548 students)

Mathematics sequence	Black	White	Total
Greater than Algebra II or geometry	46 (3.89%)	607 (6.21%)	855 (6.31%)
Algebra II and geometry	495 (8.02%)	1,553 (15.9%)	2,022 (14.92%)
Algebra II or geometry, but not both	380 (32.09%)	4,164 (42.63%)	5,414 (39.96%)
Algebra I	2,334 (28.21%)	2,021 (20.69%)	2,996 (22.11%)
Less than Algebra I	1,329 (27.79%)	1,423 (14.57%)	2,261 (16.69%)

Source: Sean Kelly, "The Black-White Gap in Mathematics Course Taking," *Sociology of Education* 82, no. 1 (January 2009): 55–56.

In particular, the US Department of Education found evidence of significant disparities in the placement of minority students in Advanced Placement (college credit) courses and other curricula deemed academically superior. In the 2011–12 school year, African Americans represented 16 percent of the national student body, but just 8 percent of enrollments in calculus (Latino figures were 21 and 12 percent).[20] There are many reasons for this, including differences in parental education that affect achievement, but schools often contribute to these patterns of distinction also.

A study in North Carolina, for instance, found that teachers in "regular" classes with larger numbers of African American students spent more time on "test prep" than in classes with "academically gifted" students, who were predominantly white and affluent. A result was that black students, on average, received significantly less instruction in mathematics than the more advanced white cohort group. In this way, tracking students into different math classes interacted with the state accountability system to produce telling instructional disparities, which can contribute directly to the racial achievement gap.[21] There is evidence that such practices are widespread today, and affect black students in particular.[22] This finding is particularly important in light of evidence, cited in the previous chapter, that most of the racial achievement gap is due to differences within schools.

Such patterns, of course, reinforce the Color of Mind, and research on tracking has uncovered a good deal of evidence regarding its existence in schools in the recent past and today. Many indicators suggest that teachers, who make many tracking recommendations in schools across the country, harbor such preconceptions. New research on implicit bias suggests that it may affect more than two-thirds of the adult population.[23] As Secretary Duncan's letter to districts implied, these ideas and the practices that they inform have very significant consequences for the distribution of educational resources within schools, and thus on the perpetuation of the racial achievement gap. It is a matter of general consensus among researchers on tracking that assigning students to the lower track has especially negative effects on their ability to learn. There is considerable evidence that placement into lower tracks, where students often experience little engagement and intellectual stimulation, contributes to alienation from school and a greater propensity to drop out. Research has found a lower proclivity to drop out in schools with greater numbers of students enrolled in academic classes, versus vocational- or "general"-level courses. Students who feel that their classes are interesting and challenging exhibit high levels of commitment to school, and are less likely to drop out. Studies have also found that students' self-esteem regarding their academic ability is also a critical element in remaining in school and enhancing their academic achievement.[24] In short, it appears that the curriculum matters, especially for students who may have fewer other reasons for engagement with the school as an institution.

The underrepresentation of African Americans in classes with the highest status, the best teachers, and the most challenging intellectual tasks is a problem with deep roots. In many cases it begins in the early grades, leaving students less prepared to succeed in such classes by the time they reach high school. But there is also evidence that black students can perform at a high level when properly supported. A recent report documents wide variation across cities and states in the number of African Americans successfully completing Advanced Placement courses, demonstrating that greater achievement is possible. But, as indicated earlier, sociological research has demonstrated that curricular differentiation still abets racial inequity in an age when most districts claim that tracking is no longer practiced, and other researchers concur.[25] The impact of this is a significant reduction in educational opportunity for African American and other disadvantaged minority students. In this respect, the Color of Mind is alive and well in American schools.

School Discipline Policies

Tracking, of course, is just one facet of school policy with important implications for dignitary justice in education. Similar patterns of racial exclusion are evident in other facets of school policies and practices; these too implicate the Color of Mind. Like tracking, these dimensions of everyday school life hinge decisively on the views and judgment of educators, who also help make decisions on curricular differentiation. Implicit racial bias undoubtedly comes into play in these instances as well. In this respect, these facets of schooling are symptomatic of an ethos of marginalization regarding racial and ethnic minority students, a long-standing set of beliefs about children of different "colors" and their ability and behavioral tendencies.

This is perhaps most graphically evident in school discipline policies, which disproportionally penalize black students for offenses generally associated with more lenient punishments for whites. Like other forms of unequal treatment in school life, this too has a history. During the 1960s and 1970s, a time of large-scale and relatively rapid desegregation, there was considerable conflict between white and black students. This generally occurred in schools that had been historically white in composition. African Americans were widely depicted as interlopers and frequently were subjected to harassment and persecution out of sight from teachers and administrators. When fighting occurred, usually instigated by whites attacking or threatening them in school, black students typically were the first to be reproved, and were disciplined more severely than their antagonists. This treatment was especially true when police became involved, as often was the case. Black students were more likely than whites to be arrested and held in jail. Much of this conflict occurred in the South, where police forces were overwhelmingly white—a pattern similar to law enforcement responses to civil rights protests during that era.[26]

To a considerable extent, this broad pattern of disproportional punishment has continued to be evident in desegregated schools up to the present. It is reflected in higher rates of suspension and expulsion for black students, conditions that contribute to lower academic achievement and higher rates of dropping out of high school. Table 2 presents data on the distribution of students in various discipline categories during the 2011–12 school year, collected from across the country by the US Department of Education's Office of Civil Rights. It shows that African American students were disproportionally represented in every category, the only group to experience this condition. Though they comprise less than a sixth of the student population, they represented more than a third of the suspensions and expulsions. Altogether, about 16 percent of elementary and secondary black students received out-of-school suspensions compared to about 5 percent of white students, making African Americans three times more likely to experience that form of discipline.[27]

A recent report by the UCLA Civil Rights Project echoes these findings, confirming that of nearly 3.5 million public school students suspended in 2011–12, whites were subject to this disciplinary action less frequently than

Table 2. **Distribution of students across disciplinary categories by race and ethnicity, 2011–12 (n = 19 million students)**

Discipline category	White	Black	Latino	Asian
Enrollment (%)	51	16	24	5
In-school suspension (%)	40	32	22	1
Out-of-school suspension (%) (single)	36	33	23	2
Out-of-school suspension (%) (multiple)	31	42	21	1
Expulsion (%)	36	34	22	1

Notes: Enrollment is 49 million students, in-school suspension is 3.5 million, single out-of-school suspension is 1.9 million, multiple out-of-school suspension is 1.55 million, and expulsion is 130,000 students.
Data were collected for the 2011–12 school year.
Totals may not add to 100 due to rounding.
Source: US Department of Education, Office of Civil Rights, Civil Rights Data Collection, Data Snapshot (School Discipline), March 21, 2014, p. 2.

any other racial or ethnic group. At the secondary level, where suspensions are far more frequent, black students were more than twice as likely to be suspended as any other such group, with nearly one in four (23 percent) punished this way during the school year. Rates of suspension have increased dramatically since the early 1970s, when less than 12 percent of black high school students were disciplined in this fashion. Tellingly, contemporary rates vary significantly from one state to another, and across districts. Ronald Ferguson has suggested that suspensions are especially high at predominantly black institutions, but other researchers have found great variability across schools with similar racial and socioeconomic profiles, suggesting a significant local policy and practice dimension to these developments.[28]

This pattern of disproportional discipline is part and parcel of the achievement gap, even if the students who are most discouraged by this aspect of school life often do not participate in achievement testing. Thousands of days in school are lost to black students as a consequence of these circumstances, which tend to underscore and reinforce the Color of Mind. The average suspension is estimated to last at least 3.5 days, and more than half of all students suspended were disciplined in this manner more than once during the academic year. The UCLA report estimates that nearly eighteen million days of instruction were lost as a consequence of these actions, with African Americans experiencing more such forfeited time than any other group. This, of course, held dire consequences for their academic performance, especially in comparison with other groups. As the authors perceptively note, "We will close the racial achievement gap only when we also address the school discipline gap." This sentiment has been confirmed in recent research finding a statistically significant negative correlation between school suspension and academic achievement, especially for African American students.[29]

In recent years, suspension has grown to be a far more widely used disciplinary measure than expulsion, which is typically associated with more combative or violent conduct. According to the US Office of Civil Rights, suspensions outnumbered expulsions nationally by about 27 to 1 in 2012. Data collected from the states indicate that the largest number of suspensions was taken as a consequence of "minor nonviolent violations of school codes of conduct, not unlawful or dangerous behavior."[30] There is considerable evidence, moreover, that black students have often been subject to "differential treatment" for such infractions, leading to higher rates of disciplinary action. Supporting this, research in the past has also found that race has been an independently significant predictor of suspension when social and economic background variables are held constant.[31] This, of course, raises the question of how and why this has been occurring.

Much of this disproportionate suspension activity appears to begin at the classroom level, where a long history of disparate responses to students linked to race, ethnicity, and socioeconomic status has been documented. As pointed out by educational researchers recently, this is also where implicit bias is likely to become manifest.[32] One team of researchers reported in 1995 that large and stable differences in school disciplinary actions suggest that "highly consistent statistical discrepancies in school punishment for black and white students are an indicator of systematic and prevalent bias in the practice of school discipline." Black and white students, moreover, were typically suspended for quite different reasons, with the largest categories for blacks being "disrespect" and "excessive noise," both largely matters of judgment on the part of authorities. As a recent study put it, black and Latino students "are often disproportionately suspended for what are minor and non-violent offenses, ones which do not require out-of-school suspensions by any state authorities but rather are applied in a discretionary manner by school or district administrators."[33] Researchers also suggest that these problems have become especially evident in the wake of so-called zero-tolerance policies associated with higher levels of suspension and other forms of school discipline.[34] In some schools, lack of engagement due to tracking and inattention to black student interests lead to minor disciplinary infractions, which in the context of such policies can lead to inappropriately severe discipline practices.[35]

As suggested above, school suspension has a negative association with academic achievement, but it is also linked to dropping out of school. Researchers have noted a relationship between high minority suspension rates, dropout behavior, and student complaints of discrimination.[36] A study of Florida schools conducted at Johns Hopkins University found that "students' associated chances of dropping out double with their first suspension," a stronger effect than even multiple disciplinary actions of that sort.[37] Studies of particular schools have shown a willingness to use disciplinary procedures to "get rid of troublemakers," often disproportionally African American. As one guidance counselor at a New York City school confessed, "We do throw students out of here for no good reasons. They feel terrible. We deny them their education. Blacks kids especially."[38]

Students who have been frequently disciplined often experience low levels of engagement with the schools, leading to higher rates of dropping out.[39] Being disciplined can lead to changes in self-image, also associated with leaving school altogether, as noted earlier. In addition, it can affect the way that teachers and peers view a particular student.[40] When African Americans are disproportionately suspended, it reinforces stereotypes, which contribute to the perceptions of teachers and administrators. This, of course, can find expression in course assignments and other key decisions related to academic opportunity. Kids viewed as troublesome often get less academic attention.[41] Given all this, there is good reason to believe that disproportionate punishment of the sort discussed earlier contributes to lower achievement and attainment for African American youth.

Racial disparity in school discipline, especially suspensions and expulsions, represents a pattern in forced or involuntary disengagement from the schools, according to educational researcher Russell Rumberger.[42] Given the extent that African Americans are likely to experience this, it too can be seen as an expression of the Color of Mind, particularly concerning the perceived moral propensities of black students, regardless of whether such perceptions are implicitly or explicitly held. If they are indeed being kicked out of school "for no good reasons," it is not clear what other factors can explain the very high level of disproportionality that characterizes these facets of school discipline. And this has a direct bearing on the achievement gap. Missing school, no matter the reason, generally harms academic performance. Disengagement from the institution altogether can lead to dropping out. As one study noted, disciplinary measures such as suspension and expulsion "may be . . . mechanism[s] through which the school helps perpetuate racial and class stratification," a problem that cries out for justice.[43]

Racial Disproportionality in Special Education

The question of mental ability and disability certainly lies at the very heart of special education (SPED) as both a field of study and a domain of educational policy and practice. As school systems developed in the late nineteenth and early twentieth centuries, children perceived to be unusually "slow" or unable to learn were often placed in separate classes, where they were taught rudimentary elements of good behavior and basic skills, or they were simply monitored for safety until they were old enough to leave the schools. This sort of segregation was undertaken largely to prevent disruption of instruction and order in other classrooms, where children learned at more or less "normal" rates. Relatively little attention was given to instructing such "retarded" children until after World War II, when research in SPED began to reveal that most of them were indeed capable of learning, and many could assume productive and fulfilling lives after leaving school. But most children enrolled in SPED remained segregated from the general student population, to one degree or another, until relatively recently.[44]

Historically, there is considerable evidence of teachers utilizing separate facilities such as "resource rooms" and alternative schools for the purpose of removing troublesome or difficult-to-teach pupils from their classes. This was evident early in the twentieth century, as urban school systems grew rapidly and depended heavily on teacher recommendations for placement of such students. This, of course, was before racial integration had become widespread, even in cities outside the South, so most children who were affected by such exclusion were the sons—and a few daughters—of immigrants. It was not until the postwar era, when the *Brown v. Board of Education* decision led to large numbers of black students entering city schools, that race became a significant factor in this practice. By the latter half of the 1960s, considerable evidence indicates that black students were assigned to so-called special classes in numbers far out of proportion to their representation in the overall student population, much of it apparently for disciplinary purposes.[45] This was an early sign of African Americans being disproportionately assigned to certain behavioral categories of disability.

Since that time, a steady stream of research has documented the disproportionality of black and other nonwhite students in various SPED programs in districts across the United States. As in the case of school discipline practices, there also is a good deal of variation from state to state, especially for categories of disability with relatively large numbers of black students. Even though some studies dispute such claims, this is widely seen as evidence of the effect of more proximate policy environments on racial disproportionality in SPED.[46]

Overall, these studies have found that black students are overrepresented in certain categories of intellectual or educational disability, particularly so-called intellectual disabilities (formerly mild mental retardation, or MMR) and emotional disorders (formerly behavioral disability, or BD). These are among the smaller categories of SPED classification, but they also are widely judged to be the least amenable to improvement, with respect to both academic achievement and eventual attainment. They are also more likely to result in students being segregated from their peers for at least a significant part of the school day. While the numbers of students in these circumstances may be relatively low, they represent a larger portion of black students than any other racial group, nearly 2 percent nationally.[47]

White and Hispanic students, on the other hand, tend to occupy categories such as learning disabilities or speech or language impairments, which are more responsive to treatment and allow for full development in intellectual or academic domains unaffected by the incapacity. These categories, consequently, enjoy somewhat higher status among both parents and many educators, often making them a favored option for children needing help with a particular learning problem. In this regard, they can serve as a means of gaining greater resources, contributing to higher achievement and improved school experiences for families savvy or influential enough to gain such a designation for their children.[48] To the extent that such children are predominantly white, and primarily black SPED categories do not function in this manner, these aspects of the system potentially widen the racial achievement gap even more. Proportionally similar numbers of African Americans are classified with learning disabilities too. The impact of this may vary a great deal from one school setting to another; and to the extent that black students are overrepresented in districts with fewer such resources, it is hardly clear that their learning disabled classifications result in advantages in the same manner as they do for white students.[49]

The distribution of students from different racial and ethnic backgrounds in the largest SPED categories is displayed in table 3, which is based on data from a survey conducted by the US Commission on Civil Rights. These figures represent "risk ratios," which are calculated to measure the degree of concentration that a group's students exhibit in each category compared with all the other groups. A value of 1 indicates that the ratio is the same as all other groups; values above that reflect a greater concentration, while those below it indicate a lower one. These data clearly show that African Americans were more likely to be classified in each of the disability categories listed. They were three times more likely than the norm to be placed in the intellectual disability category, and more than twice as likely to be labeled as having an emotionally disorder. In 2003, more than one in four black students receiving SPED services were placed in one of these two categories. Another 45 percent were diagnosed with specific learning disabilities, by far the largest category of SPED services. Even there, however, their

Table 3. Special education risk ratios by race/ethnicity, Fall 2003—ages 6 through 21

Disability	African American	Hispanic (all races)	White (non-Hispanic)
Specific learning disabilities	1.4	1.1	0.8
Speech/language impairment	1.1	0.9	1.1
Intellectual disability	3.0	0.7	0.6
Emotional disorders	2.3	0.5	0.8
Developmental delay	1.6	0.5	1.0
All disability categories	1.5	0.9	0.9

Source: US Commission on Civil Rights, *Minorities in Special Education*, briefing report, April 2009, p. 29.

numbers were proportionally greater than other groups. Overall, black students were 50 percent more likely to be declared eligible for SPED services than students in the other groups in table 3.[50]

As a general proposition, students in SPED are more likely to be associated with disciplinary action in the schools, and the disability category with the highest incidence of such measures is emotional disorders. According to a 2008 report, some 73 percent of students labeled with this disability were suspended or expelled in that year. Students with learning disabilities, on the other hand, experience a relatively low incidence of disciplinary measures. These are patterns with a long history, with black students again becoming associated with problematic behavior.[51] As such, these SPED assignments reinforce long-standing associations of race with disproportionate disciplinary action, and with certain dimensions of the Color of Mind. Stereotypes hold that black youth are more prone to disorder and misbehavior, and the intersection of SPED and school discipline, particularly suspensions and expulsions, fosters an impression that seems to bear that out.

Even if the number of black students labeled with one or another SPED category is relatively small, their historic overrepresentation in the low-status categories of intellectual disabilities and emotional disorders likely reflects the influence of the Color of Mind. As a number of researchers have pointed out, conventions for the diagnosis of these classifications are hardly clear and objective, especially for emotional disorders; a good deal of judgment is required in each case. These categories are also often associated with poverty and deprivation, especially for young children.[52] This, of course, leaves considerable room for bias of various kinds to come into play. It raises the very tangible possibility that substantial numbers of African American students are assigned this label inappropriately. Enough concern exists about this question that the US Department of Education recently proposed a new rule requiring states to identify districts where SPED classification patterns reflect "significant disproportionality."[53] Such a measure could be an important first step in preventing many black students from being separated from their peers and losing valuable instructional opportunities, direct contributions to the racial achievement gap.

Managing School Climate

Each of these sorting practices can contribute to perceptions of injustice in a school, which can adversely affect school climate. Researchers conducting case studies of particular institutions have documented the effects of such perceptions and the signals they send to a school community about race, status, and the prospects of educational success.[54] Such impressions can create a school climate, which students and teachers alike eventually become accustomed to, that sustains the Color of Mind, assails black dignity, and reinforces white superiority.

For example, the presence of relatively large numbers of black students in lower-track courses, even if classes are not formally labeled in this fashion, signals to the school community that they are academically weaker as a group. At the same time, the presence of a relatively small number of black students in advanced classes reinforces this impression, and places added pressure on those individuals to combat Color of Mind stereotypes. Some find the pressure bothersome enough to avoid such classes altogether, which of course only helps sustain stereotypes about black students and academic success.[55] It certainly does not help when white students complain about black demands for greater fairness or curriculum reform, as Prudence Carter found in her comparative study of schools in the United States and South Africa.[56]

Perceptions that school rules are not being applied fairly, or that white students benefit from partiality in their enforcement, can further damage school climate. A key factor in the creation of such patterns of unfair treatment is the willingness and ability of certain parents to intervene in the school on behalf of their children. In a series of detailed case studies, researchers have found that white middle- and upper-class parents exhibit a far greater likelihood of engaging in this sort behavior than lower-class or minority parents. Because so many of the issues involved are relatively minor, involving hall passes, loud talking, or dress code infractions, staff members often hesitate to enforce rules with students whose parents might question their judgment or even the rule itself. Parents who believe their offspring to be essentially "good kids" are sometimes quick to contest infractions that they believe threaten that reputed status. This makes some school staff members think twice before taking disciplinary action against certain individuals, essentially giving them a second (or third or fourth) chance. African American students rarely get such treatment in most schools. School staff members are reportedly quick to discipline them for such minor infractions as incidental dress code violations that white students routinely commit without repercussions. Such behavior, which typically occurs in hallways, classrooms, athletic facilities, and other public settings, can quickly lead to feelings of unfair treatment.[57]

Historically, African Americans have been the outsiders in most integrated school settings, and adverse school climate associated with sorting practices and the perceptions they generate can lower educational achievement and attainment levels for them as a group. This has contributed directly to the racial achievement gap, although the precise extent of that contribution is difficult to estimate. A recent analysis of national data, however, suggests that within-school racial disparities in achievement are greatest in the wealthiest districts.[58] To be sure, as we will make clear in the next chapter, people disagree about why schools sort kids. But this does not invalidate our argument that sorting practices are unjust. Regardless of their causes, they sustain the Color of Mind and assail black dignity.

EIGHT

Why We Sort Kids in School

There is nothing wrong with parents wanting the best school facilities, teachers, and curriculum for their kids, especially in view of education's importance for future prospects in what David Baker calls our "Schooled Society."[1] And it is understandable that teachers want to teach the "smartest" and best-behaved kids: it's more fun, it's easier, and it makes them look good. There is nothing untoward in wanting kids with disabilities to have the resources they need to make meaningful use of educational opportunity. And schools must ensure order and safety to run effectively. Tracking, special education, and discipline may make these goals easier to accomplish, but, we must ask, at what cost? This question anticipates concerns about justice. And it gains force and urgency when we consider the racial disparities inherent in these sorting practices, as described in the previous chapter.

To be sure, explanations abound for why kids get sorted in schools the way they do, and debate has swirled around these practices for many years. While some of this debate may have little to do with racial bias, there is ample evidence that race does indeed matter for understanding why disparities in sorting exist. However, we need not settle such matters to take issue with sorting on grounds of justice. In fact, we can suppose that the question of how best to justify these practices is largely a matter of personal preference. Our central claim is that as long as such practices sustain the Color of Mind and reinforce racial hierarchies, they are unjust. This is because they fail to treat black students as persons with equal dignity, and thus amount to a dignitary injustice. Before fleshing out this argument philosophically in the next chapter, we take a closer look at competing explanations of racial differences in everyday sorting practices in schools.

Explaining Tracking

Schools have a legitimate interest in challenging all students to learn, including the most gifted and talented. They may pursue this agenda by making more difficult material available in some course offerings, such as honors and Advanced Placement, but not in others. They may do this on their own accord or because some parents demand it. Still, we must ask: why do so many black kids end up in the low academic track and so few in the high one? One explanation is discrimination or racial bias. There is certainly evidence that teacher and counselor discretion plays a role in tracking placement, and with this comes the possibility of racial bias. But alternative explanations have little if anything to do with overt or even implicit racial discrimination.

For example, it might be argued that tracking promotes optimal learning environments. By placing students of similar ability and willingness to learn in the same classroom, teachers can be more effective, and learning can take place more efficiently. Rather than having lesson plans that are too fast for some and too slow for others, teachers can find one that works for all students in a given classroom. This allows them to focus more on the substance of instruction than on worrying about some kids falling behind or others not being challenged, both of which result in kids losing interest. From this perspective, finding more black students in low-track classes and fewer in high-track ones may be nothing more than a consequence of ensuring that they and other students are able to maximize their learning.

But what may start off as a legitimate academic reason for student tracking can become a rigid caste-like system *within* the school, shaping future academic and employment prospects, teacher and student expectations, self-esteem, and school climate. If tracking begins in elementary school, then students in lower tracks may find it difficult to move into a higher track later on, even when they are allowed to "choose" their classes. Black students, for instance, may feel less comfortable in these classes, because they do not have friends in them or simply because there are so few black students.[2] Furthermore, teachers and guidance counselors may be reluctant to support moves up the tracks. They may have low expectations of potential for success for all students with lower-track backgrounds.[3] In fact, evidence suggests that a combination of student choices, motivation, prior placement record, and counselor recommendations explains student track placements.[4]

While standardized ability tests may have been used in the past to make decisions about assigning students to different curricula, more recently it appears that teacher discretion has greater influence. A 1994 report by the National Center for Educational Statistics indicated that teacher recommendations and prior grades were the strongest factors in deciding which students would be placed in the highest tracks, along with student self-selection for various curricula.[5] In an important study conducted in the 1990s, Jeannie Oakes and Gretchen Guiton found that teachers and other school personnel often guided low-income and minority students in large urban high schools into lower-track classes. In multiple interviews, the research team found that a great deal of discretion rested with teachers in particular, and that biases were often expressed quite freely. As team members put it, there was a widespread belief that a student's educational prospects are "virtually set by the time he or she gets to high school." A principal told them that he could tell the future placement of a student at the end of kindergarten. In short, students were believed to have "fixed ability levels" that were not subject to change. The research team also reported that "race, ethnicity and social class signaled ability and motivation." While many teachers denied any association between race and ability, the researchers noted that their judgments "reflected stereotypical views about differences between racial groups."[6] As one researcher put it in a more recent study, "teachers did not question the deleterious effects of tracking," or their underlying assumptions about student learning.[7]

A related problem is that the "best" teachers tend to work in the higher tracks, and these classes better prepare students for postsecondary education. When lower-track placement forecloses the opportunity to work with these teachers, some students are relegated to a less optimal learning environment, while maximizing opportunities for others. This is quite different from students simply being taught at an appropriate level, and it represents an injustice, especially if most students affected adversely are black. And in addition to these aspects of tracking, there is also the concern that persistent low-status placement can negatively affect student academic self-concept.[8]

As noted in chapter 7, both middle-class and high-socioeconomic- status (SES) families can have a powerful influence on what goes on in the school building. Unfortunately, this influence is not always positive and sometimes harms less advantaged students and families.[9] One way high-SES family influence can play out is in their efforts to hoard access to high-track classes and curriculum, and to the "best" teachers who typically instruct these classes.[10] These parents cannot be faulted for wanting their kids to have every possible advantage in getting an education that best prepares them for a prosperous future and for pursuing the American Dream. All good parents should want this. Nor can the school be faulted for creating avenues for the kind of advanced coursework that can enrich students and enhance their higher-education prospects. All good schools should do this. However, where opportunities to take such classes and be taught by the "best" teachers are limited, and where future opportunities for advanced education and quality employment prospects are so extremely competitive that academic preparedness can make a difference in who gets them and who does not, allowing better-off families to hoard these valuable opportunities seems unfair to low-SES students, whose parents may lack the resources, social capital, and wherewithal to gain access to them for their children.

Some people may lament this outcome, and wish that things were different so that hoarding educational opportunity was not necessary. However, they might take this outcome to show that class, not race, explains how kids get tracked in school. But, as we know, blacks are disproportionately represented in the low-SES category, so this race-neutral proxy for explaining tracking is only one step removed from the point that race does indeed influence who ends up where. Therefore, so long as blacks remain underrepresented in the high-SES group, and this group is best situated to monopolize access to advanced educational opportunities in school, race remains a vital variable in school tracking. As noted earlier, considerable evidence indicates that racial achievement gaps are most clearly evident in wealthier school districts.[11]

Others may demur by citing a societal need to have public education structured to prepare students for productive labor befitting their talents and abilities, and for filling jobs needed to carry on the business of living together in an advanced society. These jobs vary in skill and academic knowledge requirements. Some require high proficiency in mathematics, but many do not. By creating tracks in school with advanced math that start preparing students for future jobs requiring this knowledge, and by using relevant assessments of math ability or competency to determine placement in such classes, schools are contributing to the vital societal mission of having a pool of citizens that can engage in necessary forms of productive labor. The point here is that neither class nor race should dictate which students end up in the "high" tracks. Rather, this should be settled on the basis of demonstrated ability in math, science, reading, language, or other relevant content. To this way of thinking, racial disparities in tracking merely reflect ability and have nothing to do with race, class, or parental lobbying. Moreover, so the argument goes, even if some students end up in high-track classes for the wrong reasons, they will likely not remain in them for long.

While there may be real problems—institutional and otherwise—for some students with upward track mobility, downward track mobility is decidedly meritocratic and egalitarian.

This is a potent argument. Some critics will take issue with it by arguing that tracking really serves to preserve and reproduce a structure of advantage and disadvantage in society that satisfies the interests of the affluent in maintaining their economic, social, and political dominance.[12] But it also trades on a pernicious presumption. If we accept that blacks are significantly underrepresented in high-track classes, and placements are strictly a matter of aptitude, it follows that most blacks lack the ability for advanced work. Researchers may debate whether this is due to genetics, upbringing, or laziness. However, each of these factors entails the proposition that white kids are smarter than black ones. This conclusion, of course, invokes the Color of Mind, and reveals how it can find support in routine school practices that impact academic achievement. Even if it is not often explicitly stated, the "simply aptitude" argument has no other way of accounting for racial disparities in track assignments.

There are, of course, other factors that militate against blacks ending up in high tracks. A broad category of reasons can be subsumed under the heading of choice. Suppose that middle-class blacks can make the grade in the high-track classes. Further suppose that some choose not to take these classes, and others elect to avoid the higher track. In these cases, black students might be reacting to the institutional climate or to signs that they don't belong.[13] High- and low-track classes, after all, do more than deliver differential educational content and facilitate access to other kinds of educational and employment opportunities. They also communicate messages about racial and ethnic identity and intellect, and these too often reflect the Color of Mind.

The historical construction of the Color of Mind, as we have presented it, accounts for how this began, and why certain types of academic preparation have become associated with race. Behind school doors, assumptions about identity and intellect can inform student decisions about where they do or do not belong. Classrooms are also socially significant spaces for what they indicate about their students' identities, and insofar as membership in them may constitute an existential commitment to embrace a certain social identity.[14] Although black students will act in different ways in these circumstances, some may elect to opt out of settings felt to be incongruent with their experiences. Such choices inadvertently contribute to the persistence of separate and unequal academic tracks within schools.

These decisions about whether to leave the high track may be especially consequential for students concerned with being accused of "acting white" by their black peers. Some scholars have suggested that this represents a possible explanation for why blacks underachieve in schools.[15] They argue that some of these students avoid outward signs of academic success such as studying and class participation in the interest of maintaining solidarity with their lower-achieving peers. This might explain why some black kids choose to avoid the high tracks, or to eventually leave them, even though they can succeed. But it's possible that this perspective is really a dressed-down version of the pernicious view that there's something wrong with blacks that explains their lack of achievement or ambition. It signals that they are too weak-willed to resist pressure from their anti-achievement peer-group culture.

So, on the one hand, this explanation offers a more sympathetic, black-friendly response to the tracking problem, namely that some blacks elect not to take the high tracks (even though they could succeed) because of what these classes represent politically and socially, given the dearth of black students enrolled in them. But on the other hand, it seems just as demeaning to imply that blacks as a group embrace anti-achievement norms, and that some black students lower their academic aspirations because they opt to conform to these norms. We can only hope that black solidarity and the desire to occupy spaces of respect do not require such a sacrifice. Recent research suggests that relatively few black students are subject to such pressures or respond in this manner.[16]

A recent study offers an illuminating illustration of why one high-track-capable black student in an honors math class chose to enroll in a lower-track class. As the male student recalled:

> I was swearing because I was like, "Oh man, I don't even belong in here," because it was like 30 Caucasian kids and one African student. I felt like I had to prove myself and prove that Blacks aren't stupid. [I felt like] if I were to get a problem wrong and raise my hand, they would look at me and say, "Ah, that Black." I was always under pressure, so . . . I transferred to just [the] advanced level.[17]

In this case, which is hardly an anomaly, abandoning the higher track had nothing to do with black solidarity, peer pressure, or lack of ability. Instead, it was due to burdensome classroom dynamics that left the student feeling a need to justify his presence, believing that everything he said or did was under the spotlight. He felt like a spokesperson for the entire race, as well as the expert on all things having to do with it. These are, of course, familiar sentiments for blacks finding themselves in rarified academic spaces. But more than this, the student's attempt to dodge the pernicious effects of the hierarchical tracking system was to exit the class, helping perpetuate the stigma of black intellectual inferiority. This experience also assaulted his dignity, or sense of inner worth, by placing him in the unfortunate situation of having to defend his status as a moral equal.

As we noted in chapter 2, a significant feature of eighteenth- and nineteenth-century racism, and one of the most contentious, is that physical markers of race were presumed to be a reliable basis for making inferences about non-phenotypic characteristics. This certainly has not disappeared entirely from the contemporary landscape. In *Observations on the Feeling of the Beautiful and Sublime* (1764), Kant observes that "in the lands of the black," women find themselves in the "deepest slavery." In an inflammatory connection between phenotypic blackness and intelligence, he then recounts a report about a "Negro carpenter" who called white men foolish for making concessions to their wives and then complaining about the women. Kant adds, "And it might be that there were something in this which perhaps deserved to be considered; but in short, this fellow was quite black from head to foot, a clear proof that what he said was stupid."[18] For the young black honors math student, Kant's judgment echoed down to the present.

Explaining Discipline

Schools need to maintain order, security, and safety. They cannot teach and students cannot learn unless these elements of a conducive academic environment are guaranteed in some reasonable measure. Some kids may jeopardize these aims; when that happens, disciplinary sanctions including office referrals, suspensions, and even expulsion may secure them once again. There can be less extreme methods of advancing these vital interests—some that require more resources for measures such as counseling, and others that do not. Still, proponents of harsher practices may call for a "tough on misbehavior" approach to send a strong message, to deter future misbehavior by others students, or perhaps to appease parents whose kids may have been on the receiving end of student misconduct.

Removing "bad" kids is a popular strategy. However, it has a disproportionate impact on black kids (and other students of color).[19] This discipline gap contributes to the achievement gap, often by depriving kids of instructional time.[20] This effect is magnified where the same students are disciplined more frequently than others.[21] Furthermore, apart from the direct effects of classroom exclusion on academic achievement, other consequences have indirect effects, including disengagement from school; social isolation and stigma; lack of trust; and depressed motivation to achieve, follow rules, and embrace the school community, along with increased risk of antisocial behavior.

Some suggest that race is a strong predictor of punitive disciplinary sanctions.[22] Others argue that race is merely a proxy for other factors that account for racial disparities in discipline, including residency in what Kenneth Clark called the "dark ghetto." There is reason to think that neighborhood segregation in violent poverty-stricken areas, as well as factors such as low SES, may compromise academic achievement.[23] For instance, living in a rough neighborhood may lead students to develop a "hard" persona to ward off threats there, which they then bring to school to their detriment. It can get them excluded from the classroom, negatively affecting their achievement. Some kids can drop this survival tactic when they get to school, but others cannot or choose not to.[24] It also may turn out that the conditions in school are such that the street front is also needed inside the school building to avoid bullying, in-school violence, and "getting punked."[25] Of course, this raises further questions of justice: Is it fair for students to attend schools so dangerous that they must act in antisocial ways that are more likely to get them disciplined and excluded from the classroom? And is it reasonable to expect them not to respond in ways that avoid being viewed as "soft" or an easy target for bullies or gang members?

Although this connection between neighborhood environment and academic achievement is plausible, it does not support the claim that kids exposed to violence in their neighborhood are more likely to act in ways that invite punitive discipline in school. Because the mechanisms accounting for how students are affected by neighborhood violence are unclear, further assumptions are needed to make the connection. The "hard" persona is one approach. The mental health approach is another. It is tempting to assume that students in homes with nonworking, poorly educated parents living near or below the poverty line will be more prone to behavior problems in school that result in higher rates of discipline. There is certainly evidence that children exposed to violence and drug abuse, which may be though not always is a feature of such homes, can have mental health issues with ramifications that spill over into their school and increase the prospect of disciplinary sanctions.[26]

Both of these approaches make further assumptions about kids, how they cope with exposure to violence, and the potential health effects of such exposure, to make sense of behaviors they might exhibit in school that result in discipline. But because it is implausible to think that all similarly situated students cope in the same way or suffer the same adverse health effects, we have no reason to be confident in linking neighborhood violence to the discipline gap. Moreover, even if kids coped with these things in similar ways, and had similar adverse health effects, differences in how teachers respond to misbehavior in the classroom as well as differences in school policy that impact feelings of safety could still make a difference in disproportionate disciplinary outcomes. Some schools do better than others at cultivating a climate of trust and feelings of safety. This is important, because black students have been found to feel less safe in ways that may affect the circumstances of achievement.[27]

Perhaps owing to this lack of confidence in the connection between neighborhood violence and misbehavior in school, some researchers have argued that the contribution of SES to the discipline gap is minimal, and that race remains an important predictor of who will be disciplined.[28] And this finding is strengthened by evidence that the racial discipline gap is even more pronounced in suburban schools with higher SES measures—where blacks are disciplined at higher rates than whites. This might have something to do with school climate, whether the school has been recently desegregated, school leadership, or even parental involvement.

Some kids certainly do worse in school than others. For these lower achievers, bad grades and scores are not the only negative consequences they suffer. For some, poor academic performance may have a detrimental impact on their mindset, causing them to be depressed, frustrated, aggressive, and disengaged, lowering their self-confidence and self-esteem. So, we might argue, it's not neighborhood or family characteristics but low achievement that breeds character dispositions and states of mind that invite punitive disciplinary sanctions in school.[29] Others have argued that this correlation between low achievement and behavior that invites discipline is insufficient to explain why blacks are disciplined at a much higher rate than whites.[30] After controlling for student grade-point averages, there is still evidence that race predicts suspension.[31] Furthermore, just as it is implausible to assume that all black children cope with living in a violent neighborhood in the same way, or have the same adverse mental health effects. It also is implausible to assume that all suffer the same psychological ills of low achievement.

A commonplace explanation of racial disproportionality in arrest and imprisonment rates is that blacks commit more crimes than whites. Although not without raising some eyebrows, some people might adapt this explanation to account for the school discipline gap: black students simply act out and threaten school interest in order, security, and safety more than white students, irrespective of their neighborhood or family characteristics or their level of academic achievement. There may be historical, pragmatic, psychological, or even biological explanations for this, but, they may add, whatever the reasons, the discipline gap is a product of racial differences in behavior. And this, they could argue, suffices to explain why police, surveillance cameras, drug-sniffing K-9s, metal detectors, and other exclusionary security measures are more highly concentrated in schools with higher populations of black students.[32]

However, we certainly must ask whether such an opinion is, and has been, nothing more than a pretext for overpolicing blacks—in society and in school—so that their status as full and equal members of society remains precarious. Some historians think so.[33] To hold this controversial viewpoint on racial differences accounting for misbehavior and the discipline gap, one must reckon with empirical evidence to the contrary, showing little if any differences in sanction-generating behavior and racial group membership.[34] One must also address evidence that whites seem to exhibit higher incidences of behavior meriting school discipline.[35] Moreover, one should account for differences in types of behaviors that get sanctioned, and observed correlations between whites getting disciplined for "objective" infractions and blacks for "subjective" ones. For example, one study not only failed to find evidence of differential racial behavior accounting for disciplinary office referrals, it further observed that whites were more likely to be disciplined for smoking, obscenity, and vandalism—more objective infractions—with blacks more often being referred for being disrespectful, threatening, or noisy, which are somewhat more idiosyncratic.[36] The problem is that with discipline, there is more room for discretion and thus for racial bias to operate. And as for a higher frequency of exclusionary security measures being used in predominantly black schools because blacks generally misbehave more than whites, we must consider the possibility that such a learning environment is bad for school climate, which lowers academic achievement and fosters behaviors likely to result in more school discipline.[37]

Unlike the above explanations, which leave us to speculate that certain assumptions are being relied on to explain racial differences in behavior, this differential racial behavior explanation puts the cards on the table: saying explicitly that blacks and whites are different in ways that matter. However, while this has the virtue of being direct, it has the liability of confirming our hypothesis that the Color of Mind is alive and well in contemporary America, helping to sustain school practices that exacerbate the racial achievement gap.

Explaining SPED

Public schools and their teachers must take the kids who show up on their doorstep. Some kids pose no serious issues and require no special attention or unusual resources. Other kids are a different story. Whether due to being unlucky in the natural lottery (for instance, having a genetic birth defect) or due to accident, environment, or trauma, some kids enter school with serious physical, psychological, cognitive, emotional, and behavioral challenges. The entitlement of these kids to equal educational opportunity is a matter of justice. And it is also legally required, thanks to the Education for All Handicapped Children Act of 1975. These children's needs are addressed by providing them with special education (SPED). Ideally, this should be a welcomed opportunity for all kids and families that need it. But, sadly, it isn't.

We know that black children are considerably more likely than their white peers to be identified as being intellectually disabled (formerly "mentally retarded"), emotionally disturbed, or learning disabled.[38] We also know that disabilities are distinguished in different ways; some are less demeaning and stigmatizing than others, and trigger the provision of resources rather than punitive exclusion and isolation.[39] Blacks are labeled in demeaning ways (for instance, intellectually disabled rather than learning disabled) more often than whites, and are segregated from their nondisabled peers. In everyday school practice, the SPED track for blacks is qualitatively different—less attractive and perceptibly inferior—from the one provided to whites. For many black children, SPED becomes a holding cell that sets them behind their peers academically and, in some cases, puts them on the path toward dropping out. For many white children, on the other hand, SPED creates opportunities for additional resources, services, and accommodations that afford them a better chance to realize the benefits of education.[40]

Racial discrimination is a familiar explanation for these practices, but there are certainly others, including resource-related reasons. Both general and special education require certain resources to be effective and to curtail unjust inequalities in school practices. In addition to the obvious need for money to pay for the extra care and attention necessary to accommodate children with disabilities, schools also require human capital resources. School counselors, who are responsible for knowing students, their records, and their needs and for matching them up with the proper academic and, if necessary, enrichment and SPED opportunities, are such a resource, and an important one. These counselors must be trained. They must be competent. They must be on the job and performing necessary tasks. They must also be immune from, or able to resist, administrative and parental pressures that might urge them to make improper decisions about student diagnosis, labeling, and SPED placement. Some people may argue that racial disparities in SPED result when schools lack appropriate counselors, or when they have them but for some reason the counselors cannot do their job effectively.[41] Of course, schools might provide competent counselors ready to work but nevertheless facing challenges interacting with black students, who may be unwilling to seek counseling, may not trust the counselors, or may believe that school personnel are biased and unconcerned with their welfare.

Before students make it to the counselors, however, teachers assess them and decide whether to refer black students for SPED evaluation, which will usually result in SPED placement. This is often a highly subjective matter, especially when it involves the kinds of behaviors that influence discipline referrals, such as being seen as disrespectful, threatening, shiftless, or disruptive. Both counselor evaluation and teacher assessment and referral are stages in the process where biased beliefs about black behavior, character, and intelligence can contribute to racially disproportionate SPED placement outcomes.[42]

Many people believe that children's scores on standardized assessments can provide evidence of a problem that requires SPED placement. Indeed, some studies find that when controlling for demographic and economic factors, student academic achievement remains a strong predictor of SPED referral and placement.[43] When the evaluation and referral process is working correctly, these assessments play a vital role in the final judgment. However, as critics point out, such assessments can be somewhat idiosyncratic and arbitrary, often not accounting for the contextual factors that influence behavior and might shape SPED placement. There is also the possibility of bias in psychological assessments, not to mention student disinterest in completing them, which suggests that these "objective" assessments often serve simply to legitimize segregating kids for different educational experiences.[44]

But what about poverty and its adverse effects? Might poverty best explain racial disparities in SPED placement? Some kids grow up in deprivation and live in segregated neighborhoods that are unstable, violent, and blighted, and in many cases are also food deserts. In addition, they are often exposed to environmental hazards such as lead paint, contaminated water, and other toxins. These structural factors within the context of concentrated poverty are known to have adverse physical, psychological, cognitive, and emotional effects.[45] And their impact may account for why some children show up at school with higher disability rates that require SPED. Schools are certainly not responsible for these larger social problems, and they cannot fix them, as we suggested in chapter 6. Yet they must find suitable arrangements for kids who come to school with these problems. Black children are disproportionately affected by poverty and related perils, but proponents of the poverty explanation suggest that it is economic deprivation, not racial discrimination, that makes the biggest difference to SPED placement.[46] This is a familiar and rather potent line of argument, one that is often espoused by teachers and administrators.[47] It is not without problems, however.

We can distinguish between disabilities directly caused by racial discrimination, and those indirectly caused by it. Suppose that black children have higher rates of certain disabilities stemming from poverty and related ills, and that diagnosis of these disabilities accounts for why they are placed in SPED at higher rates. Even if this were true, because poverty and many of its adverse effects—including living in segregated communities—are associated with the legacy of racial discrimination in the United States and its impact on the construction of segregated dark ghettos, these disabilities and SPED are indirectly due to this legacy.[48] To be sure, this is a weaker claim, but it nevertheless situates the problem of certain disabilities within the broader context of a history that cannot be ignored.

Another problem with the poverty argument, as suggested earlier, is that it requires us to assume that all black kids will respond to poverty in the same way, and will suffer the same physical, psychological, cognitive, and emotional ill effects. But this is implausible.[49] Labels placed on SPED children vary from the most stigmatizing (intellectually disabled) to the least stigmatizing (learning disabled), with emotional disturbance falling somewhere in between. The poverty argument cannot account for why black children are identified as intellectually disabled—the most stigmatizing SPED label—at substantially higher rates than white children. One study reports that nationwide, they are almost three times more likely than their white peers to receive that label.[50] Another shortcoming of the poverty argument is that it does not capture what goes on in wealthier communities with higher-SES blacks, whose children are not only disproportionately placed in SPED but also disproportionately labeled as intellectually disabled and segregated from their nondisabled peers at higher rates than white students.[51] This and other evidence suggest that the cause of racial disproportionality in the SPED track is more complex than a mere lack of resources or counselors or the effects of poverty.[52]

We can consider additional factors to explain the phenomenon, including school discipline practices, school organizational strategies, teachers' level of sensitivity to racial injustice, student's academic achievement level at school entry, the degree of school segregation or desegregation (that is, the percentage of enrolled minority students), and middle-class parental advantage (or lack of it). However, it is likely, as one study concludes, that the "factors that create and maintain racial disparities in special education referral and placement are highly complex and interactive. Therefore, it is critical to avoid simplistic or linear solutions in addressing these issues."[53] A similar point can obviously be made about tracking and discipline practices as well.

A Question of Justice?

Explanations are extensive for the persistence of racial disparities in school practices of special education, discipline, and tracking. We can critically evaluate them and assess the weight of evidence in their favor. While we believe that some explanations are more plausible than others, our argument does not require a resolution of this matter. Indeed, for the sake of argument we can assume that what constitutes the best empirical explanation for these practices remains an open question. Still, there are reasons to take issue with their outcomes on grounds of justice. Having black children in low-track classes, disciplining them disproportionally, and placing them in certain categories of special education at higher rates than whites is manifestly unjust, irrespective of the reasons. This is especially so in light of the history of racially unequal education in the United States, and its role in sustaining the Color of Mind. Explaining why these everyday school practices are unjust and outlining the steps school leaders might take to undo them, and how this bears on closing the racial achievement gap, are the final tasks to which we now turn.

NINE

Unjust Schools: Why the Origins of the Achievement Gap Matter

Recall Jesse's observation in chapter 1 that the hardest part of growing up in Port Clinton, Ohio, during the 1950s was not being accepted as a human being. He and other African Americans—including those from previous generations, such as the aspiring art student that Anna Julia Cooper brought to our attention in the introduction—were deprived of certain educational opportunities, and experienced the denial of their dignity, or inner worth as persons. The construction of racial differences in intellect, character, and conduct, or what we have called the Color of Mind, and its role in establishing racial inequality of educational opportunities and other opportunity gaps, has had a profound impact in shaping the racial achievement gap. The history of its origins and evolution demonstrates that the ignoble American legacy of viewing blacks as inferior remains a problem in education today. And, as the evidence reviewed in chapter 7 shows, the contemporary legacy extends far beyond the fact that some schools remain segregated by race.

With evidence that the Color of Mind still thrives in well-funded, desegregated schools, manifest in routine sorting practices like tracking, school discipline policies, and special education assignments, affronts to black dignity associated with past subjugation endure in new forms. No matter how these sorting practices are explained, as we argue in this chapter, they are a dignitary injustice that school leaders are obligated to address. Some educators already believe that interventions to close the achievement gap ought to be guided by social justice. Others should consider this in reflecting on their professional roles and duties. We believe that if school leaders do what they can to expel the Color of Mind—a persistent affront to black dignity—their efforts will contribute to closing the racial achievement gap. In closing, we propose that these leaders measure their efforts against a Color of Mind Index, and we identify concrete steps which some have taken to improve their results. This will complete our argument that appreciating the historical origins of the racial achievement gap is vital for our ongoing progress toward dignitary justice in education.

Dignitary Injustice in Schools

A cursory examination of egalitarian social movements, such as the abolitionist, women's suffrage, civil rights, and anti-apartheid movements, reveals their varied goals for equality. Sometimes they have sought equal treatment before the law (*procedural equality*); at other times they have advocated for an equal voice for all in lawmaking and in governance (*political equality*); and at yet other times they stood for giving everyone an equal opportunity to attain food, shelter, education, and other necessities for survival or human flourishing (*opportunity equality*). There has also been the goal of recognizing every person, regardless of national origin, religion, race, gender, or class, as having equal moral worth (*status equality*). Demands for status equality have been central to the contemporary, post-Ferguson Black Lives Matter campaign, for instance. These varied goals intersect in certain ways, and clearly there can be arguments over how to prioritize them; but status equality, which can be fruitfully connected with the notion of dignity, is especially germane to our argument.

A long tradition of philosophical thought highlights the ethical significance of viewing individuals as equal persons who should have their dignity recognized and be afforded equal concern and respect.[1] We follow the lead of African American voices of dissent in associating dignitary injustice with failing to regard persons as having equal status. The realization of this status, or what W. E. B. Du Bois called relations between persons based on perfect social equality, is an aspirational ideal. To be sure, there is philosophical work that must be done to flesh out how to understand this ideal, and to clarify what it looks like on the ground in our everyday lives. One way to proceed is to specify ways of relating to one another that are incompatible with relations based on perfect social equality. In other words, we can identify the variety of ways in which we insult, demean, or degrade persons, thereby denying them social recognition of their dignity. Numerous thinkers within the tradition of black social and political thought, including Dr. Martin Luther King Jr., proceeded in this fashion by specifying, in plain terms, the indignities that blacks and other disadvantaged persons have endured in the United States. For instance, King called racial segregation and racial discrimination "evil monsters," and contended that they have stripped "millions of Negro people of their sense of dignity."[2] Sadly, given our American history, this list of evil monsters is shamefully long. To be numbered among them is the Color of Mind and the school practices informed by it, which we have discussed throughout this book, as they too have assailed black dignity.

Schooling practices—whether mandating that black kids and white kids attend "separate and unequal" schools or placing them in integrated schools but sorting them by race in ways that send the pernicious message that black kids are inferior to white ones in intelligence, character, and conduct—clearly do not allow students to look each other in the eye as moral and social equals, notwithstanding any individual differences in talents, interests, and dispositions. Consequently, these too are among the evil monsters constituting dignitary injustice. And, as we noted in chapter 4, going as far back as Frances Ellen Watkins Harper, status equality has informed critical thought about what is owed African Americans as a matter of justice in the domain of education. In theory, this ideal calls for pursuing a social arrangement in which persons can relate to each other not as superiors and inferiors but as moral and social equals. In practice, it entails ordering social practices and institutions to enable such interactions. Historically, philosophers and other thinkers have identified the various mechanisms that have caused society to fall short of status equality.

For philosopher Elizabeth Anderson and other contemporary thinkers who focus attention on asymmetrical relations of power and authority, egalitarian social arrangements should ensure that persons can relate to each other not in terms of oppression, domination, or subordination, but so that "each adult meets every other adult member of society eye to eye, as an equal."[3] Black chattel slavery and Jim Crow are, of course, paradigmatic examples of failures to realize this ideal. Anderson has done much to advance status equality in the egalitarian philosophical tradition, and recently drew from that ideal to argue that racial integration is an imperative of justice. Although we have problems with integration idealism, as we noted in chapter 6, her analysis in her book *The Imperative of Integration* nonetheless offers an illuminating way to make explicit just what status inequality, or being held in lower regard, looks like in practice. Moreover, it provides valuable insights about why this is generally unjust, which we now adapt to assess racial sorting practices within schools.

Anderson begins her argument with the observation that social relations—rule-governed practices or processes that facilitate interaction and ways of affecting interests—between groups of people are a primary concern of justice.[4] It is the character of these social relations, rather than claims to a share of goods or opportunities, that provides a focal point for justice-based moral assessment. People can, of course, organize themselves and be sorted into various kinds of groups, including racial categories. But in the case of black and white racial groups, the claim is that egalitarian justice demands assessing whether blacks and whites are relating to one another as equals. And whether this is the case in practice will turn on whether black citizens are being held in lower regard than whites by being demeaned and stigmatized within rule-governed practices. If it is so, and blacks thus do not stand in relations of equality with whites, then their just claim to be regarded as equals is being violated.

Anderson presumes that racial inequalities, spanning many dimensions of well-being, are not necessarily unjust. Indeed, her view is compatible with persistent material inequalities between racial groups. To assess black-white racial inequality from the standpoint of her relational approach to justice, we must consider three factors: whether this inequality *embodies, causes,* or *is caused by* unjust relations between blacks and whites.

For example, distributing education based on race so that whites are permitted to learn to read and blacks are not *embodies* unjust social relations. This practice in and of itself expresses and entrenches the perception that blacks are intellectually inferior to whites, or do not need the skills of literacy. Distributing a quality education, or one necessary to flourish in today's society, based on either costly and limited school choice options or residency in neighborhoods assessed high property taxes *causes* unjust social relations. It does this by denying some groups a right to an adequate education, as well as a fair opportunity to develop their talents. Anderson claims that recognizing this right is necessary to "enable them to participate as equals in society,"[5] and to "appear in public without shame."[6] A fair opportunity to develop talents is necessary so that groups are not "relegated to an inferior status, confined to menial, servile occupations."[7] Unfair distribution of a good, including education, can be *caused by* unjust social relations in different ways: (1) when it stems from a failure to respect equal rights to a minimal share of a good necessary for interacting with others on equal terms; (2) when it is due to not guaranteeing fair equality of opportunity, or (3) when it results from allowing overt or implicit discrimination against a group.

Of course, inequalities in the distribution of some good, resource, or opportunity can be unjust on all three counts. While the crucial point is that each of these possibilities represents intergroup relations premised on status inequality, Anderson's argument against racial segregation does indeed draw from all three. De jure and de facto segregation, as currently realized in the United States, are unjust forms of social exclusion. She argues that they embody, cause, and are caused by unjust relations between blacks and whites, which makes them inherently unjust. These forms of exclusion involve dominant groups controlling and hoarding resources and opportunities, such as education, through spatial segregation in ways that perpetuate advantage. For Anderson, these are especially important forms of social closure. Segregation, she says, "is the linchpin of categorical inequality, since it is needed to keep critical goods preferentially circulating within the dominant social group and out of the hands of the subordinate group, except on disadvantageous terms."[8]

There is nothing inherently wrong with groups favoring their own members. Indeed, social psychologists have long established that social groups may show favoritism by self-segregation, and perhaps by promulgating positive stories about themselves. But concerns of justice arise when group self-interest manifests itself in dominant in-groups seeking to hoard resources and opportunities by relying, in part, on stigmatizing subordinate out-groups. Among other things, this behavior may reinforce spatial and social boundaries between an in-group and an out-group, and it may be used to explain and rationalize inequalities between the two.[9]

Social psychologists have developed a rich theoretical framework for thinking about inegalitarian group-based social hierarchies. While whites, the dominant racial group in the United States, enjoy a larger share of all the benefits of wealth, education, power, and status, subordinate racial groups such as African Americans have a disproportionately lower share of these, as well as a higher share of burdens such as punishment.[10] One important element of this social dominance orientation is the mechanisms that hold the race-based social hierarchies and attending social inequalities in place. A pertinent example is a "hierarchy-legitimizing myth," which "consists of attitudes, values, beliefs, stereotypes, and ideologies that provide moral and intellectual justification for the social practices that distribute social value within the social system."[11] While some myths—such as the idea of God-given natural rights to freedom—seek to foster greater social equality, others aim to entrench hierarchies and promote social inequality. These are called "hierarchy-enhancing legitimizing myths." The Color of Mind is an archetypal example of just such a myth, representing beliefs about racial differences in intelligence as well as temperament and character that have, and continue to, justify ways of educating children to sustain a racial status hierarchy. It is antithetical to viewing blacks as moral and social equals and contributes directly to harmful stigma.[12]

Stigma plays a crucial role in Anderson's story, and in ours about why school sorting practices are unjust. It captures the essential dignitary injustice involved in group-based status inequality. Relying on stigmatizing stories or stereotypes, or on hierarchy-enhancing myths, to rationalize educational or other forms of opportunity hoarding by whites over blacks is both inherently unjust and instrumentally unjust. Anderson makes the point this way: "Conduct grounded in group prejudice or stigma toward racial, gender, ethnic, and similar groups is always unjust because it *assaults the dignity of groups that do not deserve to be demeaned* [our emphasis], and it usually also impairs their access to important goods on unjustified grounds. Those disadvantaged by such conduct have a moral claim that the actors moved by prejudice or stigma stop."[13]

Appealing to such stigmatizing stories constitutes an expressive harm to out-group members, and offers a pretext for flouting principles of antidiscrimination and justice as fairness. Anderson contends that the liberal state should take action to block these outcomes. While she acknowledges the importance of respecting the boundaries between the public and private domains as well as the differences between the legal and moral realms, she cautions against allowing "the seeds of injustice," such as out-group stigmatizing stories and stereotypes, to grow outside these relations. She thinks that this worry calls for preemptive and robust measures to offset or counteract the use of stigmatizing stereotypes in private ethnocentric relations. As she puts it, "Because such affiliation contains the seeds of injustice, the state should take steps to prevent ethnocentric patterns of affiliation from reproducing themselves in institutions of civil society such as public schools."[14]

The notion of status inequality offers a compelling rationale for assessing the school sorting practices we have considered. We can ask whether they *sustain* or *reinforce* the perception that black students are inferior in intellect, character, and conduct to whites. Do they, in other words, sustain the Color of Mind? We suggest that they do so unavoidably. Much like the historical denial of education to blacks in the past, and the establishment of separate and inferior education, these contemporary sorting practices—whatever their causes—serve to sustain and reinforce invidious racial stereotypes about blacks. Insofar as school sorting practices have this consequence, they constitute a dignitary injustice. Perpetuating these stigmatizing stereotypes is an affront to the dignity of African American students, violating their just claim to be treated as equal persons. These everyday systemic sorting practices, which also affect black student achievement, run afoul of Harper's imperative of reverence for black dignity, which is not only a moral imperative but also a demand of dignitary justice.

Thus, each of the systemic sorting practices we have considered, along with the racial disparities associated with them, do indeed suffice to sustain the Color of Mind. Racially disproportionate tracking, school discipline, and special education practices inflict an expressive harm on the dignity of black students, sending a clear message that impugns their inner worth as persons. As a result, they constitute a dignitary injustice, which is distinct from other injustices associated with the adverse material consequences these sorting practices may have on African American educational attainment, job prospects, and wealth accumulation, along with self-concept. They also undermine fair opportunity to black students to compete for resources and opportunities to live not just a satisfactory life but also a meaningful and rewarding one. To be sure, as we acknowledged in the previous chapter, there is considerable disagreement over why black kids and white kids ultimately get sorted in schools. Yet the dignitary injustice of these practices is settled, in our view, without resting on any particular explanation of racial sorting disparities, and this is a virtue.[15]

Of course, the dignity of African American students is also at risk in highly segregated and under-resourced inner-city schools, even if racial sorting is not as plainly evident. In predominantly black urban schools, kids clearly see the gross disparities in educational resources, facilities, teacher quality, curricular and extracurricular opportunities, and the like. And these disparities cannot help but reinforce the Color of Mind. To be sure, these resource and opportunity gaps may generate differences in achievement between black kids in these schools and their white counterparts. But unless we are in the grip of the Color of Mind, there is no reason to attribute these to innate racial differences in ability. And, as W. E. B. Du Bois observed during his day, blacks themselves are not immune from this way of thinking.[16] They too can come to believe that "multiplication is for white people," or to believe that they must flee black schools and attend integrated ones if they want to be educated. A society with racially separate schools, where black schools are grossly under-resourced relative to predominantly white or racially mixed schools, bears a striking resemblance to the pre-*Brown* era. To the extent that it does, the Color of Mind will operate the way it did then, and will constitute a dignitary injustice, just as it did then.

So although sorting practices are not at issue in majority black urban schools, where these schools are under-resourced and "inferior," some black kids cannot help but conclude that they are not regarded as having equal worth. Addressing this dignitary harm informed the Supreme Court's decision to overturn *Plessy* and to "save hearts and minds" in *Brown*. And nearly two decades earlier, when America was tightly in the grip of Jim Crow education, confronting the ramifications of the Color of Mind loomed large in Du Bois's arguments for separate black schools in a society rife with racial prejudice and intractable race-based opportunity gaps. We must remain realistic about what urban school leaders can accomplish in closing opportunity gaps between their schools and others. Still, they can certainly find ways to address the Color of Mind and the dignitary harms it perpetuates on kids. For instance, as Du Bois and many others have proposed, leaders of predominantly black schools can support a curriculum that provides the kind of cultural perspectives that can offset the impression that black kids do not have the same worth as kids in "better" schools.[17] Such curriculum reform is but one of several innovative strategies adopted by social justice school leaders in racially segregated schools to expel the Color of Mind.

A Color of Mind Index

We have not written this book to offer sweeping policy recommendations for closing the black-white achievement gap. School leaders, other educators, and policymakers are in the best position to do this, though they must rely on evidence and knowledge. To date, they have largely relied on data and ideas supplied by the social and behavioral sciences, especially economics, sociology, and psychology. We have, however, provided another layer of understanding—not available in the social science domain—regarding the origins of racial educational opportunity and achievement gaps and why they persist in the United States. Consequently, our humanistic collaboration between history and philosophy has brought additional insight and knowledge to light that can inform school reform in the interest of justice. Exposing the Color of Mind as the rotten root of these problems also suggests a useful accountability tool that may be helpful to school leaders wishing to expel the Color of Mind from their schools, and make further progress in closing the racial achievement gap.

One way to help ensure a degree of accountability for school leaders, other educators, parents, and students is to monitor the way that schools address disproportionate treatment of students along racial lines. As we have already shown, there are many reasons for black children to be excluded from the most demanding classes, to be subject to the harshest disciplinary measures, and to be assigned to certain special education categories—but if these different forms of treatment affect black students in numbers out of proportion to their share of the school population and that of its community, questions of dignitary justice arise. The disparate impact of such racialized sorting practices serves to legitimize the Color of Mind daily, reinforcing noxious stereotypes with deep historical roots and undermining the prospects of black students being treated with dignity. For these reasons, it is essential that schools that are serious about addressing dignitary injustice work to end these sorting practices and prevent them from reoccurring.

A concrete approach to operationalizing what we call a *Color of Mind Index*—a school accountability tool—might be to frame it as a ratio, similar to the "risk ratios" presented in our earlier discussion of disproportionality in special education. The same type of assessment could be made to estimate the comparative likelihood of black students being placed in lower-track classrooms and being subjected to the most severe forms of punitive discipline. So, for example, if black students in a school were twice as likely as other students to be in a particular class, or subject to a certain form of discipline, the risk ratio would be 2. On the other hand, if there was no difference, the ratio would be 1. Obviously, the role of a school leader concerned about the dignitary injustice associated with the Color of Mind would be to reduce the risk of black students experiencing any of these forms of indignity to 1, if not lower.

With respect to tracking, a big step in accomplishing this risk reduction would be to ensure that the numbers of black students in higher-track courses approximate the same percentage of those classes as their share of the school population. This may not be easy to do at first, and it may encounter resistance from parents and others concerned with "standards" and other issues. But it is a critically important goal for the school as a whole to strive for. It might require additional academic support for students who want to take these classes and whose record indicates the possibility of success. It may require active recruitment of promising students to participate in such preparation. But in all such efforts, it will be necessary to maintain a critical mass of these students and provide the support and encouragement of the entire school community. And this can be accomplished only by explicitly addressing the Color of Mind as a formidable obstacle.

Another step, which pertains to school discipline, is to closely monitor disciplinary policies and practices to ensure that African American students are not more likely than other groups to be subjected to detentions, suspensions, expulsions, and other forms of punitive discipline. As noted earlier, national data and case studies of particular schools suggest that black students are punished more severely for relatively minor infractions than other students. They are widely perceived to "lack respect" or "respond inappropriately" to school authorities, behavior which may well be conditioned by their experiences. School personnel should be prepared to react responsibly and professionally when interacting with black students, seek their perspective on circumstances in which they find themselves, and treat them with the same dignity and sense of fairness afforded other students.

Additionally, black students should not be overrepresented in special education classifications that cause them to be segregated from their peers in everyday classrooms and other school activities. In particular, they should not be classified as intellectually or emotionally disabled without clear, indisputable evidence, and not simply the impressions or judgments of school personnel based on previous experience or interaction with the individuals concerned. These often are decisions with highly significant consequences for the students who are assigned such potentially stigmatizing labels, and when large numbers of black students receive such treatment it further reinforces the Color of Mind. The historical and social implications of such classifications should be carefully explained to parents and students before these classifications are utilized, which also could help decrease these problematic placements.

As a consequence of measures such as these, the disproportionate representation of black students being assigned to lower-track classes, facing punitive discipline, and being relegated to the most stigmatizing special education classifications ought to diminish substantially. When black students are no more likely than other students in the school to experience these forms of indignity, and the Color of Mind Index (or risk ratio) stands at 1, the conditions for expelling the Color of Mind exist, as does the resulting contribution this will make to closing the racial achievement gap. Progress may not happen right away, of course, and it must be subject to constant monitoring and correction; but using such an accountability tool could mark the beginning of the end for the racialization of sorting practices in schools, and a significant step toward expelling the Color of Mind from school.

Expelling the Color of Mind

Numerous case studies show that some school leaders concerned about dignitary injustice have already taken steps within their schools that seem to make a difference in tackling racialized sorting practices that sustain the Color of Mind. While we leave it to others to assess these efforts, here we merely cite them as ways in which some school leaders have proceeded, noting that much of what they have done does not require a windfall of additional resources, and lies well within their power and authority.

Perhaps the greatest attention has been given to tracking, and to the social dimension of "detracking" as an answer to the problems it poses. It is fundamentally a human process rather than a technical one. In her compelling description of detracking efforts in several schools in the Northeast, Carol Corbett Burris discusses seven steps:

1   Establish a stable and committed leadership.
2   Eliminate low-track classes first (level up rather than down).
3   Build support structures for struggling learners.
4   Support and engage the staff, especially in curriculum planning.
5   Start small and build outward.
6   Collect and disseminate achievement data regularly.
7   Respond to the concern of parental and other external parties.

Burris suggests additional points, but these steps seem essential and quite workable. To be sure, none of this will occur if students, parents, and (most significantly) teachers do not want it to happen; it necessarily begins with hearts and minds.[18] And equipping school leaders with a historically grounded account of the origins of the racial achievement gap can aid detracking, particularly by breaking down resistance rooted in ignorance of the Color of Mind and how it thrives in school sorting practices.

As Burris notes, some parents and teachers believe that intelligence is a hereditable and immutable human attribute, and that racial differences in mental ability are innate and generally impervious to the efforts of educators. Adults with these attitudes tend to be opponents of detracking, asserting that measurable ability levels should be the principal criteria for admission to high-track classes. They are likely to be white, relatively affluent, and well educated. Some reportedly declared outright that they did not want their children attending class with "those kids," or, more explicitly, "with the black kids."[19] Experienced teachers who enjoy working with upper-track kids often oppose changes that threaten their comfortable routine.[20] Clearly, if attitudes such as these are prevalent, detracking is highly unlikely to succeed. Here our analysis can be instructive.

Burris suggests that parental anxieties can be managed by demonstrating that the education of high-achieving kids will not be compromised with the end of tracking, that in fact detracking can occur without undermining the academic performance of the school's best students. This means that standards must be maintained, and reliable, wholehearted support provided for struggling students. The latter may require a reallocation of resources, or additional funds from grants or other sources, but it is an essential part of the process. And it too is unlikely to succeed if teachers and other members of the school community do not believe that African American and other minority students can flourish in a demanding academic environment. Successful detracking also requires renewed attention to instruction for most teachers, utilizing constructivist approaches to help students engage with difficult material in ways that are helpful to them.[21] As Burris and others have discovered, the results can be quite remarkable. There are ample cases where detracking has been accomplished, demonstrating that students from all kinds of backgrounds can respond positively to it.[22]

Leadership is clearly a key element to such a process of transformation. And Burris notes that changes of principals or superintendents can derail a promising plan of change very quickly. As a number of scholars have pointed out, schools are highly resistant to institutional change, and teachers in particular are often skeptical about reforms that demand changes to their familiar instructional routines. Teaching is a highly personal endeavor, so its practitioners are naturally suspicious of new ideas espoused by leaders who may leave at any time. Consequently, it is critically important for all members of the school community to be involved in planning for reforms such as these. Without such involvement, meaningful change is unlikely to occur.[23]

George Theoharis, in another study, focuses on seven school principals who have undertaken social justice reform measures at schools across the American Midwest. A former principal himself, Theoharis covers much of the same ground as Burris, but focuses less on discrete steps to realizing change. The Color of Mind looms large in this account also, as each of the school leaders in his book made regular discussions of race and racism a centerpiece of the change process. This was essential to establishing the importance of reform of existing practices from the standpoint of social justice. Each of these leaders recognized the critical human dimension of change in schools, and that staff members would have to share a common vision of justice concerns for the process to succeed. Common values and a commitment to eliminating injustice by transforming the school climate were key in each case. This proved to be very hard work, but each of the principals discussed in the book made considerable headway.[24]

Each principal took different paths, but all started with identifying key teacher-leaders who could help begin a process of change from the bottom up. Steps undertaken resembled those described by Burris in most cases, but Theoharis focuses on the role of the building leader as offering a vision, organizing opportunities for collaboration and planning, smoothing obstacles, providing incentives and rewards, involving parents, and negotiating with district administrators. Each leader struggled to navigate the tide of administrative tasks in order to focus on instruction and curricular change, and detracking in particular. They also addressed discipline disparities (crucial to lowering the discipline risk ratio), working with parents and community members to be sure that their concerns about fairness were considered in the change process. It was exhausting work, but driven by a genuine commitment to stamping out dignitary injustice and improving school climate. It was that moral commitment to dignitary justice as a fundamental value that pushed the reform process forward.[25] These case studies provide examples of how substantial progress can be made toward expelling the Color of Mind from schools in a practical and effective manner.

Theoharis also offers examples of how principals reorganized school resources to enable teachers to transition successfully to a detracked instructional regime. This involved defining new roles for support personnel, special education teachers, and other staff members to create classroom environments where differentiated learning could be managed effectively. To be sure, these changes required the enthusiastic affirmation of everyone involved in order to succeed, and did not occur overnight. But the ability of school leaders to offer a vision of how the work of teaching could be arranged differently was a key component of the process. It pointed to a way out of the "business as usual" mindset that often prevails in educational institutions, and the narrowly prescribed roles that educators sometimes define for themselves. By focusing attention on the problem of dignitary injustice, a critical task of the school leader became one of removing institutional barriers to black and white students relating to one another as moral and social equals.[26] This allowed the whole school community to address the systemic practices that served to sustain the Color of Mind.

In the end, as Theoharis notes, this type of institutional change is less about particular steps or administrative adjustments. Instead, it is a matter of changing school climate from one of preferences and privilege for some students, to one of equal commitment to the dignity and success of all. At the heart of this process is enlightening school community members about the Color of Mind, its origins, and why understanding these origins matters for making schools just. Teachers and other members of the staff must confront their own beliefs about race and education, and confront the terrible history of those beliefs, to anchor their commitment to change and to dignitary justice in education. As each of these school leaders recognized, without such reflection and understanding, lasting reform was unlikely to occur. A school climate of dignitary justice requires the Color of Mind to stop at the building's doors, however much havoc it may be causing beyond the schoolyard. Whatever the rest of the world may think or do, school leaders and educators can take control of what happens in their schools, and resolve not to let the Color of Mind run wild on their watch. This is not only a critical step in creating schools that provide equality of educational opportunity for everyone,[27] but an imperative of dignitary justice, which has implications for closing the racial achievement gap.

Institutional transformation on this scale is not easy, of course, and simply doing away with one or more tracks is unlikely to produce dramatic change right away. In some cases, careful intermediate steps may be necessary, such as mandatory high-track assignments for capable minority students.[28] But whatever these steps happen to be, only by deliberately and comprehensively confronting sorting practices can conditions that help sustain the Color of Mind be altered. School districts and state education authorities can aid in the process. For instance, they can sponsor workshops led by educators who have succeeded in creating an antiracist school climate. They can also support the preparation and distribution of relevant readings and other professional development materials. While the impetus for changes such as these must occur at the building level, other educational leaders need to be proactively supportive as well.[29]

While the foregoing has focused on detracking, similar considerations apply to discipline and special education sorting. In the end, efforts to dismantle pernicious sorting practices are part and parcel of creating a more positive and hospitable school climate for black students, providing them equal opportunities for academic success. This must be accomplished without resentment or resistance from other students, or from adults associated in one way or another with public schools. Such a climate, after all, is what all children should be offered by educational institutions. The fact that this needs explicit articulation, along with a proviso about the possibility of hostility or resentment, is evidence of the continuing power of the Color of Mind.

There is a difference between putting bodies in a classroom or school, which idealistic integrationists have long proposed, and dismantling—root and branch—the systemic practices steeped in a long history of irreverence for black dignity. As race-sensitive yet realistic integrationists, we believe that bringing black and white students together within schools, formally and socially, must work in tandem with contravening the Color of Mind. Our historical argument shows that the two have worked together, and so they must be dealt with together. Social justice school leadership must therefore be mindful of the complicated relationship between systemic practices and racial ideology.

Closing the Racial Achievement Gap

We certainly do not assume that there is widespread agreement on how to close the achievement gap. On the contrary, we admit that there is sharp disagreement, especially between conservatives and liberals. The former typically say that we need to fix black kids, their families, and their culture. They say we need to stop making excuses for bad behavior, incompetent teachers, and failing schools; advocate the use of carrots and sticks to improve individual performance for students and teachers alike; and provide private and semiprivate alternatives to "failing" public schools. Incentives, accountability, and choice are the conservatives' keys to closing the achievement gap. Meanwhile, liberals say we need to end racial discrimination (overt and implicit) and create genuine equality of educational opportunity. They call for more resources and for redistributing existing assets to students and schools with the greatest needs. Many also decry the retreat from *Brown*'s promise, and renew calls for school integration. Antidiscrimination, resources, and integration are archetypal liberals' keys to closing the achievement gap.[30]

These competing strategies correspond to contrasting accounts of the achievement gap. A focus on factors *internal* to black children, their families, and their communities, as conservatives often do, favors certain kinds of interventions. Looking to *external* factors to explain the achievement gap, the preferred liberal approach, points to other solutions. Given today's polarized political debates (often framed in these stark terms), policymakers frequently settle on partisan solutions to intricate social problems, and more elaborate proposals fail to gain traction. However, closing the black-white achievement gap, and addressing the host of problems associated with it, is a deeply rooted problem with a long history demanding a multifaceted solution.

As a starting point, certain essential expectations must be established. Teachers should be held responsible for teaching, school principals should be answerable for cultivating a climate for learning and trust, and students should be rewarded for good behavior and penalized for serious misconduct. At the same time, as suggested in our discussion of the Color of Mind Index, explicit and implicit forms of racial bias in schools should not be tolerated, nor should harmful racial stereotypes be permitted to impair academic achievement. Furthermore, schools should not be asked to make straw with insufficient water: resources should suffice to meet student needs, and schools with populations of students whose needs are more costly should be funded accordingly. When politics and ideology take a backseat to ensuring equality of educational opportunity, the wisdom of crafting interventions that draw from a variety of perspectives can prevail. However, meager resources and disagreements on these points need not stand in the way of school leaders carrying out their duty to expel the Color of Mind from their schools, or so we have argued.

We do not offer or pretend to have a comprehensive solution to the racial achievement gap. But we do believe that school leaders taking responsibility to change unjust school practices that sustain the Color of Mind can contribute a great deal to closing it. What is generally missing in the social science and policy domains, in addition to careful reflection on the historical origins of the achievement gap, is philosophical reflection on what justice in education demands. This includes determining the responsibilities entailed in closing the achievement gap, and who should bear them. Maintaining a historical sense of perspective is important here. Preoccupation with proximate causes and targeted interventions, whether piecemeal or multifaceted, may foreclose reflection on connections between past and present. This can contribute to neglect of important questions of justice, and the answers, informed by awareness of the Color of Mind and its dreadful history.

Not all school leaders are concerned with justice, but many current and aspiring ones most certainly are. Social justice school leaders want to bring academic achievement with dignity to their schools. The Color of Mind Index may be a helpful means of getting this work started. In this book, relying on a history of the origins of the achievement gap, we have argued that closing the black-white achievement gap and fostering respect for the dignity of black students must go hand in hand. The history shows that the Color of Mind and the color of schooling have worked in tandem to constrain educational opportunities and achievement for African Americans in the United States. It also shows that black dignity—reviled or revered—has been, from the very beginning, centrally at stake in defenses of the racial status quo as well as in efforts to challenge it and reverse its impact on black educational achievement and attainment.

There are, of course, important differences between today and the time when Du Bois wrote about the possibility of blacks experiencing "perfect social equality" in their own schools. Many changes have occurred, including the accomplishments of the civil rights movement and the formal desegregation of many American schools. But history has also shown that blacks and whites have continued to receive unequal educational opportunities based on constructed racial differences in intelligence, character, and conduct—from yesterday's desegregated schools to the in-school sorting practices of today. History has also revealed that these sorting practices have sustained and reinforced these purported racial differences, creating a pernicious mutually reinforcing cycle denigrating black dignity.

The origins of the black-white achievement gap can be traced to the beginning of formal education in the United States, and its roots extend to the foundations of European Enlightenment philosophy. The racial ideology of this era planted the seeds from which the Color of Mind sprung. And from its very beginning, this conception that skin color and certain other outward physical traits are linked to behavior and mental capabilities represented a dreadful, debilitating deceit, intended to warrant the servile status of all people racialized as black. It thus became a fountainhead from which continuing degradation of blacks in America continues to flow today.

In the end, this is why the origins of the achievement gap matter for justice. Until its beginnings are readily acknowledged, identified in everyday school practices and policies, and resisted vigorously, the power of the Color of Mind is unlikely to disappear. This too is what history teaches us, and it is a lesson all educators should heed earnestly. The school leaders our children deserve must be aware of this, and work to ensure that black dignity does not remain denigrated in their schools, as it does in other domains beyond the schoolyard, where black lives still seem not to matter. Those of us who care about dignity, justice, and equity in academic achievement should make every effort to help current and future generations of educators advance this urgent and noble cause. Without this effort, we are unlikely to see substantial progress in closing the racial achievement gap.

Scholarship is a collective enterprise, and many people have supported us, in large and small ways, in writing this book. We are especially grateful to Jon Zimmerman and Randall Curren; without them our collaboration would not have happened. They invited us to write about the achievement gap for this book series on the history and philosophy of education. In addition to providing written feedback on multiple occasions, and supporting our American Council of Learned Societies (ACLS) fellowship application, they afforded us wonderful opportunities to meet with other authors in the series to discuss work in progress. We benefited immensely from these occasions in New York City and Rochester, New York, and we are grateful to the participants for giving us terrific feedback during the early stages of our work. We owe a special debt to Paula McAvoy for comments that helped us identify our target audience for the book, an invaluable contribution indeed.

We are fortunate to have had generous financial support for our research and writing from the Spencer Foundation and ACLS. Spencer provided the resources for our initial research forays and preliminary drafting of the first half of the book, and a 2014 joint research presentation at the International Standing Conference on the History of Education. A collaborative research fellowship from ACLS gave us an academic year to complete the research and finish the book, along with additional research and travel support. And our home institutions—the University of Michigan and the University of Kansas—were entirely supportive of our leaves. These grants were absolutely essential to the process of melding history and philosophy in a cohesive narrative. We are most grateful to both organizations for their confidence in us, and for the resources to make our collaboration so fruitful. We could not have written this book independently of each other.

We would also like to thank students, staff, and audiences at various institutions with which we shared parts of the book. KU graduate students Katy Merriweather and Jennifer Hurst were intrepid research assistants: they dug up old ideological tracts and tracked down more contemporary information; they also provided feedback on matters of style, including citation formatting. Kristie Faust in the College of Literature, Science, and the Arts at the University of Michigan and Kathy Porsch at the KU Hall Center for the Humanities were indispensable in helping us with our successful grant applications and their management. We benefited from discussion at seminars on parts of our manuscript held at New York University's Steinhardt School and Columbia University's Teachers College, and from additional research presentations at the University of Pennsylvania (the Graduate School of Education and the Department of Philosophy); the University of Chicago School of Law; Georgia State University; King's College; and the University of Illinois at Chicago.

We have used material from the following articles with permission from the publishers and editors: John L. Rury and Derrick Darby, "War and Education in the United States: Racial Ideology and Inequality in Three Historical Episodes," *Paedagogica Historica* 52, nos. 1–2 (February–April 2016): 8–24; and Sylvia L. M. Martinez and John L. Rury, "From 'Culturally Deprived' to 'At Risk': The Politics of Popular Expression and Educational Inequality in the United States, 1960–1985," *Teachers College Record* 114, no. 6 (June 2012): 1–31.

Academic life keeps us all very busy. We thus are extremely grateful for the generous colleagues who supported us by reading and commenting on early drafts of our entire manuscript. Our deepest gratitude is owed to Shawn Alexander, Prudence Carter, Thomas McCarthy, and two anonymous readers for the University of Chicago Press. They have all helped us write a better book.

We would also like to thank our editor at the press, Elizabeth Branch Dyson, for all her encouragement and support of this project, which included very helpful comments regarding the manuscript. Along with Jon and Randy, she has been a steadfast and enthusiastic advocate of our vision for this book, which made the process of bringing it to publication especially rewarding. Copy editor Sandra Hazel did a terrific job of improving our prose and finding innumerable errors and omissions in the manuscript. Hannah Bailey skillfully and cheerfully produced the index..

The task of academic research and writing is often a lonely one, although in this case we did a great deal of the work together, which has been immensely rewarding. Still, when off on our own, doing the solitary reading, research, and writing needed to finish the job, we benefited from the patience, understanding, and support of our wonderful partners, Angela and Aïda, to whom we dedicate this book as a small token of our heartfelt gratitude.

NOTES

INTRODUCTION

1. *The Voice of Anna Julia Cooper, Including "A Voice from the South" and Other Important Essays, Papers, and Letters*, ed. Charles Lemert and Esme Bhan (Lanham, MD: Rowman and Littlefield, 1998), p. 103.

2. W. E. Burghardt Du Bois, "Does the Negro Need Separate Schools?," *Journal of Negro Education* 4, no. 3 (1935): 328–35.

3. Ibid., p. 328. It was not unheard of for whites and blacks to relate on terms of equality, as Cooper notes: "A noble army of Christian workers and helpers have gone to the South ever since the [Civil] War, have lived with [Negroes] on terms of Christian sympathy and perfect social equality." *The Voice of Anna Julia Cooper*, p. 211. But this certainly has been the exception rather than the rule, and it has not been a feature of schooling in America.

4. Important work has been done on the importance of closing opportunity gaps and achievement gaps. See, for example, Prudence L. Carter and Kevin G. Welner, eds., *Closing the Opportunity Gap: What America Must Do to Give Every Child an Even Chance* (New York: Oxford University Press, 2013). What we add to this debate is the insight that the Color of Mind underwrites both, and so taking on racial ideology directly is indispensable for closing both gaps.

5. For an account of how this kind of injustice, of not being related to as a social equal, contributes to racial injustice beyond the schoolyard, see Elizabeth S. Anderson, *The Imperative of Integration* (Princeton, NJ: Princeton University Press, 2010).

6. For instance, thinkers have asked whether justice demands that persons have an equal share of distributable goods or resources such as income or wealth. For some of them, distributive injustice results when persons have unequal shares of these things, but for others it obtains only when they have unequal shares unrelated to how hard a person works, the choices they make, or their preferences.

7. Within philosophy the idea that humanity has an inner worth is now a familiar one thanks partly to Immanuel Kant. A rich tradition of secular and religious thought has contributed to our understanding of the concept of dignity. See Michael Rosen, *Dignity: Its History and Meaning* (Cambridge, MA: Harvard University Press, 2012).

8. For instance, arguing for the equal dignity of persons of all races, Cooper calls attention to the conceptual link between equality and dignity: "The concept of Equality as it is the genuine product of the idea of inherent value in the individual derived

from the essential worth of Humanity," Cooper contends, "must be before all else unquestionably of universal application." *The Voice of Anna Julia Cooper*, p. 297.

9. Avishai Margalit, *The Decent Society* (Cambridge, MA: Harvard University Press, 1996).

10. Donna Hicks, *Dignity: Its Essential Role in Resolving Conflicts* (New Haven, CT: Yale University Press, 2011).

11. For a philosophical elaboration of this ideal, see Samuel Scheffler, "The Practice of Equality," in *Social Equality: On What It Means to Be Equals*, ed. Carina Fourie, Fabian Schuppert, and Ivo Wallimann-Helmer (Oxford: Oxford University Press, 2015), pp. 21–44.

12. Jeremy Waldron, *Dignity, Rank, and Rights* (New York: Oxford University Press, 2012), p. 60.

13. David P. Baker, *The Schooled Society: The Educational Transformation of Global Culture* (Palo Alto, CA: Stanford University Press, 2014).

14. One could, for instance, associate dignitary injustice with inequitable distributions of goods such as income, wealth, and education or with the unequal opportunity to acquire them, and then ask whether these inequalities can be justified to persons who take themselves to have equal dignity.

15. W. E. Burghardt Du Bois, "The Conservation of Races," in *The American Negro Academy Occasional Papers, no. 2* (Washington, DC: The Academy, 1897), pp. 3–15.

16. Ibid., p. 5.

17. Ibid., p. 7.

18. See, for example, Anthony Appiah, "The Uncompleted Argument: Du Bois and the Illusion of Race," *Critical Inquiry* 12 (1985): 21–37; Paul Taylor, "Appiah's Uncompleted Argument: Du Bois and the Reality of Race," *Social Theory and Practice* 26 (2000): 103–28.

19. Dorothy Roberts, *Fatal Invention: How Science, Politics, and Big Business Re-Create Race in the Twenty First Century* (New York: New Press, 2011).

20. Khalil Gibran Muhammad, *The Condemnation of Blackness: Race, Crime, and the Making of Modern Urban America* (Cambridge, MA: Harvard University Press, 2010).

21. Ivan Hannaford, *Race: The History of an Idea in the West* (Washington, DC: Woodrow Wilson Center Press, 1996).

22. For discussion of this, see Robert Wald Sussman, *The Myth of Race: The Troubling Persistence of an Unscientific Idea* (Cambridge, MA: Harvard University Press, 2014), introduction.

23. Christopher Jencks and Meredith Phillips, eds., *The Black-White Test Score Gap* (Washington, DC: Brookings, 1998).

24. Grace Kao and Jennifer S. Thompson, "Racial and Ethnic Stratification in Educational Achievement and Attainment," *Annual Review of Sociology* 29 (2003): 417–42.

25. See discussion of these points in chapter 3.

26. Monica Anderson, "A Rising Share of the U.S. Black Population Is Foreign Born," Pew Research Center, Social and Demographic Trends, April 9, 2015, available at http://www.pewsocialtrends.org/2015/04/09/a-rising-share-of-the-u-s-black-population-is-foreign-born/.

27. Kevin J. A. Thomas, "Familial Influences on Poverty among Young Children in Black Immigrant, U.S. Born and Non-Black Immigrant Families," *Demography* 48, no. 2 (May 2011): 456. Also see V. Bashi and A. McDaniel, "A Theory of Immigration and Racial Stratification," *Journal of Black Studies* 27 (1997): 668–82; J. Gela and D. Dixon, "Detailed Characteristics of the Caribbean Population in the United States," Migra-

tion Policy Institute, accessed April 19, 2017, http://www.migrationpolicy.org/article
/detailed-characteristics-caribbean-born-united-states; and E. Grieco, "The African
Foreign Born in the United States," Migration Policy Institute, accessed April 19,
2017, http://www.migrationpolicy.org/article/african-foreign-born-united-states.

28. The Broad Foundation, "New Education R&D Lab Aims to Advance Innovations in
Public Education," news release, September 25, 2008, http://www.broadfoundation
.org/asset/1165-0-080924edlabspressreleasefinal.pdf.

29. Alan Vanneman, Linda Hamilton, Janet Baldwin Anderson, and Taslima Rahman,
*Achievement Gaps: How Black and White Students in Public Schools Perform in Mathe-
matics and Reading on the National Assessment of Educational Progress; Statistical Analysis
Report* (Washington, DC: National Center for Educational Statistics, 2009).

30. Alfinio Flores, "Examining Disparities in Mathematics Education: Achievement Gap
or Opportunity Gap?," *High School Journal* 91, no. 1 (October–November 2007):
29–42; Fan French, "Closing Opportunity and Cultural Competency Gaps," *ASCD:
Disrupting Inequality* 12, no. 6 (November 2016); available at http://www.ascd.org
/ascd-express/vol12/1206-french.aspx.

31. Carter and Welner, *Closing the Opportunity Gap*, p. 9.

32. See, for instance, Patricia Cohen, "I.Q. Debate Adds a Chapter Online," *New York
Times*, December 1, 2007, available at http://www.nytimes.com/2007/12/01/books
/01race.html.

33. On this point, see National Center for Educational Statistics, *School Composition and
the Racial Achievement Gap*, September 22, 2015, p. 22; available at https://nces.ed.gov
/nationsreportcard/studies/gaps/.

34. Lisa Delpit, *"Multiplication Is for White People": Raising Expectations for Other People's
Children* (New York: New Press, 2012).

35. George Theoharis, *The School Leaders Our Children Deserve: Seven Keys to Equity, Social
Justice, and School Reform* (New York: Teachers College Press, 2009).

CHAPTER ONE

1. Allen Vaneman, Linda Hamilton, Janet Baldwin Anderson, and Taslima Rahman,
*Achievement Gaps: How Black and White Students in Public Schools Perform in Mathe-
matics and Reading on the National Assessment of Educational Progress* (Washington, DC:
National Center for Educational Statistics, 2009), pp. 6–11.

2. Paul E. Barton and Richard J. Coley, *The Black White Achievement Gap: When Progress
Stopped*, Policy Information Report (Princeton, NJ: Policy Information Center, Educational Testing Service, 2010), passim. A 2010 report used NAEP data to document a
substantially shrinking achievement gap from the early 1970s through the late 1980s,
stalled progress during the 1990s, modest narrowing from 1999 to 2004, and slowed
progress after that. In short, the nation never made better progress in closing racial
achievement gaps in mathematics and reading than during the 1970s and 1980s.
For discussion of state assessments, see Nancy Kober, Victor Chudowsky and Naomi
Chudowski, "Slow and Uneven Progress in Narrowing Achievement Gaps on State
Tests," in *Narrowing the Achievement Gap: Perspectives and Strategies for Challenging
Times*, ed. Thomas B. Timar and Julie Maxwell-Jolly (Cambridge, MA: Harvard Edu-
cation Press, 2012), pp. 11–33.

3. Ronald F. Ferguson, "What Doesn't Meet the Eye: Understanding and Addressing Racial
Disparities in High-Achieving Suburban Schools " *NCREL Policy Issues* 13 (2002):
1–39. Big-city public schools come to mind when thinking about the achievement
gap, but significant racial disparities exist elsewhere too. Public schools in suburban

areas where resources are plentiful and schools are reputedly excellent certainly have their own problems with raising the academic achievement of black students to a level comparable to that of their white peers. Even in these schools we find that blacks (and Hispanics) are overrepresented at the bottom of the achievement distribution and underrepresented at the top of it. See, for example, R. L'Heureux Lewis-McCoy, *Inequality in the Promised Land: Race, Resources, and Suburban Schooling* (Stanford, CA: Stanford University Press, 2014), chap. 3, "Segmented Suburbia."

4. Katherine Magnuson and Jane Waldfogel, eds., *Steady Gains and Stalled Progress: Inequality and the Black-White Test Score Gap* (New York: Russell Sage Foundation, 2008). See Sean F. Reardon, "Differential Growth in the Black-White Achievement Gap during Elementary School among Initially High- and Low-Scoring Students," Working Paper no. 2008–07 (Palo Alto, CA: Stanford University Institute for Research on Education Policy and Practice, 2008); and see Eric A. Hanushek and Steven G. Rivkin, "School Quality and the Black-White Achievement Gap," Working Paper no. 1265 (Cambridge, MA: National Bureau of Economic Research, 2006). Also see Jonathan Jacobson, Cara Olsen, Jennifer King Rice, Stephen Sweetland, and John Ralph, *Educational Achievement and Black-White Inequality*, NCES 2001–061 (Washington, DC: Government Printing Office, 2001), and Robert K. Ream, Sarah Ryan and Jose A. Espinoza, "Reframing the Ecology of Opportunity and Achievement Gaps: Why 'No Excuses' Reforms Have Failed to Narrow Student Group Differences in Educational Outcomes," in Timar and Maxwell-Jolly, *Narrowing the Achievement Gap*, pp. 35–56.

5. Daniel Losen, Cherl Hodson, Michael A. Keith, Katrina Morrison and Shakti Belway, *Are We Closing the School Discipline Gap?* (Los Angeles: Center for Civil Rights Remedies, the Civil Rights Project at UCLA, February 2015), http://civilrightsproject.ucla.edu/resources/projects/center-for-civil-rights-remedies/school-to-prison-folder/federal-reports/are-we-closing-the-school-discipline-gap/.

6. James J. Heckman and Paul A. LaFontaine, "Graduation Rate: Trends and Levels," discussion paper (Bonn: Institute for the Study of Labor, 2007).

7. Anne Gregory, Russell J. Skiba, and Pedro A. Noguera, "The Achievement Gap and the Discipline Gap: Two Sides of the Same Coin?," *Educational Researcher* 39, no. 59 (2010): 59–68; American Psychological Association, *Facing the School Dropout Dilemma* (Washington, DC: APA, 2012), http://www.apa.org/pi/families/resources/school-dropout-prevention.aspx.

8. Spyros Konstantopoulos and Geoffrey Borman, "Family Background and School Effects on Student Achievement: A Multilevel Analysis of the Coleman Data," *Teachers College Record* 113, no. 1 (2011): 97–132, http://www.tcrecord.org.www2.lib.ku.edu/library/content.asp?contentid=15989.

9. Adam Gamoran and David A. Long, "*Equality of Educational Opportunity*: A Forty Year Retrospective," WCER Working Paper no. 2006–9 (Madison: Wisconsin Center for Educational Research, 2006).

10. Jaekyung Lee, "Racial and Ethnic Achievement Gap Trends: Reversing the Progress toward Equity?," *Educational Researcher* 31, no. 1 (January 2002): 3–12.

11. Both quotes can be found in George Frederickson, *The Black Image in the White Mind: The Debate on Afro-American Character and Destiny, 1817–1914* (New York: Harper and Row, 1971). The first can be found on p. 83 and is taken from E. N. Elliot, *Cotton Is King and Pro-Slavery Arguments* (Augusta, GA: Pritchard, Abbott and Loomis, 1860), p. xiii. The Channing quote can be found on p. 103 and is taken from William Ellery Channing, *The Works of William Ellery Channing* (Boston: J. Munro, 1849), 2:12–14.

12. James D. Anderson, *The Education of Blacks in the South, 1860–1935* (Chapel Hill: University of North Carolina Press, 1988), p. 92.

13. John T. Morgan, "The Race Question in the United States," *Arena* 2, no. 10 (September 1890): 392.

14. Ronald F. Ferguson, *Toward Excellence with Equity: An Emerging Vision for Closing the Achievement Gap* (Cambridge, MA: Harvard Education Press, 2007), p. 124. Still, there is uneasiness associated with attributing racial differences in intelligence to genetic differences, not to mention the fact that the very idea of race as a biological category is fraught with controversy. There are books such as Dorothy Roberts's *Fatal Invention: How Science, Politics, and Big Business Re-create Race in the Twenty-First Century* (New York: New Press, 2011) that argue against understanding race in biological terms and make the case that doing so serves certain interests. And there are ones such as Nicholas Wade's *A Troublesome Inheritance: Genes, Race and Human History* (New York: Penguin Press, 2014), which hold the line on the biological reality of race and defend the impolite view that some intellectual traits, such as literacy and numeracy, do have a genetic basis, although Wade denies evidence of genetically based racial differences in intelligence.

15. Lawrence D. Bobo, Camille Z. Charles, Maria Krysan, and Alicia D. Simmons, "The Real Record on Racial Attitudes," in *Social Trends in American Life: Findings from the General Social Survey Since 1972*, ed. Peter V. Marsden (Princeton, NJ: Princeton University Press, 2012), p. 59.

16. Ronald F. Ferguson, *Aiming Higher Together: Strategizing Better Educational Outcomes for Boys and Young Men of Color* (Washington, DC: Urban Institute, 2016), pp. 10–18.

17. Robert Putnam, *Our Kids: The American Dream in Crisis* (New York: Simon and Schuster, 2015), p. 15.

18. Ibid., p. 18.

19. Michael Hilton, "Residential Segregation and Brain Development: Implications for Equitable Educational Opportunities," in *School Integration Matters: Research-Based Strategies to Advance Equity*, ed. Erica Frankenberg, Lilliana M. Garces, and Megan Hopkins (New York: Teachers College Press, 2016), pp. 73–87.

20. William Julius Wilson, *More than Just Race: Being Black and Poor in the Inner City* (New York: W. W. Norton, 2009); Douglas S. Massey, *Categorically Unequal: The American Stratification System* (New York: Russell Sage Foundation, 2007); Bruce Western, *Punishment and Inequality in America* (New York: Russell Sage Foundation, 2006).

21. A classic statement of the discrimination perspective is Douglas S. Massey and Nancy A. Denton, *American Apartheid: Segregation and the Making of the Underclass* (Cambridge, MA.: Harvard University Press, 1993).

22. For discussion of the psychological, philosophical, and legal obstacles to redistributive remedies that are race-specific, see Derrick Darby and Richard E. Levy, "Postracial Remedies," *University of Michigan Journal of Law Reform* 50, no. 2 (2017): 387–488.

23. Gloria Ladson-Billings, "From the Achievement Gap to the Education Debt: Understanding Achievement in U.S. Schools," *Educational Researcher* 35, no. 7 (2006): 3–12.

24. Linda Darling-Hammond, *The Flat World and Education: How America's Commitment to Equity Will Determine Our Future* (New York: Teachers College Press, 2010), chap. 2.

25. James D. Anderson, *The Education of Blacks in the South, 1860–1935* (Chapel Hill: University of North Carolina Press, 1988).

26. On this point, see Norton Grubb, *The Money Myth: Schools, Resources, Outcomes and Equity* (New York: Russell Sage Foundation, 2009), p. 95.

27. Ladson-Billings, "From the Achievement Gap to the Education Debt," p. 6, quoting

figures from Jonathan Kozol, *The Shame of the Nation: The Restoration of Apartheid Schooling in America* (New York: Three Rivers Press, 2005), introduction.

28. John L. Rury and Jeffrey E. Mirel, "The Political Economy of Urban Education," *Review of Research in Education* 22 (1997): 49–110.

29. Natasha Warikoo and Prudence Carter, "Cultural Explanations for Racial and Ethnic Stratification in Academic Achievement: A Call for a New and Improved Theory," *Review of Educational Research* 79, no. 1 (2009): 366–94.

30. On cash for grades, see Eric Bettinger, "Paying to Learn: The Effect of Financial Incentives on Elementary School Test Scores," Working Paper no. 16333 (Cambridge, MA: National Bureau of Economic Research, September 2010); on moving to better opportunities, see Raj Chetty, Nathaniel Hendren, and Lawrence Katz, "The Effects of Exposure to Better Neighborhoods on Children: New Evidence from the Moving to Opportunity Experiment," Working Paper no. 21156 (Cambridge, MA: National Bureau of Economic Research, 2015), http://www.nber.org/papers/w21156; and on the benefits of integration, see Anderson, *The Imperative of Integration*, conclusion.

31. Anne Phillips, "Defending Equality of Outcome," *Journal of Political Philosophy* 12, no. 1 (2004): 1–19.

32. Immanuel Kant, *Practical Philosophy*, trans. and ed. Mary J. Gregor (Cambridge: Cambridge University Press, 1996), p. 557.

33. If we acknowledge that even the most celebrated Enlightenment thinkers such as Kant are themselves capable of self-deception and can suffer from cognitive deficiencies, deeply rooted in their racism, then this paradox between Kant's moral philosophy and Kant's racism is much less puzzling. For an insightful development of this claim, see Lucy Allais, "Kant's Racism," *Philosophical Papers* 45 (2016): 1–36.

34. Thomas Jefferson, *Notes on Virginia*, 8th American ed. (Boston: David Carlisle, 1801), p. 208. Also see Henry Louis Gates Jr., *The Trials of Phillis Wheatley: America's First Black Poet and Her Encounters with the Founding Fathers* (New York: Civitas Books, 2003), p. 42.

35. Ralph Waldo Emerson, *Emerson in His Journals*, ed. Joel Porte (Cambridge, MA: Belknap Press of Harvard University Press, 1982), p. 19.

36. G. Bohrnstedt, S. Kitmitto, B. Ogut, D. Sherman, and D. Chan, *School Composition and the Black-White Achievement Gap*, NCES 2015–018, U. S. Department of Education (Washington, DC: National Center for Education Statistics, 2015), p. 2, http://nces.ed.gov/pubsearch.

CHAPTER TWO

1. Daniel J. Hemel, "Summers' Comments on Women and Science Draw Ire," *Harvard Crimson*, January 14, 2005, http://www.thecrimson.com/article/2005/1/14/summers-comments-on-women-and-science/.

2. Ralph Waldo Emerson, *Emerson in His Journals*, ed. Joel Porte (Cambridge, MA: Belknap Press of Harvard University Press, 1982), p. 21.

3. Charlotte Hunt-Grubble, "The Elementary DNA of Dr. Watson," *Times* (London), October 14, 2007, http://www.thesundaytimes.co.uk/sto/culture/books/article73186.ece; also see Rajeev Syal, "Nobel Scientist Who Sparked Race Row Says Sorry—I Didn't Mean It," *Times* (London), October 19, 2007, http://www.thetimes.co.uk/tto/news/world/article1966680.ece.

4. Mrs. M. B. Moore, *The Geographical Reader for the Dixie Children* (Raleigh, NC: Braneon, Farrar, 1863), p. 10.

5. George Frederickson, "Science, Polygenesis, and the Proslavery Argument," chap. 3

in *Black Image in the White Mind: The Debate on Afro-American Character and Destiny, 1817–1914* (New York: Harper and Row, 1971); Reginald Horsman, *Race and Manifest Destiny: The Origins of American Racial Anglo Saxonism* (Cambridge, MA: Harvard University Press, 1981), chaps. 7 and 8.

6. George Fitzhugh, *Cannibals All! Or, Slaves without Masters* (Richmond, VA: A. Morris, 1857), pp. xxi–xxii.

7. For an illuminating discussion of how the ancient Greeks thought about race and racial differences, see Denise Eileen McCoskey, *Race: Antiquity and Its Legacy* (New York: Oxford University Press, 2012).

8. Julie K. Ward, "Ethnos in the Politics: Aristotle and Race," in *Philosophers on Race: Critical Essays*, ed. Julie K. Ward and Tommy L. Lott (Oxford: Blackwell, 2002), pp. 14–37. Ward argues that the textual evidence in Aristotle's *Politics* is ambiguous as to whether he had racial or ethnic groups in mind when discussing "natural slavery," notwithstanding the fact that proponents of racial hierarchy and slavery have long cited him as a source of authority.

9. Aristotle, *Politics*, bk. 1, chap. 5, 1254b20–23.

10. Ivan Hannaford, *Race: The History of an Idea in the West* (Washington, DC: Woodrow Wilson Center Press, 1996). Aristotle did not make contributions to the idea of race as we understand it today. Hannaford dates the "pre-idea" of race with specific ethnic group connotations to the late seventeenth century, but argues that the idea of race, as we understand it in the West, was not fully conceptualized until after the French and American Revolutions.

11. Fitzhugh believed that poor white workers were subject to even worse exploitation than black slaves; *Cannibals All!!*, p. 25.

12. Charles W. Mills, *The Racial Contract* (Ithaca, NY: Cornell University Press, 1997).

13. Hilary J. Moss, "The Emergence of White Opposition to African American Education," chap. 1 in *Schooling Citizens: The Struggle for African American Education in Antebellum America* (Chicago: University of Chicago Press, 2009).

14. On these themes, see Leon Litwack, *North of Slavery: The Negro in the Free States, 1790–1860* (Chicago: University of Chicago Press, 1965), chaps. 5 and 8.

15. Ibid., p. 116; Moss, "The Emergence of White Opposition to African American Education"; Carl F. Kaestle, "Ins and Outs: Acquiescence, Ambivalence, and Resistance to Common-School Reform," chap. 7 in *Pillars of the Republic: Common Schools and American Society, 1780–1860* (New York: Hill and Wang, 1983).

16. There is evidence that after courts started to enforce *Brown*, desegregation did indeed lower property values as urban whites in major Northern city school districts fled to bordering suburbs not under desegregation orders. See Leah Platt Boustan, "School Desegregation and Urban Change: Evidence from City Boundaries," *American Economic Journal: Applied Economics* 4, no. 1 (2012): 85–108.

17. Litwack, "Education: Separate and Unequal," chap. 4 in *North of Slavery*; Moss, *Schooling Citizens*, pp. 18–20.

18. Emmanuel Chukwudi Eze, ed., *Race and the Enlightenment: A Reader* (Malden, MA: Blackwell, 1997). These ideas and the suggestion that such differences necessitated educating the two races differently were not a wholly American invention, though it certainly came to have a profound practical impact here. These contributions to what Eze has described as the "race idea" were also a legacy of early modern European philosophy.

19. Thomas McCarthy, *Race, Empire, and the Idea of Human Development* (Cambridge: Cambridge University Press, 2009).

. Hannaford, *Race*, pp. 203–4.
21. Ibid., p. 204.
22. Ibid., p. 206.
23. David Hume, "Of National Characters," in *Essays Moral, Political, and Literary* (London: A. Millar, 1744), pt. 1, essay 21, p. 208.
24. Robert Bernasconi, ed., "Who Invented the Concept of Race? Kant's Role in the Enlightenment Construction of Race," *Race* (Oxford: Blackwell, 2001), pp. 11–36; and Robert Bernasconi, "Kant as an Unfamiliar Source of Racism," in Ward and Lott, *Philosophers on Race*, pp. 145–66; also see McCarthy, *Race, Empire, and the Idea of Human Development*. For additional reflections on Kant's views on race, see Emmanuel Chuckwudi Eze, "The Color of Reason: The Idea of 'Race' in Kant's Anthropology," in *Postcolonial African Philosophy: A Reader*, ed. Eze (Oxford: Blackwell, 1997), pp. 103–40; Thomas Hill and Bernard Boxill, "Kant and Race," in *Race and Racism*, ed. Bernard Boxill (Oxford: Oxford University Press, 2001), pp. 448–71. On the absolute inferiority of blacks and Africans on every measure of personhood, Hume and Kant agreed; however, one of their main disagreements was over whether the English or the Germans were atop the human hierarchy. In his 1764 work *Observations on the Feelings of the Beautiful and Sublime*, Kant, a German, distinguished nations of the world by their aesthetic and moral sensibilities, which require both a refined intellect and a refined character. Not surprisingly, in his classification the Germans came out on top (with the English and the French following) and the Africans were at the bottom.
25. Immanuel Kant, *Observations on the Feeling of the Beautiful and Sublime*, trans. John T. Goldthwait (Berkeley: University of California Press, 2004), p. 110. It has been argued that Kant eventually retreated from his defense of the superiority of whites over nonwhites; see, for example, Pauline Kleingeld, "Kant's Second Thoughts on Race," *Philosophical Quarterly* 57, no. 229 (2007): 575–92. Even if this is true, the ideas he expressed before this retreat were nonetheless part of, and helped to buttress, the prevailing racist ideology at the time; and it was these ideas that proved fertile for imperialism, colonialism, and the justification of New World racial slavery.
26. Hannaford, *Race*, p. 150.
27. Quoted in Eze, *Race and the Enlightenment*, p. 63.
28. Ibid., p. 64.
29. Hume, "Of National Characters," in *David Hume*, p. 207.
30. Hill and Boxill, "Kant and Race," p. 449. According to Hume, the superiority of England's form of political association accounted for the superiority of its natural character to that of the people who lived at the Poles. Thus for Hume, the presumed inability of the "Negroes" to erect and sustain the requisite forms of rule accounted for their alleged intellectual inferiority.

It is, of course, important not to assume that the contributions of Hume and Kant to Enlightenment racial ideology diminish the value and utility of their contributions to shaping broad universal, humanistic, and egalitarian visions of what human beings owe one another as a matter of morality. In the case of Kant, for example, we should not assume that Kant the man was himself so racist and sexist that his ideal categorical moral imperative to treat humanity as an end in itself and never only as a mere means should be dismissed as a consequence.
31. For a philosophical analysis of the relationship between race and rights, see Derrick Darby, *Rights, Race, and Recognition* (Cambridge: Cambridge University Press, 2009).
32. Thomas Jefferson, *Notes on the State of Virginia*, 8th American ed. (Boston: David Carlisle, 1801), pp. 205–6.

33. Ibid., p. 206. Jefferson was willing to recognize the musical talents of blacks but not without a qualification that further disparaged their intellectual ability. As he noted, "In music [blacks] are more generally gifted than the whites with accurate ears for tune and time. . . . Whether they will be equal to the composition of a more extensive run of melody, or of complicated harmony, is yet to be proved" (pp. 207–8). Although Jefferson foresaw the possibility of a great civil war to free the slaves, he clearly didn't anticipate the rise of composer Duke Ellington, saxophonist John Coltrane, and MC Rakim (aka William Michael Griffin Jr.).

34. Frederickson, "Science, Polygenesis, and the Proslavery Argument."

35. Dred Scott v. Sandford, 60 U.S. 19 How. 393, 407 (1856).

36. Stephen J. Gould, *The Mismeasure of Man*, rev. and exp. ed. (New York: W. W. Norton, 1996), chaps. 2–4.

37. Pilar Ossario, "Myth and Mystification: The Science of Race and IQ," in *Race and the Genetic Revolution: Science, Myth and Culture*, ed. Sheldon Krimsky and Kathleen Sloan (New York: Columbia University Press, 2011), p. 190. The field of behavioral genetics has long been concerned with the biological foundations of human intelligence. Historically, such work was strictly correlational, statistically controlling for environmental influences and treating the remaining association of test scores across generations as hereditary. Studies of identical twins also provided natural experiments on the presumption of shared genetic endowment. This line of research indicated that both genetic and environmental factors account for observed differences in IQ and other cognitive measures *between individuals*, but it could not conclusively address the question of racial differences. Inferences drawn from this sort of evidence regarding race and IQ were largely speculation, regardless of how persistent and large the test score averages may have been.

   With the development of the Human Genome Project, it became possible in theory to link particular genes to variation in test scores, although studies have failed to reliably identify such connections. By and large, there remains a broad consensus that both biological and environmental factors contribute to variation in performance on such tests, although the precise combination of these factors is subject to wide debate. More recently, researchers have focused on the interaction of genes and the environment, noting that certain conditions can affect the role of genetic factors in influencing behavior. These interactions can be quite complex and are still not well understood. But even the non-replicated observation of genetic variation that can be statistically linked to test score differences, amounting to minor differences, does not approach the magnitude of racial variation in IQ or achievement. This suggests that the vast bulk of interracial difference on this count is in fact environmental in origin. See Robert J. Sternberg, Elena L. Grigorenko, Kenneth K. Kidd, and Steven E. Stemler, "Intelligence, Race and Genetics," in Krimsky and Sloan, *Race and the Genetic Revolution*, pp. 195–240; and I. J. Dreary, W. Johnson, and L. M. Houlihan, "Genetic Foundations of Human Intelligence," *Human Genetics* 126 (2009): 215–32.

38. Sylvia L. M. Martinez and John L. Rury, "From 'Culturally Deprived' to 'At Risk': The Politics of Popular Expression and Educational Inequality in the United States, 1960–1985," *Teachers College Record* 114, no. 6 (2012): 1–31.

39. For a biographical account of Smith's life and a collection of his writings, see John Stauffer, ed., *The Works of James McCune Smith: Black Intellectual and Abolitionist* (New York: Oxford University Press, 2006).

40. John Stauffer, "Smith, James McCune," *American National Biography Online*, October 2008, http://www.anb.org.www2.lib.ku.edu:2048/articles/16/16-01529.html.

41. Litwack, "Slavery of Freedom," chap. 1 in *North of Slavery*; Stephen Kantrowitz, *More than Freedom: Fighting for Black Citizenship in a White Republic, 1829–1889* (New York: Penguin, 2012), pt. 1; Patrick Rael, "A Different Measure of Oppression: Leadership and Identity in the Black North," chap. 1 in *Black Identity and Black Protest in the Antebellum North* (Chapel Hill: University of North Carolina Press, 2002); Benjamin Quarles, *Black Abolitionists* (Cambridge, MA: Da Capo Press, 1991), chaps. 1 and 2.

42. Roy E. Finkenbine, "Nell, William Cooper," *American National Biography Online, 2000*, Oxford University Press, accessed April 6, 2017, http://www.anb.org.www2.lib.ku .edu/articles/16/16-01194.html; Martin Burt Pasternak, "Rise Now and Fly to Arms: The Life of Henry Highland Garnet" (PhD diss., University of Massachusetts, 1981); Darlene Clark Hine, Elsa Barkley Brown, and Rosalyn Terborg-Penn, "Sarah Parker Redmond (1826–1894)," in *Black Women in America: An Historical Encyclopedia* (Indianapolis: Indiana University Press, 1993), 2:972–74.

43. Quoted in David W. Blight, *Frederick Douglass' Civil War: Keeping the Faith in Jubilee* (Baton Rouge: Louisiana State University Press, 1991), p. 55.

44. *Frederick Douglass: Selected Speeches and Writings*, ed. Philip S. Foner (Chicago: Lawrence Hill, 1999), p. 194.

45. Frederick Douglas, *The Claims of the Negro Ethnologically Considered; An Address Before the Literary Societies of Western Reserve College at Commencement, July 12, 1854* (Rochester: Lee, Mann, 1854).

46. Ibid., p. 15.

47. Ibid., p. 34.

48. Eric Foner, *Reconstruction: America's Unfinished Revolution, 1863–1877*, updated ed. (New York: Harper and Row, 2014), chaps. 2 and 6.

49. Pat Shipman, *The Evolution of Racism: Human Differences and the Use and Abuse of Science* (Cambridge, MA: Harvard University Press, 1994).

50. Lawrence D. Bobo, Camille Z. Charles, Maria Krysan, and Alicia D. Simmons, "The Real Record on Racial Attitudes," in *Social Trends in American Life: Findings from the General Social Survey since 1972*, ed. Peter V. Marsden (Princeton, NJ: Princeton University Press, 2012), pp. 38–83.

51. Prudence L. Carter and Kevin G. Welner, eds., *Closing the Opportunity Gap: What America Must Do to Give Every Child an Even Chance* (New York: Oxford University Press, 2013).

52. David F. Labaree, *Someone Has to Fail: The Zero-Sum Game of Public Schooling* (Cambridge, MA: Harvard University Press, 2010), p. 1.

CHAPTER THREE

1. Hilary J. Moss, *Schooling Citizens: The Struggle for African American Education in Antebellum America* (Chicago: University of Chicago Press, 2009), chap. 5.

2. Boston Primary School Committee, *Report to the Primary School Committee on the Abolition of the Schools for Colored Children, with the City Solicitor's Opinion* (Boston: J. H. Eastburn, Printer, 1846), p. 7.

3. Ibid., p. 29.

4. Quoted in Carl F. Kaestle, *Pillars of the Republic: Common Schools and American Society, 1780–1860* (New York: Hill and Wang, 1983), p. 179.

5. Leon Litwack, *North of Slavery: The Negro in the Free States, 1790–1860* (Chicago: University of Chicago Press, 1965), p. 113; Hilary J. Moss, "Common Schools, Revolutionary Memory, and the Crisis of Black Citizenship in the Mid-Nineteenth Century," chap. 6 in *Schooling Citizens*; Stanley K. Schultz, "Separate but Equal Schools?

White Abolitionists and Black Education," chap. 8 in *The Culture Factory: Boston Public Schools, 1789–1860* (New York: Oxford University Press, 1973); Kaestle, "Ins and Outs: Acquiescence, Ambivalence and Resistance to Common School Reform," chap. 7 in *Pillars of the Republic.*

6.   "The Black Laws: Speech of Hon. B. W. Arnett of Greene County and Hon. J. A. Brown of Cuyahoga County, in the Ohio House of Representatives, March 10, 1886," in Stephen Middleton, *The Black Laws: Race and the Legal Process in Early Ohio* (Athens: Ohio University Press, 2005), p. 3; also see Stephen Middleton, "The Limits of Freedom," chap. 8 in ibid.

7.   Joel Perlmann, "The Blacks," chap. 5 in *Ethnic Differences: Schooling and Social Structure among the Irish, Italians, and Blacks in an American City, 1880–1935* (New York: Cambridge University Press, 1988).

8.   Charles W. Mills, *The Racial Contract* (Ithaca, NY: Cornell University Press, 1997), pt. 2; on loss of political rights for African Americans during this era, see Eric Foner, "Redemption and After," chap. 12 in *Reconstruction: America's Unfinished Revolution, 1863–1877* (New York: Harper and Row, 2014).

9.   George McKenna, ed., *A Guide to the Constitution: That Delicate Balance* (New York: McGraw-Hill, 1984), p. 385.

10.   Quoted in James D. Anderson, *The Education of Blacks in the South, 1860–1935* (Chapel Hill: University of North Carolina Press, 1988), p. 82.

11.   Emmanuel Chukwudi Eze, *Achieving Our Humanity: The Idea of the Postracial Future* (New York: Routledge, 2001), p. 99.

12.   Edward E. Baptist, *The Half Has Never Been Told: Slavery and the Making of American Capitalism* (New York: Basic Books, 2014), chaps. 4 and 5; Kenneth Stamp, "Between Two Cultures," chap. 8 in *The Peculiar Institution: Slavery in the Ante-Bellum South* (New York: Alfred A. Knopf, 1956).

13.   Thomas L. Webber, *Deep Like the Rivers: Education in the Slave Quarter Community, 1831–1865* (New York: W. W. Norton, 1978); also see Leslie Howard Owens, "The Shadow of the Slave Quarters," chap. 7 in *This Species of Property: Slave Life and Culture in the Old South* (New York: Oxford University Press, 1976); and Herbert G. Gutman, "The Birthpangs of a World," pt. 1 in *The Black Family in Slavery and Freedom, 1750–1925* (New York: Vintage Books, 1977).

14.   Thanks to James Tappenden for the pointer to Burke on this issue.

15.   Edmund Burke, *Miscellaneous Writings, 1729–1797*, found on the Library of Economics and Liberty website, accessed April 19, 2017, http://www.econlib.org/library/LFBooks/Burke/brkSWv4c7.html, §4.79.

16.   Stamp, "Chattels Personal," chap. 5 in *The Peculiar Institution*; Peter Kolchin, "Antebellum Slavery: Organization, Control, Paternalism," chap. 4 in *American Slavery: 1619–1877* (New York: Hill and Wang, 2003); also see Eugene Genovese, *Roll Jordan Roll: The World the Slaves Made* (New York: Vintage Books, 1976), bk. 1, pt. 2.

17.   Richard H. Steckel, "Work, Disease, and Diet in the Health and Mortality of American Slaves," in *Without Consent or Contract: The Rise and Fall of American Slavery; Technical Papers*, edited by Robert W. Fogel and Stanley L. Engermen (New York: W. W. Norton, 1992), 2:489–507.

18.   William J. Reese, *The Origins of the American High School* (New Haven, CT: Yale University Press, 1995), pp. 231–34; Moss, "Education's Divide: Boston, Massachusetts," pt. 3 in *Schooling Citizens.*

19.   On this point, see Perlmann, "The Blacks," chap. 5 in *Ethnic Differences.*

20.   On these early institutions, see Roger Geiger, "Land Grant Colleges and the Practical

Arts," chap. 7 in *The History of American Higher Education: Learning and Culture from the Founding until World War Two* (Princeton, NJ: Princeton University Press, 2014).

21. On these developments, see Stanley Lieberson, "Education," chap. 6 in *A Piece of the Pie: Blacks and White Immigrants Since 1880* (Berkeley: University of California Press, 1980); and David B. Tyack, *The One Best System: A History of American Urban Education* (Cambridge, MA: Harvard University Press, 1974), p. 123.

22. Heather Andrea William, *Self-Taught: African American Education in Slavery and Freedom* (Chapel Hill: University of North Carolina Press, 2005), chaps. 3, 4, and 8.

23. Steven Hahn, *A Nation under Our Feet: Black Political Struggles in the Rural South from Slavery to the Great Migration* (Cambridge, MA: Harvard University Press, 2003), pp. 276–77.

24. Anderson, "Education and the Race Problem in the New South: The Struggle for Ideological Hegemony," chap. 3 in *The Education of Blacks in the South*; a detailed accounting can also be found in Louis R. Harlan, "The Uses of Adversity: An Introduction," chap. 1 in *Separate and Unequal: Public School Campaigns and Racism in the Southern Seaboard States, 1901–1915* (Chapel Hill: University of North Carolina Press, 1958).

25. James D. Anderson, "A Long Shadow: The American Pursuit of Political Justice and Education Equality," *Educational Researcher* 44, no. 6 (August/September 2015): 319–35; also see Robert A. Margo, "Race and Schooling in the South: A Review of the Evidence," chap. 2 in *Race and Schooling in the South, 1880–1950: An Economic History* (Chicago: University of Chicago Press, 1994).

26. Harlan, *Separate and Unequal*, p. 14.

27. Anderson, *The Education of Blacks in the South*, chaps. 2 and 3; William H. Watkins, "The Phelps Stokes Family, Friends, and Fund: Adventures in Philanthropy," chap. 5 in *The White Architects of Black Education: Ideology and Power in America, 1865–1954* (New York: Teachers College Press, 2001).

28. Anderson, "The Hampton Model of Normal School Industrial Education, 1868–1915," chap. 2 in *The Education of Blacks in the South*; Louis R. Harlan, "The Burning Bush," chap. 5 in *Booker T. Washington: The Making of a Black Leader* (New York: Oxford University Press, 1975); Raymond W. Smock, "The Tuskegee Idea," chap. 3 in *Booker T. Washington: Black Leadership in the Age of Jim Crow* (Chicago: Ivan R. Dee, 2009).

29. Washington's position on these issues can be found in *Negro Education Not a Failure: Address by Booker T. Washington in the Concert Hall of Madison Square Garden, New York, Lincoln's Birthday, February 12, 1904* (Tuskegee, AL: Tuskegee Institute Steam Print, 1904), pp. 6–7.

30. *The Voice of Anna Julia Cooper, Including A Voice from the South and Other Important Essays, Papers, and Letters*, ed. Charles Lemert and Esme Bhan (Lanham, MD: Rowman and Littlefield, 1998), p. 175.

31. Ibid., p. 251.

32. William Edward Burghardt Du Bois, *The Souls of Black Folk: Essays and Sketches*, 2nd ed. (Chicago: A. C. McClurg, 1903), p. 54.

33. Anderson, "Education and the Race Problem in the New South: The Struggle for Ideological Hegemony," chap. 3 in *The Education of Blacks in the South*; David Levering Lewis, *W. E. B. Du Bois, 1868–1919: Biography of a Race* (New York: Henry Holt, 1994), chap. 10; Derrick P. Alridge, *The Educational Thought of W. E. B. Du Bois: An Intellectual History* (New York: Teachers College Press, 2008), pp. 53–55.

34. Du Bois's ideas changed with time; see Alridge, *The Educational Thought of W. E. B. Du Bois*, 5–8.

35. Horace Mann Bond, *Negro Education in Alabama: A Study in Cotton and Steel* (New York: Octagon Books, 1939), chaps. 10–14; Anderson, "A Long Shadow"; Anderson, "The Black Public High School and the Reproduction of Caste in the Urban South, 1880–1935," chap. 6 in *Education of Blacks in the South.*

36. Ida B. Wells, in *Southern Horrors and Other Writings: The Anti-Lynching Campaign of Ida B. Wells, 1892–1900*, ed. Jacqueline Jones Royster (Boston: Bedford/St. Martins, 1997), pp. 52 and 61.

37. Hahn, *A Nation under Our Feet*, pp. 426–27.

38. Quoted in *Biennial Report of the Department of Education of the State of Alabama for the Scholastic Year Ending, September 30, 1899 and 1900* (Montgomery, AL: State Printing Office, 1900), pp. 57–58.

39. Anderson, "The Black Public High School and the Reproduction of Caste in the Urban South, 1880–1935," chap. 6 in *The Education of Blacks in the South.*

40. Thomas Jefferson, *Notes on the State of Virginia*, 8th Am. ed. (Boston: David Carlisle, 1801), p. 210.

41. Iver Bernstein, "Draft Riots and the Social Order," pt. 1 in *The New York City Draft Riots: Their Significance for American Society and Politics in the Age of the Civil War* (Lincoln, NE: Bison Books, 2010); P. J. Staudenraus, *The African Colonization Movement, 1816–1865* (New York: Columbia University Press, 1961).

42. Stephen Kantrowitz, *More than Freedom: Fighting for Black Citizenship in a White Republic, 1829–1889* (New York: Penguin, 2012), p. 384.

43. John H. Van Evrie, *White Supremacy and Negro Subordination* (New York: Van Evrie, 1868), p. 221. This book was an expanded version of his earlier work, *Negros, a Subordinate Race, and So-Called Slavery Its Normal Condition* (New York: Van Evrie, 1853).

44. Ibid., p. 219.

45. Ibid., p. 221.

46. Laten Ervin Bechtel, *"That's Just the Way It Was": A Chronological and Documentary History of African American Schools in Staunton and Augusta County* (Staunton, VA: Lot's Wife, 2010), pp. 47–48.

47. On this point, see Glenn Feldman, *The Irony of the Solid South: Democrats, Republicans and Race, 1865–1944* (Tuscaloosa: University of Alabama Press, 2013), p. 9.

48. Leon F. Litwack, *Trouble in Mind: Black Southerners in the Age of Jim Crow* (New York: Vintage Books, 1998), p. 52. Litwack was writing about the slave-era South, but the logic of these concerns extended to later decades as well.

49. Tillman is quoted in Edward Byerly, *Divided We Stand: Jim Crow Education in Victoria, Texas, 1901–1966* (College Station: Texas A&M Press, 2011), p. 179. The fact that Tillman was quoted in a Texas newspaper is evidence of his influence in the region, and agreement with his concerns.

50. Professor Kelly Miller, *"The Primary Needs of the Negro Race": An Address Delivered before the Alumni Association of the Hampton Normal and Agricultural Institute* (Washington, DC: Howard University Press, 1899), pp. 7–8.

51. Anderson, *The Education of Blacks in the South*, p. 39.

52. Ibid.

53. Quotes are taken from Curry's report, included in the *Proceedings of the Trustees of the John F. Slater Fund for the Education of Freedmen* (Baltimore: John Murphy, 1891), pp. 14, 19, 18, and 25 respectively.

54. Perlmann, "The Blacks," chap. 5 in *Ethnic Differences*; also see Lieberson, "Education," chap. 6 in *A Piece of the Pie.*

55. Perlmann, "The Blacks."

56. Quoted in John L. Rury, "Race, Region, and Education: An Analysis of Black and White Scores on the 1917 Army Alpha Intelligence Test," *Journal of Negro Education* 57, no. 1 (Winter 1988): 52. Yerkes did not take the length of school terms into consideration for his analysis, which would have raised the correlation of test scores and schooling even higher.

57. On the history of the psychological testing movement, and the Army IQ test in particular, see Stephen J. Gould, "The Hereditarian Theory of IQ: An American Invention," chap. 5 in *The Mismeasure of Man*, rev. and exp. ed. (New York: W. W. Norton, 1996).

58. Fred J. Galloway, "Inferential Sturdiness and the 1917 Army Alpha: A New Look at the Robustness of Educational Quality Indices as Determinants of Interstate Black-White Score Differentials," *Journal of Negro Education* 63, no. 2 (Spring 1994): 266; also see Rury, "Race, Region, and Education," pp. 51–66.

59. On the link between the 1917 test and contemporary achievement tests, James Popham has argued that "today's standardized achievement tests are patterned directly after the Army Alpha, a group-administered intelligence test used in World War I to identify potential officers." See W. James Popham, "Standardized Achievement Tests: Misnamed and Misleading," *Education Week* 21, no. 3 (September 19, 2001): 35. Also see W. James Popham, "The Mystique of Standardized Measuring Instruments," chap. 3 in *The Truth about Testing: An Educator's Call to Action* (Washington, DC: Association for Supervision and Curriculum Development [ASCD], 2001).

60. Galloway, "Inferential Sturdiness and the 1917 Army Alpha," p. 265.

61. David Walker, *David Walker's Appeal in Four Articles: An Address to the Slaves of the United States of America* (Boston: D. Walker, 1829), p. 73.

CHAPTER FOUR

1. Carl C. Brigham, *A Study of American Intelligence* (Princeton, NJ: Princeton University Press, 1923), pp. 192, 194, and xi.

2. Ibid., p. xi.

3. W. E. Burghardt Du Bois, "Does the Negro Need Separate Schools?," *Journal of Negro Education* 4, no. 3 (1935): 332.

4. Brigham, *A Study of American Intelligence*, p. 205.

5. Roger Daniels, "The 1920s: The Triumph of the Old Nativism," chap. 2 in *Guarding the Golden Door: American Immigration Policy and Immigrants Since 1882* (New York: Hill and Wang, 2004).

6. Leonard Dinnerstein and David Reimers, "Ethnic Conflict and Immigration Restriction," chap. 4 in *Ethnic Americans: A History of Immigration*, 5th ed. (New York: Columbia University Press, 2009). On school attendance and social standing, see James S. Pula, "Image, Status, Mobility and Integration in American Society: The Polish Experience," *Journal of American Ethnic History* 16, no. 1 (1996): 74–95; and Dorothee Schneider, "Polish Peasants into Americans: U.S. Citizenship and Americanization among Polish Immigrants in the Inter-war Era," *Polish Sociological Review*, no. 158 (2007): 159–71. On ethnic test scores, see Andrew W. Brown and Carol B. Cotton, "A Study of the Intelligence of Italian and Polish School Children from Deteriorated and Non-deteriorated Areas of Chicago as Measured by the Chicago Non-verbal Examination," *Child Development* 12, no. 1 (1941): 21–30.

7. David R. Roediger, "Entering the White House," pt. 3 in *Working toward Whiteness: How America's Immigrants Became White* (New York: Basic Books, 2005).

8. Nicholas Lemann, *The Big Test: The Secret History of the American Meritocracy* (New

York: Farrar, Straus and Giroux, 2000), p. 32; for additional problems with the test, see Carl C. Brigham, "Intelligence Tests of Immigrant Groups," *Psychological Review* 37, no. 2 (1930): 158–65; and Rudolph Pintner, *Intelligence Testing: Methods and Results*, rev. ed. (New York: Henry Holt, 1923), p. 448.

9. Lothrop Stoddard, *The Rising Tide of Color: The Threat against White World Supremacy* (New York: Charles Scribner and Sons, 1920), p. 88.

10. Quoted in Francis Smith Foster, *A Brighter Coming Day: A Frances Ellen Watkins Harper Reader* (New York: Feminist Press, 1990), p. 4.

11. Ibid., p. 205.

12. Ibid., p. 103.

13. Ibid., p. 104.

14. Ibid., pp. 220–21.

15. Ibid., p. 220.

16. Hilary J. Moss, "African American Educational Activism under the Shadow of Slavery," chap. 4 in *Schooling Citizens: The Struggle for African American Education in Antebellum America* (Chicago: University of Chicago Press, 2009). Also see Leon Litwack, "Education: Separate and Unequal," chap. 4 in *North of Slavery: The Negro in the Free States, 1790–1860* (Chicago: University of Chicago Press, 1965).

17. Patricia Hill Collins, "Distinguishing Features of Black Feminist Thought," chap. 2 in *Black Feminist Thought: Knowledge, Consciousness, and the Politics of Empowerment* (New York: Routledge, 2008).

18. Anderson, "The Hampton Model of Normal School Industrial Education, 1868–1915," chap. 2 in *The Education of Blacks in the South*; Rackham Holt, *Mary McLeod Bethune: A Biography—a Life Devoted to the Cause of Racial Equality* (New York: Doubleday, 1964).

19. Anderson, "Common Schools for Black Children: The Second Crusade, 1900–1935," chap. 5 in *The Education of Blacks in the South*; Robert A. Margo, *Race and Schooling in the South, 1880–1950: An Economic History* (Chicago: University of Chicago Press, 1994), chaps.1 and 2; Daniel Aaronson and Bhashkar Mazumder, "The Impact of the Rosenwald Schools on Black Achievement," Working Paper no. 2009–26 (Chicago: Federal Reserve Bank of Chicago, September 2011), pp. 6–8. Also see Peter Ascoli, *Julius Rosenwald: The Man Who Built Sears, Roebuck and Advanced the Cause of Black Education in the South* (Bloomington: Indiana University Press, 2006); and John J. Donohue, James J. Heckman, and Petra E. Todd, "The Schooling of Southern Blacks: The Roles of Legal Activism and Private Philanthropy, 1910–1960," *Quarterly Journal of Economics* 117, no. 1 (2002): 225–68.

20. Adam Fairclough, "Teachers Organize," chap. 8 in *A Class of Their Own: Black Teachers in the Segregated South* (Cambridge, MA: Harvard University Press, 2007).

21. Margo, "The Political Economy of Segregated Schools: Explaining the U-Shaped Pattern," chap. 3 in *Race and Schooling in the South, 1880–1950*; John L. Rury and Shirley A. Hill, "The South in the 1940s," chap. 1 in *The African American Struggle for Secondary Schooling, 1940–1980: Closing the Graduation Gap* (New York: Teachers College Press, 2012).

22. Alison Stewart, "It's the Principal," chap. 4 in *First Class: The Legacy of Dunbar, America's First Black Public High School* (Chicago: Chicago Review Press, 2015); Vanessa Siddle Walker, "Valued Segregated Schools for African American Children in the South, 1935–1969: A Review of Common Themes and Characteristics," *Review of Educational Research* 70, no. 3 (2000): 253–85.

23. Rury and Hill, "The South in the 1940s"; Anderson, "The Black Public High School

and the Reproduction of Caste in the Urban South, 1880–1935," chap. 6 in *The Education of Blacks in the South*; Margo, *Race and Schooling in the South, 1880–1950*.

24. Anderson, "The Black Public High School and the Reproduction of Caste in the Urban South, 1880–1935," chap. 6 in *The Education of Blacks in the South*.
25. Rury and Hill, "The South in the 1940s."
26. Ibid.; Aaronson and Mazumder, "The Impact of the Rosenwald Schools on Black Achievement," pp. 3–4.
27. Rury and Hill, *The African American Struggle for Secondary Schooling*, p. 38.
28. Anderson, "Training the Apostles of Liberal Culture: Black Higher Education, 1900–1934," chap. 7 in *Education of Blacks in the South*.
29. During the Civil War, border states were those slave states that refused to secede from the Union and did not join the Confederacy.
30. John L. Rury, "Growth in African-American High School Enrollment, 1950–1970: An Under-Appreciated Legacy of the Brown Era," *Washburn Law Journal* 53, no. 3 (2014): 479–507.
31. Rury and Hill, "Inequality, Discrimination, and Growth Outside the South, 1948–1960," chap. 3 in *The African American Struggle for Secondary Schooling*.
32. James Gregory, *The Southern Diaspora: How the Great Migrations of Black and White Southerners Transformed America* (Chapel Hill: University of North Carolina Press, 2005), pp. 12–17.
33. Rury and Hill, "Inequality, Discrimination, and Growth Outside the South, 1948–1960."
34. Rury and Hill, "The South in the 1940s"; Anderson, "Training the Apostles of Liberal Culture: Black Higher Education, 1900–1934," chap. 7 in *Education of Blacks in the South*.
35. Quoted in Moss, *Schooling Citizens*, p. 194.
36. For example, see W. S. Armistead, *The Negro Is a Man: A Reply to Professor Charles Carroll's Book, "The Negro Is a Beast or in the Image of God"* (Tifton, GA: Armistead and Vickers, 1903).
37. Douglas Cole, *Franz Boas: The Early Years, 1858–1906* (Seattle: University of Washington Press, 1999); also see Lee D. Baker, "Rethinking Race at the Turn of the Century: W. E. B. Du Bois and Franz Boas," chap. 5 in *From Savage to Negro: Anthropology and the Construction of Race, 1896–1954* (Berkeley: University of California Press, 1998).
38. These quotes are from Boas's short foreword to Mary White Overton, *Half a Man: The Status of the Negro in New York* (New York: Longman, Green, 1911); also see Vernon J. Williams, *Rethinking Race: Franz Boas and His Contemporaries* (Lexington: University Press of Kentucky, 1996), which demonstrates these convictions despite the influence of nineteenth-century ideology on Boas's thought.
39. A concise overview of Boas's career and influence can be found in Melville Herskovitz, *Franz Boas: The Science of Man in the Making* (New York: Charles Scribner and Sons, 1953). Also see Baker, "Unraveling the Boasian Discourse," chap. 8 in *From Savage to Negro*; and Elazar Barkin, "American Diversity," chap. 2 in *The Retreat of Scientific Racism: Changing Concepts of Race in Britain and the United States between the World Wars* (New York: Cambridge University Press, 1992).
40. A helpful account of Benedict and Mead and their influence on discussions of race can be found in Zoe Burkholder, "Ruth Benedict and Margaret Mead: Teaching Teachers; Race and Culture," chap. 3 in *Color in the Classroom: How American Schools Taught Race, 1900–1954* (New York: Oxford University Press, 2011).
41. Harvard Sitkoff, *A New Deal for Blacks: The Emergence of Civil Rights as a National Issue*;

The Depression Decade, classic edition (New York: Oxford University Press, 2008), chaps. 6–8.

42. For an overview, see Steven Watson, *The Harlem Renaissance: Hub of African American Culture, 1920–1930* (New York: Pantheon, 1996); also see Nathan Irvin Huggins, *Harlem Renaissance*, updated ed. (New York: Oxford University Press, 2007), chaps. 3–5.

43. W. E. B. Du Bois, "Race Relations in the United States," *Annals of the American Academy of Political and Social Science* 140, no. 3 (November 1928): 9.

44. Donald Young, foreword, *Annals of the American Academy of Political and Social Science* 140, no. 3 (November 1928): viii.

45. On this point specifically, see Charles H. Thompson, "The Educational Achievements of Negro Children," *Annals of the American Academy of Political and Social Science* 140, no. 3 (November 1928): 193–208; and Baker, "The New Negro and Cultural Politics of Race," chap. 6 in *From Savage to Negro.*

46. Lewis Copeland, "The Negro as a Contrast Conception," in *Race Relations and the Race Problem: A Definition and Analysis*, ed. Edgar T. Thompson (Durham, NC: Duke University Press, 1939), pp. 157–69. Also see Charles S. Johnson, "Race Relations and Social Change," in the same volume, pp. 292–302. Du Bois, "Does the Negro Need Separate Schools?"

47. Doris Kearns Goodwin, "No Ordinary Time," chap. 5 in *No Ordinary Time: Franklin and Eleanor Roosevelt; The Home Front in World War Two* (New York: Simon and Schuster, 1994); John W. Jeffries, "New Circumstances, Old Patterns: Women and the War; African Americans and the War," chap. 5 in *Wartime America: The World War II Home Front* (Chicago: Ivan R. Dee, 1996).

48. John Morton Blum, "Black America: The Rising Wind," chap. 6 in *V Was for Victory: Politics and American Culture during World War II* (New York: Harcourt, 1976); David M. Kennedy, "The Cauldron of the Home Front," chap. 8 in *The American People in World War II: Freedom from Fear; Part II* (New York: Oxford University Press, 1999).

49. Roger Daniels, *Prisoners without Trial: Japanese Americans in World War II* (New York: Hill and Wang, 1993); Ronald Takaki, "'Bomb the Color Line': The War against Jim Crow," chap. 3 in *Double Victory: A Multicultural History of America in World War II* (Boston: Little, Brown, 2000).

50. Michael C. C. Adams, "Mythmaking and the War," chap. 1 in *The Best War Ever: America and World War II* (Baltimore: Johns Hopkins University Press, 1994); Studs Terkel, introduction to *The Good War: An Oral History of World War Two* (New York: New Press, 1984).

51. Takaki, "'Bomb the Color Line.'"

52. Stefan Kuhl, *The Nazi Connection: Eugenics, American Racism, and German National Socialism* (New York: Oxford University Press, 1994), chaps. 2, 3, and 5; Richard Polenberg, "The Struggle for Equal Rights," chap. 4 in *War and Society: The United States 1941–1945* (New York: Lippincott, 1972).

53. Glenda Elizabeth Gilmore, *Defying Dixie: The Radical Roots of Civil Rights: 1919–1950* (New York: W. W. Norton, 2008), chap. 4.

54. Tom Engelhardt, "Containments (1945–1962)," pt. 2 in *The End of Victory Culture: Cold War America and the Disillusioning of a Generation* (New York: Basic Books, 1995); James T. Patterson, *Grand Expectations: The United States, 1945–1974* (New York: Oxford University Press, 1996), chaps. 4 and 5. On these points, also see John L. Rury and Derrick Darby, "War and Education in the United States: Racial Ideology and Inequality in Three Historical Episodes," *Paedagogica Historica* 52, nos. 1–2 (February–April 2016): 8–24.

55. Gunnar Myrdal, *An American Dilemma: The Negro Problem and Modern Democracy* (New York: Harper and Row, 1944), p. 75; Burkholder, "Conclusion: Race and Educational Equality after Brown v. Board of Education," in *Color in the Classroom*. On the limitations of this viewpoint, see Leah N. Gordon, *From Power to Prejudice: The Rise of Racial Individualism in Midcentury America* (Chicago: University of Chicago Press, 2015), chap. 1.

56. Nicholas Lemann, *The Promised Land: The Great Black Migration and How It Changed America* (New York: Knopf, 1992), p. 16; Isabel Wilkerson, *The Warmth of Other Suns: The Epic Story of America's Great Migration.*(New York: Vintage Books, 2010), pt. 4.

57. Robert J. Cottrol, Raymond T. Diamond, and Leland B. Ware, "From Scientific Racism to Uneasy Egalitarianism: One Nation's Troubled Odyssey," chap. 4 in *Brown v. Board of Education: Caste, Culture, and the Constitution* (Lawrence: University Press of Kansas, 2003); Barkin, *The Retreat of Scientific Racism*, p. 341.

58. Philip A. Klinkner and Rogers M. Smith, "Hearts and Minds: The Cold War and Civil Rights, 1946–1954," chap. 7 in *The Unsteady March: The Rise and Decline of Racial Equality in America* (Chicago: University of Chicago Press, 1999); Gilbert G. Gonzales, "De Jure Segregation," chap. 7 in *Chicano Education in The Era of Segregation* (Philadelphia: Balch Institute Press, 1990); Michael J. Klarman, *Brown v. Board of Education and the Civil Rights Movement* (New York: Oxford University Press, 2007), chaps. 1–3.

59. *Brown v. Board of Education of Topeka*, 347 U.S. 483, 494 (1954).

60. Richard Kluger, *Simple Justice: The History of Brown v. Board of Education and Black America's Struggle for Equality* (New York: Vintage, 1975).

61. *Brown v Board of Education of Topeka*, 347 U.S. 483, 490 (1954).

62. Meyer Weinberg, "The Relationship between School Desegregation and Academic Achievement: A Review of the Research," *Law and Contemporary Problems* 39, no. 2 (1975): 241–70; Robert L. Crain and Rita E. Mahard, "Desegregation and Black Achievement: A Review of the Research," *Law and Contemporary Problems* 42, no. 3 (1978): 17–56; Greg Wiggan, "Race, School Achievement, and Educational Inequality: Toward a Student-Based Inquiry Perspective," *Review of Educational Research* 77, no. 3 (2007): 310–33.

CHAPTER FIVE

1. Lee Rainwater and William L. Yancey, *The Moynihan Report and the Politics of Controversy: A Trans-action Social Science and Public Policy Report* (Cambridge, MA: MIT Press, 1967); also see Alice O'Connor, "Poverty's Culture Wars," chap. 8 in *Poverty Knowledge: Social Science, Social Policy and the Poor in Twentieth Century U.S. History* (Princeton, NJ: Princeton University Press, 2002); and James T. Patterson, *Freedom Is Not Enough: The Moynihan Report and America's Struggle over Black Family Life from LBJ to Obama* (New York: Basic Books, 2010).

2. Sylvia L. M. Martinez and John L. Rury, "From 'Culturally Deprived' to 'At Risk': The Politics of Popular Expression and Educational Inequality in the United States, 1960–1985," *Teachers College Record* 114, no. 6 (June 2012): 16–17.

3. Kenneth B. Clark, "How Children Living in Ghettos Should Be Taught," *Chicago Tribune*, September 11, 1971; For an earlier critique, see Kenneth B. Clark, *Dark Ghetto: Dilemmas of Social Power* (Hanover, NH: University Press of New England, 1965), pp. 129–30.

4. Oscar Lewis, *Five Families: Mexican Case Studies in the Culture of Poverty* (New York: Basic Books, 1975); James B. Conant, *Slums and Suburbs: A Commentary on Schools in Metropolitan Areas* (New York: McGraw-Hill, 1961); Frank Riessman, *The Cultur-*

ally Deprived Child (New York: Harper, 1962); Harrington, *The Other America*; Oscar Lewis, *La Vida: A Puerto Rican Family in the Culture of Poverty—San Juan and New York* (New York: Random House, 1966).

5. Leon Kamin, *The Science and Politics of IQ* (New York: Lawrence Erlbaum, 1974); Adam Miller, "The Pioneer Fund: Bankrolling the Professors of Hate," *Journal of Blacks in Higher Education*, no. 6 (1994): 58–61.

6. Steven Fraser, ed., *The Bell Curve Wars: Race, Intelligence, and the Future of America* (New York: Basic Books, 1995).

7. Martinez and Rury, "From 'Culturally Deprived' to 'At Risk,'" passim.

8. Riessman, *The Culturally Deprived Child*, passim.

9. Quoted in Martinez and Rury, "From 'Culturally Deprived' to 'At Risk,'" 8–10.

10. Gareth Davies, "Race and Poverty: Redefining Equality, 1964–1965," chap. 3 in *From Opportunity to Entitlement: The Transformation and Decline of Great Society Liberalism* (Lawrence: University Press of Kansas, 1996).

11. This explanation was clearly evident in the attitudes of whites who left city schools during the 1960s. See Donna Gardner and John L. Rury, "Suburban Resistance to District Reorganization: The 1968 Spainhower Commission and Metropolitan Kansas City and St. Louis," *Urban Review* 46, no. 1 (2014): 125–45.

12. Patricia Sullivan, *Lift Every Voice: The NAACP and the Making of the Civil Rights Movement* (New York: New Press, 2010), chaps. 8 and 9; Michael J. Klarman, *From Jim Crow to Civil Rights: The Supreme Court and the Struggle for Racial Equality* (New York: Oxford University Press, 2006), chaps. 4 and 5; Robert J. Cottrol, Raymond T. Diamond, and Leland B. Ware, *Brown v Board of Education: Caste, Culture, and the Constitution* (Lawrence: University Press of Kansas, 2003), chaps. 4 and 5.

13. John L. Rury and Shirley A. Hill, "Sea Change: 'Equalization' and Secondary Schooling," chap. 2 in *The African American Struggle for Secondary Schooling, 1940–1980: Closing the Graduation Gap* (New York: Teachers College Press, 2012).

14. Ibid.; also see Vanessa Siddle Walker, "Meeting Needs," chap. 4 in *Their Highest Potential: An African American School Community in the Segregated South* (Chapel Hill: University of North Carolina Press, 1996).

15. James T. Patterson, *Brown v Board of Education: A Civil Rights Milestone and Its Troubled Legacy* (New York: Oxford University Press, 2002), chaps. 4 and 5; Klarman, *Brown v Board of Education and the Civil Rights Movement*, chaps. 5–7.

16. "A Southern Manifesto," *Congressional Record*, 84th Cong. 2nd Sess.; vol. 102, pt. 4, March 12, 1956 (Washington, DC: Government Printing Office, 1956), pp. 4459–60.

17. John L. Rury, "Growth in African-American High School Enrollment, 1950–1970: An Under-Appreciated Legacy of the Brown Era," *Washburn Law Journal* 53, no. 3 (2014):488–92; Patterson, *Brown v Board of Education*, chap. 4.

18. Diane Ravitch, "Race and Education: Social Science and the Law," chap. 5 in *The Troubled Crusade: American Education, 1945–1980* (New York: Basic Books, 1983); also see Harvard Sitkoff, *The Struggle for Black Equality* (New York: Hill and Wang, 2008), chaps. 1 and 2.

19. Patterson, "Southern Whites Fight Back," chap. 5 in *Brown v Board of Education*; Karen Anderson, *Little Rock: Race and Resistance at Central High School* (Princeton, NJ: Princeton University Press, 2010), chaps. 3 and 4; Ira Wilmer Counts, *Life Is More than a Moment: The Desegregation of Little Rock's Central High* (Bloomington: Indiana University Press, 2007).

20. Patterson, *Brown v Board of Education*, p. 94; Klarman, "Brown's Backlash," chap. 7 in *Brown v Board of Education and the Civil Rights Movement*; Charles Clotfelter, "The

Legacies of *Brown* and *Milliken*," chap. 2 in *After "Brown": The Rise and Retreat of School Desegregation* (Princeton, NJ: Princeton University Press, 2004).

21. Patterson, *Brown v Board of Education*, chaps. 5–7.

22. Rury and Hill, *The African American Struggle for Secondary Schooling*, 149–50.

23. Frank McGurk, "A Scientist's Report on Race Differences," *U.S. News and World Report* 41 (September 21, 1956), pp. 92–98; the quote is on p. 96.

24. William H. Tucker, "Our Source of Funds: The Campaign against Civil Rights," chap. 3 in *The Funding of Scientific Racism: Wickliffe Draper and the Pioneer Fund* (Urbana: University of Illinois Press, 2002).

25. John P. Jackson, *Science for Segregation: Race, Law and the Case against Brown v. Board of Education* (New York: New York University Press, 2005), chaps. 4 and 5; Carleton Putnam, *Race and Reason: A Yankee View* (Washington, DC: Public Affairs Press, 1961), p. 44.

26. Jackson, "Organizing Massive Resistance and Organizing Science," chap. 5 in *Science for Segregation*.

27. I. A. Newby, *Challenge to the Court: Social Scientists and the Defense of Segregation, 1954–1966* (Baton Rouge: Louisiana State University Press, 1969), chaps.7 and 8.

28. Ibid., chap. 8; Jackson, "The Attack on *Brown*," chap. 6 in *Science for Segregation*.

29. Klarman, *Brown v Board of Education and the Civil Rights Movement*, chaps. 6 and 7; Sullivan, *Lift Every Voice*, chaps. 8 and 9.

30. Clotfelter, "The Legacies of *Brown* and *Milliken*"; Rury and Hill, "Battling Segregation," chap. 5 in *The African American Struggle for Secondary Schooling*.

31. On this point, see Nicholas Lemann, *The Promised Land: The Great Black Migration and How It Changed America* (New York: Vintage, 1992).

32. Rury, "Growth in African-American High School Enrollment, 1950–1970," 488–92.

33. Clotfelter, *After "Brown*," chaps. 2 and 3; Rury and Hill, "Battling Segregation."

34. Patterson, "Stalemates," chap. 8 in *Brown v Board of Education*; quote is from U.S. Supreme Court, 413 U.S. 189, Keyes v. School District No. 1, Denver, Colorado (no. 71–507).

35. Jennifer Hochschild, "Eradicating Racism," chap. 2 in *The New American Dilemma: Liberal Democracy and School Desegregation* (New Haven, CT: Yale University Press, 1984).

36. "Integration Plans Fraught with Emotion," *Wednesday Magazine*, October 20, 1965, p. 1.

37. Clotfelter, "Residential Segregation and 'White Flight,'" chap. 3 in *After "Brown"*; David Armor, "Desegregation Policy and the Law," chap. 1 in *Forced Justice: School Desegregation and the Law* (New York: Oxford University Press, 1996); on the success of George Wallace, see Patterson, *Brown v Board of Education*, p. 132.

38. Harvey Kantor and Barbara Brenzel, "Urban Education and the 'Truly Disadvantaged': The Historical Roots of the Contemporary Crisis, 1945–1990," *Teachers College Record* 94, no. 2 (1992): 278–314.

39. Jeffrey Mirel, "The Rise of the Liberal-Labor-Black Coalition, 1949–64," chap. 5 in *The Rise and Fall of an Urban School System: Detroit, 1907–1981* (Ann Arbor: University of Michigan Press, 1993); John L. Rury, "Race, Space and the Politics of Chicago's Public Schools: Benjamin Willis and the Tragedy of Urban Education," *History of Education Quarterly* 39, no. 2 (Summer 1999): 117–42; Peter William Moran, "Too Little, Too Late: The Elusive Goal of School Desegregation in Kansas City, Missouri, and the Role of the Federal Government," *Teachers College Record* 107, no. 9 (2005): 1933–55; for an overview, see John L. Rury, "The Changing Social Context of Urban

Education: A National Perspective," in *Seeds of Crisis: Public Schooling in Milwaukee since 1920*, ed. J. L. Rury and F. A. Cassel (Madison: University of Wisconsin Press, 1993), pp. 10–41.

40. Clotfelter, "The Legacies of *Brown* and *Milliken*"; Joyce A Baugh, *The Detroit School Busing Case: Milliken v Bradley and the Controversy over Desegregation* (Lawrence: University Press of Kansas, 2011).

41. Patterson, "The Burger Court Surprises," chap. 7 in *Brown v Board of Education*; Stephen Samuel Smith, *Boom for Whom?: Education, Desegregation, and Development in Charlotte* (Albany: State University of New York Press, 2004), chaps. 1 and 2.

42. Ravitch, "Race and Education: Social Science and the Law," chap. 5 in *The Troubled Crusade*; Martinez and Rury, "From 'Culturally Deprived' to 'At Risk,'" passim.

43. John L. Rury, "Attainment amidst Adversity: Black High School Students in the Metropolitan North, 1940–1980," in *Clio at the Table: History and Educational Policy*, ed. Kenneth Wong and Robert Rothman (New York: Peter Lang, 2009), pp. 37–58.

44. Gareth Davies, *See Government Grow: Educational Politics from Johnson to Reagan* (Lawrence: University Press of Kansas, 2007), pts. 2 and 3; Maris Vinovskis, "The Charlottesville Education Summit and the National Educational Goals," chap. 1 in *From a Nation at Risk to No Child Left Behind: National Education Goals and the Creation of Federal Education Policy* (New York: Teachers College Press, 2008); Clotfelter, "Residential Segregation and 'White Flight'"; Armor, "Desegregation Policy and Law."

45. Jennifer Hochschild, "Where Do We Go from Here?," chap. 6 in *The New American Dilemma*; Gary Orfield and Susan Eaton, eds., "Turning Back to Segregation," in *Dismantling Desegregation: The Quiet Reversal of Brown v Board of Education* (New York: New Press, 1996).

46. Elizabeth H. Debray, "Education Policy and Politics, 1990–2004," pt. 1 in *Politics, Ideology and Education: Federal Policy during the Clinton and Bush Administrations* (New York: Teachers College Press, 2006); Vinovskis, *From a Nation at Risk to No Child Left Behind*, chaps. 3 and 4.

47. Mark Berends, Samuel R. Lucas, and Roberto V. Peñaloza, "How Changes in Families and Schools Are Related to Trends in Black-White Test Scores," *Sociology of Education* 81, no. 4 (October 2008): 313–44; Derek Neal, "How Families and Schools Shape the Achievement Gap," in *Generational Change: Closing the Test Score Gap*, ed. Paul E. Peterson (Lanham, MD: Rowman and Littlefield, 2006), pp. 26–46; also see Jonathan Guryan, "Desegregation and Black Dropout Rates," *American Economic Review* 94, no. 4 (2004): 919–43; and Rucker C. Johnson, "Long-Run Impacts of School Desegregation and School Quality on Adult Attainments," Working Paper no. 16664 (Cambridge, MA: National Bureau of Economic Research, 2015), http://www.nber.org/papers/w16664.

48. William Julius Wilson, "The New Urban Poverty," pt. 1 in *When Work Disappears: The World of the New Urban Poor* (New York: Vintage Books, 1997); Douglas S. Massey and Nancy A. Denton, *American Apartheid: Segregation and the Making of the Underclass* (Cambridge, MA: Harvard University Press, 1993), pt. 1.

49. Michelle Alexander, "The Lockdown," chap. 2 in *The New Jim Crow: Mass Incarceration in the Age of Colorblindness* (New York: New Press, 2012); Michael Javen Fortner, *Black Silent Majority: The Rockefeller Drug Laws and the Politics of Punishment* (Cambridge, MA: Harvard University Press, 2015); Judith Kafka, *The History of "Zero Tolerance" in American Public Schooling* (New York: Palgrave Macmillan, 2011).

50. Rury and Hill, "Conclusion: The African American High School Experience in Perspective," in *The African American Struggle for Secondary Schooling*.

51. John L. Rury, "Historians and Policymaking," *American Journal of Education* 112, no. 3 (Summer 1999): 321–27.

52. Christopher Jencks and Meredith Phillips, eds., *The Black-White Test Score Gap* (Washington, DC: Brookings Institution Press, 1998), introduction.

53. Debray, "Implications for Education Policy: 2002 and Beyond," pt. 4 in *Politics, Ideology and Education*; Michael Rebell and Jessica R. Wolf, eds., *NCLB at the Crossroads: Reexamining the Federal Effort to Close the Achievement Gap* (New York: Teachers College Press, 2009).

54. On this point, see Katherine Magnuson and Jane Waldfogel, eds., "A Long-Term View," pt. 1 in *Steady Gains and Stalled Progress: Inequality and the Black-White Test Score Gap* (New York: Russell Sage Foundation, 2008); and Derek Neal, "Why Has Black-White Skill Convergence Stopped?," in *Handbook of the Economics of Education*, ed. Eric Hanushek and Finis Welch (New York: Elsevier, 2006), 1: 511–76.

55. John Rawls, *A Theory of Justice* (Cambridge, MA: Belknap Press of Harvard University Press, 1971).

56. Bernard R. Boxill, *Blacks and Social Justice* (Totowa, NJ: Rowman and Allanheld, 1984); Charles W. Mills, *The Racial Contract* (Ithaca, NY: Cornell University Press, 1997); Howard McGary, *Race and Social Justice* (Malden, MA: Blackwell, 1999); Derrick Darby, *Rights, Race, and Recognition* (Cambridge: Cambridge University Press, 2009); Tommie Shelby, *Dark Ghettos: Injustice, Dissent, and Reform* (Cambridge, MA: Belknap Press of Harvard University Press, 2016).

57. Natasha Warikoo and Prudence Carter, "Cultural Explanations for Racial and Ethnic Stratification in Academic Achievement: A Call for a New and Improved Theory," *Review of Educational Research* 79, no. 1 (2009): 366–94.

58. Claude Steele, "A Threat in the Air: How Stereotypes Shape Intellectual Ability and Performance," *American Psychologist* 52, no. 6 (1997): 613–29.

59. For influential conservative thinkers, see, for instance, Stephen and Abigail Thernstrom, *America in Black and White: One Nation, Indivisible* (New York: Simon and Schuster, 1999); and Thomas Sowell, *The Vision of the Anointed: Self Congratulation as a Basis for Social Policy* (New York: Basic Books, 1996).

CHAPTER SIX

1. On the urban crisis of the 1960s, see John L. Rury and Shirley A. Hill, *The African American Struggle for Secondary Schooling, 1940–1980: Closing the Graduation Gap* (New York: Teachers College Press, 2012), chap. 4, "Black Youth and the Urban Crisis."

2. The most thorough research on the benefits of living in an integrated setting comes from the Moving to Opportunity Project. For the most recent assessment of this large-scale experiment, see Raj Chetty, Nathaniel Hendren, and Lawrence Katz, "The Effect of Exposure to Better Neighborhoods on Children: New Evidence from the Moving to Opportunity Experiment," Working Paper no. 21156 (Cambridge, MA: National Bureau of Economic Research, 2015); also see Douglas S. Massey and Nancy A. Denton, *American Apartheid: Segregation and the Making of the Underclass* (Cambridge, MA: Harvard University Press, 1993). On the positive impact of desegregation, see Rucker C. Johnson, "Long-Run Impacts of School Desegregation and School Quality on Adult Attainments," Working Paper no. 16664 (Cambridge, MA: National Bureau of Economic Research, 2015).

3. For an overview, see the essays in Katherine Magnuson and Jane Waldfogel, eds., *Steady Gains and Stalled Progress: Inequality and the Black-White Test Score Gap* (New York: Russell Sage Foundation, 2008).

4. On this point, see Massey and Denton, *American Apartheid*, pt. 1, for a contemporary account of these developments. On the question of segregation and its effect on these communities, see ibid., chaps. 1 and 2.

5. On this point, see Spyros Konstantopoulos and Geoffrey Borman, "Family Background and School Effects on Student Achievement: A Multilevel Analysis of the Coleman Data," *Teachers College Record* 113, no. 1 (2011): 97–132, http://www.tcrecord.org.www2.lib.ku.edu/library/content.asp?contentid=15989.

6. Derrick Darby and Argun Saatcioglu, "Race, Inequality of Opportunity, and School Choice," *Theory and Research in Education* 13 (2015): 56–86.

7. Greg J. Duncan and Richard J. Murnane, "Economic Inequality: The Real Cause of the Urban School Problem," *Chicago Tribune*, October 6, 2011, available at http://articles.chicagotribune.com/2011–10–06/opinion/ct-perspec-1006-urban-20111006_1_poor-children-graduation-rate-gap.

8. A good recent exposition of these points can be found in Robert Putnam, *Our Kids: The American Dream in Crisis* (New York: Simon and Schuster, 2015).

9. For an overview, see the Urban League, *2015 State of Black America*, accessed April 19, 2017, http://soba.iamempowered.com/.

10. On these points, see CensusScope, "United States, Segregation: Dissimilarity Indices, 2000," Social Sciences Data Analysis Network, available at http://www.censusscope.org/us/rank_dissimilarity_white_black.html, accessed April 19, 2017; Alexander Kent and Thomas C. Frohlich, "America's Most Segregated Cities," 24/7 Wall Street, August 19, 2015, available at http://247wallst.com/special-report/2015/08/19/americas-most-segregated-cities/; Tamy Lubi, "Chicago: America's Most Segregated City," CNN Money, January 5, 2016, available at http://money.cnn.com/2016/01/05/news/economy/chicago-segregated/.

11. For an overview of these factors, see Eric Jensen, *Teaching with Poverty in Mind* (Washington, DC: Association for Supervision and Curriculum Development [ASCD], 2009) chap. 2.

12. Richard Rothstein, *Class and Schools: Using Social, Economic, and Educational Reform to Close the Black-White Achievement Gap* (New York: Teachers College Press and Economic Policy Institute [EPI], 2004), pp. 37–45.

13. Will Dobbie and Roland Fryer Jr., "Are High Quality Schools Enough to Close the Achievement Gap? Evidence from a Social Experiment in Harlem," Working Paper no. 15473 (Cambridge, MA: National Bureau of Economic Research, 2009).

14. Michelle Alexander, *The New Jim Crow: Mass Incarceration in the Age of Colorblindness* (New York: New Press, 2012); Becky Pettit, "Illusions of Progress," chap. 4 in *Invisible Men: Mass Incarceration and the Myth of Black Progress* (New York: Russell Sage, 2012).

15. Statistics on family structure were drawn from Child Trends Databank, *Family Structure*, accessed April 19, 2017, http://www.childtrends.org/?indicators=family-structure; On unemployment and family structure, see William Julius Wilson, "The Fading Inner-City Family," chap. 4 in *When Work Disappears: The World of the New Urban Poor* (New York: Vintage Books, 1997).

16. Wendy D. Manning and Kathleen A. Lamb, "Adolescent Well Being in Cohabitating, Married and Single Parent Families," *Journal of Marriage and Family* 65, no. 4 (November 2003): 876–93; Sheila Fitzgerald Krein and Andrea H. Beller, "Educational Attainment of Children from Single-Parent Families: Differences by Exposure, Gender, and Race," *Demography* 25, no. 2 (May 1988): 221–34.

17. These figures are taken from Monique W. Morris, "Education," chap. 2 in *Black Stats: African Americans by the Numbers in the Twenty First Century* (New York: New Press,

2014); on composition effects, see G. Bohrnstedt, S. Kitmitto, B. Ogut, D. Sherman, and D. Chan, *School Composition and the Black-White Achievement Gap*, NCES 2015–018 (Washington, DC: National Center for Education Statistics, U. S. Department of Education, 2015), p. 5, accessed April 19, 2017, from http://nces.ed.gov/pubsearch. Also see Janie Boschma and Ronald Brownstein, "The Concentration of Poverty in American Schools," *Atlantic*, February 29, 2016, available at http://www.theatlantic.com/education/archive/2016/02/concentration-poverty-american-schools/471414/.

18. Robert Balfanz and Nettie Legters, "Locating the Dropout Crisis: Which High Schools Produce the Nation's Dropouts? Where Are They Located? Who Attends Them?" (Baltimore: Center for Research on the Education of Students Placed at Risk [CRESPAR], Johns Hopkins University, 2004), accessed at http://web.jhu.edu/CSOS/graduation-gap/power.html.

19. On this point, see Rothstein, "Schools That 'Beat the Demographic Odds,'" chap. 2 in *Class and Schools*.

20. Brian Jacob, "The Challenges of Staffing Urban Schools with Effective Teachers," *Future of Children*, 17, no. 1 (Spring 2007): 129–53.

21. On class size, see Barbara Nye, Larry V. Hedges, and Spyros Konstantopoulos, "The Effects of Small Classes on Academic Achievement: The Results of the Tennessee Class Size Experiment," *American Educational Research Journal* 37, no. 1 (January 2000): 123–51; and Michael Boozer and Cecelia Rouse, "Intraschool Variation in Class Size: Patterns and Implications," *Journal of Urban Economics* 50, no. 1 (July 2001): 163–89.

22. Jacob, "The Challenges of Staffing Urban Schools with Effective Teachers," p. 131.

23. Vanessa Coca, David W. Johnson, Thomas Kelley-Kemple, Melissa Roderick, Eliza Moeller, Nicole Williams, and Kafi Moragne, *Working to My Potential: The Postsecondary Experiences of CPS Students in the International Baccalaureate Diploma Programme* (Chicago: Consortium on Chicago School Research, March 2012), available at https://consortium.uchicago.edu/publications/working-my-potential-postsecondary-experiences-cps-students-international-baccalaureate; on magnet schools, see Maureen Kelleher, "Magnet Focus Shifts from Diversity to Choice," CatalystChicago, January 22, 2016, available at http://catalyst-chicago.org/2016/01/magnet-school-focus-shifts-from-diversity-to-choice/.

24. Anthony S. Bryk, Penny Bender Sebring, Elaine Allensworth, Stuart Luppescu, and John Q. Easton, *Organizing Schools for Improvement: Lessons from Chicago* (Chicago: University of Chicago Press, 2010). On comparison of the HCZ with other schools, see Michelle Croft and Grover J. "Russ" Whitehurst, *The Harlem Children's Zone, Promise Neighborhoods, and the Broader, Bolder Approach to Education*, Brookings Institution Report, July 20, 2010, accessed at http://www.brookings.edu/research/reports/2010/07/20-hcz-whitehurst.

25. Jennifer O'Day and Marshall S. Smith, "Quality and Equity in American Education: Systemic Problems, Systemic Solutions," in *The Dynamics of Opportunity in America: Evidence and Perspective*, ed. Irwin Kirsch and Henry Braun (New York: Springer, 2016), pp. 297–358.

26. Charles M. Payne, *So Much Reform, So Little Change: The Persistence of Failure in Urban Schools* (Cambridge, MA: Harvard Education Press, 2008).

27. Massey and Denton, *American Apartheid*, chaps. 4–6.

28. On the attitudes of employers who discriminate against blacks because of supposed moral problems or character flaws, see Wilson, *When Work Disappears*, chaps. 5 and 6.

29. Diane Whitmore Schanzenbach, David Boddy, Megan Mumford, and Greg Nantz, *Fourteen Facts on Education and Economic Opportunity*, the Hamilton Project, Brookings Institution, March 2016, available at http.EconomicFacts-Educ&Economic Opportunity-Brookings2016.pdf.

30. On the need for such reforms, and how to achieve them, see Jean Anyon, *Radical Possibilities: Public Policy, Urban Education, and a New Social Movement* (New York: Routledge, 2014), chaps. 4, 9, and 10. Also see Helen Ladd, Pedro Noguera, Paul Reville, and Joshua Starr, "Student Poverty Isn't an Excuse: It's a Barrier," *Education Week*, May 11, 2016, accessed at http://www.edweek.org/ew/articles/2016/05/11/student-poverty-isnt-an-excuse-its-a.html?cmp=eml-enl-eu-news2.

31. For a somewhat critical account of the history of school choice, see Diane Ravitch, "Choice: The Story of an Idea," chap. 7 in *The Death and Life of the Great American School System: How Testing and Choice Are Undermining Education* (New York: Basic Books, 2011).

32. Citizens Research Council of Michigan, "Public School Enrollment Trends in Detroit," Memorandum 1141, June 2016, available at www.crcmich.org/PUBLICAT/2010s/2016/enrollment_trends_in_detroit-2016.pdf; Center for Research on Educational Outcomes, "Charter School Performance in Michigan," November 2013, available at https://credo.stanford.edu/ . . . /MI_report_2012_FINAL_1_11_2013_no_watermark.pdf; Kate Zernike, "A Sea of Charter Schools in Detroit Leaves Students Adrift," *New York Times*, June 26, 2016, available at http://www.nytimes.com/2016/06/29/us/for-detroits-children-more-school-choice-but-not-better-schools.html.

33. A useful compendium of essays examining the research on charter schools can be found in Christopher Lubienski and Peter Weitzel, eds., *The Charter School Experiment: Expectations, Evidence, and Implications* (Cambridge, MA: Harvard Education Press, 2010), see chaps. 1, 4, and 5 in particular. Also see Martin Carnoy, Rebecca Jacobson, Lawrence Mishel, and Richard Rothstein, *The Charter School Dust-up: Examining the Evidence on Enrollment and Achievement* (New York: Teachers College Press and EPI, 2005); and Priscilla Wohlstetter, Joanna Smith, and Caitlin Farrel, *Choices and Challengers: Charter School Performance in Perspective* (Cambridge, MA: Harvard Education Press, 2013), chaps. 2, 3, and 7.

34. For a study of the experiences of inner-city African American students in suburban schools, see Amy Stuart Wells and Robert Crain, *Stepping over the Color Line: African American Students in White Suburban Schools* (New Haven, CT: Yale University Press, 1999); on suburban resistance to such ideas in the past, see Donna Gardner and John L. Rury, "Suburban Resistance to District Reorganization: The 1968 Spainhower Commission and Metropolitan Kansas City and St. Louis," *Urban Review* 46, no. 1 (2014): 125–45.

35. Erin Einhorn, "The Extreme Sacrifice Detroit Parents Make to Access Better Schools," *Atlantic*, April 11, 2016, available at http://www.theatlantic.com/education/archive/2016/04/the-extreme-sacrifice-detroit-parents-make-to-access-better-schools/477585/.

36. Eric A. Hanushek, John F. Kain, and Steven G. Rivkin, "New Evidence about Brown v. Board of Education: The Complex Effects of School Racial Composition on Achievement," *Journal of Labor Economics* 27, no. 3 (2009): 352; Jonathan Guryan, "Desegregation and Black Dropout Rates," *American Economic Review* 94, no. 4 (2004): 919–43; and Rucker C. Johnson, "Long-Run Impacts of School Desegregation and School Quality on Adult Attainments," Working Paper no. 16664 (Cambridge, MA: National Bureau of Economic Research, 2015), http://www.nber.org/papers/w16664.

37. Ronald F. Ferguson, *Aiming Higher Together: Strategizing Better Educational Outcomes for Boys and Young Men of Color* (Washington, DC: Urban Institute, 2016), p. 58.

38. Jeremy E. Fiel has demonstrated that between 1993 and 2010, "whites and minorities actually became more evenly distributed across schools, helping increase minority students' exposure to whites" (p. 1). Jeremy E. Fiel, "Decomposing School Resegregation: Social Closure, Racial Imbalance, and Racial Isolation," *American Sociological Review* 78, no. 5 (2013): 1–21.

39. On the unpopularity of busing, see Matthew F. Delmont, *Why Busing Failed: Race, Media, and the National Resistance to School Desegregation* (Berkeley: University of California Press, 2016). Regarding the Civil Rights Project at UCLA, see the Civil Rights Project, Mission Statement, available at https://civilrightsproject.ucla.edu/about-us/mission-statement; on research about segregation, Massey and Denton, *American Apartheid*.

40. Sean F. Reardon, "School Segregation and Racial Academic Achievement," paper prepared for the Russell Sage Foundation Conference, "The Coleman Report at Fifty: Its Legacy and Enduring Value," Johns Hopkins University, Baltimore, April 2016, p. 26.

41. On this point, for instance, see Halley Potter and Kimberly Quick, "The Secret to School Integration," *New York Times*, February 23, 2016, accessed at http://www.nytimes.com/2016/02/23/opinion/the-secret-to-school-integration.html.

42. Elizabeth Anderson, *The Imperative of Integration* (Princeton, NJ: Princeton University Press, 2010).

43. Bohrnstedt et al., *School Composition and the Black-White Achievement Gap*, p. 23; also see William H. Schmidt, Nathan A. Burroughs, Pablo Zoido, and Richard T. Houang, "The Role of Schooling in Perpetuating Educational Inequality: An International Perspective," *Educational Researcher* 44, no. 7 (2015): 1–16; and C. C. Burris and K. G. Welner, "Closing the Achievement Gap by Detracking," *Phi Delta Kappan* 86, no. 8 (2005): 594–98.

44. On tracking, see the next chapter, and Samuel Roundfield Lucas, *Tracking Inequality: Stratification and Mobility in American High Schools* (New York: Teachers College Press, 1999) chaps. 1 and 2; on the politics of urban education, see Jeffrey R. Henig, Richard C. Hula, Marion Orr, and Desiree S. Pedescleaux, "The Role of External Actors," chap. 7 in *The Color of School Reform: Race, Politics and the Challenge of Urban Education* (Princeton, NJ: Princeton University Press, 2001).

45. See, for example, Amy L. Wax, *Race, Wrongs and Remedies: Group Justice in the Twenty First Century* (Lanham, MD: Rowman and Littlefield, 2009).

46. Anna Maria Barry-Jester, "Attitudes toward Racism and Inequality Are Shifting," *FiveThirtyEight Politics*, June 23, 2015, http://fivethirtyeight.com/datalab/attitudes-toward-racism-and-inequality-are-shifting/.

CHAPTER SEVEN

1. Anderson, *The Imperative of Integration*, p. 116.

2. For a summary of much of this body of research, see Amanda Lewis and John B. Diamond, "Introduction," chap. 1 in *Despite the Best Intentions: How Racial Inequality Thrives in Good Schools* (New York: Oxford University Press, 2015).

3. Joel Perlmann, "The Russian Jews," chap. 4 in *Ethnic Differences: Schooling and Social Structure among the Irish, Italians, Jews and Blacks in an American City, 1880–1935* (New York: Cambridge University Press, 1988).

4. Jeannie Oakes, "Unlocking the Tradition," chap. 2 in *Keeping Track: How Schools Structure Inequality*, 2nd ed. (New Haven, CT: Yale University Press, 2005).

5. Diane Ravitch, "Race and Education: The Brown Decision," chap. 4 in *The Troubled Crusade: American Education, 1945–1980* (New York: Basic Books, 1983).

6. John L. Rury and Shirley A. Hill, "Inequity, Discrimination and Growth," chap. 3 in *The African American Struggle for Secondary Schooling, 1940–1980: Closing the Graduation Gap* (New York: Teachers College Press, 2012).

7. For a summary of this research, see Jeannie Oakes, "Keeping Track: Structuring Equality and Inequality in an Era of Accountability," *Teachers College Record* 110, no. 3 (March 2008): 700–712.

8. Rury and Hill, "The Black Youth and the Urban Crisis," chap. 4 in *The African American Struggle for Secondary Schooling*.

9. Oakes, "Keeping Track," pp. 700–710; Samuel Roundfield Lucas, *Tracking Inequality: Stratification and Mobility in American High Schools* (New York: Teachers College Press, 1998), chap. 1; also see Samuel R. Lucas and Aaron D. Good, "Race, Class, and Tournament Track Mobility," *Sociology of Education* 74, no. 2 (April 2001): 139–56.

10. Lucas, *Tracking Inequality*, 36.

11. John Tierney, "AP Classes Are a Scam," *Atlantic*, October 13, 2012, http://www.theatlantic.com/national/archive/2012/10/ap-classes-are-a-scam/263456/.

12. Lucas, *Tracking Inequality*, chaps. 3 and 4; also see Adam Gamoran and Robert D. Mare, "Secondary School Tracking and Educational Equality: Compensation, Reinforcement or Neutrality?," *American Journal of Sociology* 94, no. 5 (1989): 1146–83; and Sean Kelly, "The Black-White Gap in Mathematics Course Taking," *Sociology of Education* 82, no. 1 (January 2009): 47–69.

13. Rury and Hill, "Black Youth and the Urban Crisis."

14. On this point, see Mark Berends, Samuel R. Lucas, and Roberto V. Peñazola, "How Changes in Families and Schools Are Related to Trends in Black-White Test Scores," *Sociology of Education* 81, no. 4 (October 2008): 313–44.

15. For an overview of this, see "Stereotype Threat Widens Achievement Gap," Research in Action, American Psychological Association, accessed April 19, 2017, at http://www.apa.org/research/action/stereotype.aspx.

16. Adam Gamoran, "Alternative Uses of Ability Grouping in Secondary Schools: Can We Bring High Quality Instruction to Low Ability Classes?," *American Journal of Education* 102, no. 1 (1993): 1–22.

17. Samuel R. Lucas and Mark Berends, "Sociodemographic Diversity, Correlated Achievement, and De Facto Tracking," *Sociology of Education* 75, no. 4 (October 2002): 328–48; Kelly, "The Black-White Gap in Mathematics Course Taking," 47–69.

18. Karolyn Tyson, *Integration Interrupted: Tracking, Black Students and Acting White after Brown* (New York: Oxford University Press, 2011), p. 51.

19. Kelly, "The Black-White Gap in Mathematics Course Taking."

20. Quotes and figures from Sonali Kohli, "Modern-Day Segregation in Public Schools," *Atlantic*, November 18, 2014, http://www.theatlantic.com/education/archive/2014/11/modern-day-segregation-in-public-schools/382846/.

21. Maika Watanabe, "Tracking in the Era of High Stakes State Accountability Reform: Case Studies of Classroom Instruction in North Carolina," *Teachers College Record* 110, no. 3 (2008): 489–534; for additional information on curricular differentiation by race in North Carolina, see Roslyn Arlin Mickelson and Bobbie J. Everett, "Neotracking in North Carolina: How High School Courses of Study Reproduce Race and Class-Based Stratification," *Teachers College Record* 110, no. 3 (2008): 535–70.

22. Audrey Devine-Eller, "Timing Matters: Test Preparation, Race, and Grade Level," *Sociological Forum* 27, no. 2 (June 2012): 458–80; for a closer look at a single urban

district, see Al Baker, "Test Prep Endures in New York Schools, Despite Calls to Ease It," *New York Times*, May 1, 2014.

23. On this point, see Elizabeth Covay Minor, "Racial Differences in Teacher Perceptions of Student Ability," *Teachers College Record* 116, no. 10 (October 2014): 1–22. On implicit bias, see Natasha Warikoo, Stacey Sinclair, Jessica Fei, and Drew Jacoby-Senghor, "Examining Racial Bias in Education: A New Approach," *Educational Researcher* 45, no. 9 (December 2016): 508–14.

24. Russell Rumberger, "Predictors of Dropping Out," chap. 7 in *Dropping Out: Why Students Drop Out of High School and What Can Be Done about It* (Cambridge, MA: Harvard University Press, 2011).

25. Michael Q. McShane, *The Path Forward: Improving Opportunities for African American Students* (Washington, DC: U.S. Chamber of Commerce Foundation, 2015), p. 6, https://www.uschamberfoundation.org/sites/default/files/The_Path_Forward_Report_Final.pdf; Lucas, conclusion to *Tracking Inequality*; Adam Gamoran and Robert D. Mare, "Secondary School Tracking and Educational Inequality: Compensation, Reinforcement, or Neutrality?," *American Journal of Sociology* 94, no. 5 (March 1989): 1146–83.

26. Rury and Hill, *The African American Struggle for Secondary Schooling*, 168–71.

27. U.S. Department of Education, Office of Civil Rights, Civil Rights Data Collection: Data Snapshot (School Discipline), March 21, 2014, available at ocrdata.ed.gov /Downloads/CRDC-School-Discipline-Snapshot.pdf.

28. Ronald F. Ferguson, *Aiming Higher Together: Strategizing Better Educational Outcomes for Boys and Young Men of Color* (Washington, DC: Urban Institute, 2016), pp. 50–56; Daniel Losen, Cheri Hodson, Michael A. Keith II, Katrina Morrison, and Shakti Belway, *Are We Closing the School Discipline Gap?* (Los Angeles: Center for Civil Rights Remedies, the Civil Rights Project at UCLA, February 2015), http://civilrightsproject .ucla.edu/resources/projects/center-for-civil-rights-remedies/school-to-prison-folder /federal-reports/are-we-closing-the-school-discipline-gap; Robert Balfanz, Vaughan Byrnes, and Joanna Fox, "Sent Home and Put Off-Track: The Antecedents, Disproportionalities, and Consequences of Being Suspended in the Ninth Grade" (Baltimore: Everyone Graduates Center, Johns Hopkins University, 2012), p. 7.

29. Losen et. al, *Are We Closing the School Discipline Gap?*, "Introduction and Overview." Edward W. Morris and Brea L. Perry, "The Punishment Gap: School Suspension and Racial Disparities in Achievement," *Social Problems* 63 (January 2016): 68–86.

30. Losen et al., *Are We Closing the School Discipline Gap?*, p. 10; also see Balfanz, Byrnes, and Fox, "Sent Home and Put Off-Track."

31. S. C. Wu, W. T. Pink, R. L. Crain, and O. Moles, "Student Suspension: A Critical Reappraisal," *Urban Review* 14, no. 4 (1982): 245–303; for a more recent analysis with similar findings, see Balfanz, Byrnes, and Fox, "Sent Home and Put Off-Track," 7.

32. Russell J. Skiba, Robert S. Michael, Abra Carroll Nardo, and Reece L. Peterson, "The Color of Discipline: Sources of Racial and Gender Disproportionality in School Punishment," *Urban Review* 34, no. 4 (December 2002): 317–42. For a historical perspective, see Joseph A. Tropea, "Bureaucratic Order and Special Children: Urban Schools, 1950s–1960s," *History of Education Quarterly* 27, no. 3 (Fall 1987): 339–61. On implicit bias in classroom settings, see Warikoo et al., "Examining Racial Bias in Education," 509–10.

33. Skiba et al., "The Color of Discipline," 338, 332. The second quote is from Balfanz, Byrnes, and Fox, "Sent Home and Put Off-Track," 6.

34. Russell J. Skiba and Reece L. Peterson, "School Discipline at the Crossroads: From

Zero Tolerance to Early Response," *Exceptional Children* 66, no. 3 (April 2000): 335–46; Gale M. Morrison and Barbara D'Incau, "The Web of Zero-Tolerance: Characteristics of Students Who Are Recommended for Expulsion from School," *Education and Treatment of Children* 20, no. 3 (August 1997): 316.

35. Matthew C. Williams, "A Normative Ethical Analysis of School Discipline Practices" (Ph.D. diss., University of Rochester, 2013), chaps. 1 and 5.

36. L. G. Falice, "Black Student Dropout Behavior: Disengagement from School, Rejection and Racial Discrimination," *Journal of Negro Education* 50, no. 4 (1981): 415–24.

37. Balfanz et al., "Sent Home and Put Off-Track," 8.

38. Quoted in Rumberger, *Dropping Out*, 199.

39. Christine Bowditch, "Getting Rid of Troublemakers: High School Disciplinary Procedures and the Production of Dropouts," *Social Problems* 40, no. 4 (1993): 493–509; Isabelle Archambault, Michael Janosz, Jean-Sebastian Fallu, and Linda S. Pagani, "Student Engagement and Its Relationship to Early High School Dropout," *Journal of Adolescence* 32, no. 3 (June 2009): 651–70.

40. Rumberger, *Dropping Out*, 170.

41. Lewis and Diamond, "The Road to Detention Is Paved with Good Intentions: Race and Discipline Expectations," chap. 3 in *Despite the Best Intentions*.

42. Rumberger, *Dropping Out*, 197.

43. Bowditch, "Getting Rid of Troublemakers."

44. Robert L. Osgood, *The History of Special Education: A Struggle for Equality in American Public Schools* (Westport, CT: Praeger, 2008), chaps. 4 and 5.

45. Ibid.; Tropea, "Bureaucratic Order and Special Children," pp. 348–49.

46. M. Suzanne Donovan and Christopher T. Cross, eds., "Influences on Cognitive Behavioral Development," chap. 3 in *Minority Students in Special and Gifted Education* (Washington, DC: National Academies Press, 2002). On debates over this, see Russell Skiba, Alfredo Artilles, Elizabeth B. Kozleski, Daniel J. Losen, and Elizabeth G. Henry, "Risks and Consequences of Oversimplifying Educational Inequalities: A Response to Morgan et al.," *Educational Researcher* 45, no. 3 (April 2016): 221–25; and Paul L. Morgan and George Farkas, "Are We Helping All the Children That We Are Supposed to be Helping?" in the same issue, pp. 226–28.

47. Paul L. Morgan, George Farkas, Marianne M. Hillemeier, Richard Mattison, Steve Maczuga, Hui Li, and Michael Cook, "Minorities Are Disproportionally Underrepresented in Special Education: Longitudinal Evidence across Five Disability Conditions," *Educational Researcher* 44, no. 5 (2015): 284. These figures are estimates based on a nationally representative sample of elementary schoolchildren. For similar data from a slightly earlier point in time, see Donovan and Cross, *Minority Students in Special and Gifted Education*, especially chapter 2; also see Christopher B. Swanson, *Special Education in America: The State of Students with Disabilities in the Nation's High Schools* (Washington, DC: Editorial Projects in Education, 2008), p. 10.

48. On the history of this, see Christine E. Sleeter, "Learning Disabilities: The Social Construction of a Special Education Category," *Exceptional Children* 53, no. 1 (1986): 46–54; also see Argun Saatcioglu and Thomas Skrtic, "Categorical Manipulation in Formal Organization: The Case of Racial Inequality in Mild Disabilities" (unpublished paper, University of Kansas, July 2015), pp. 8–10.

49. Russell J. Skiba, Lori Poloni-Staudinger, Sarah Gallini, Ada B. Simmons, and Renae Feggins-Azziz, "Disparate Access: The Disproportionality of African American Students with Disabilities across Educational Environments," *Exceptional Children* 72, no. 4 (2006): 411–24; also see Alfredo J. Artiles, Beth Harry, Daniel J. Reschly, and

Philip C. Chinn, "Over-Identification of Students of Color in Special Education: A Critical Overview," *Multicultural Perspectives* 4, no. 1 (2002): 3–10.

50. U.S. Commission on Civil Rights, *Minorities in Special Education*, briefing report, April 2009, available at www.usccr.gov/pubs/MinoritiesinSpecialEducation.pdf. For a more recent accounting, looking at individual states, see Office of Special Education and Rehabilitative Services, U. S. Department of Education, *Racial and Ethnic Disparities in Special Education: A Multi-Year Disproportionality Analysis by State, Analysis Category, and Race/Ethnicity*, February 2016, available at http://www2.ed.gov/programs/osepidea/618-data/LEA-racial-ethnic-disparities-tables/index.html.

51. Swanson, *Special Education in America*, p. 14; on the history, see Russell J. Skiba, "Special Education and School Discipline: A Precarious Balance," *Behavioral Disorders* 27, no. 2 (February 2002): 81.

52. Artiles et al., "Over-Identification of Students of Color in Special Education," 4; Justin J. W. Powell, *Barriers to Inclusion: Special Education in the United States and Germany* (Boulder, CO: Paradigm, 2011); also see Hugh Mehan, Alma Hertweck, and J. Lee Meihls, *Handicapping the Handicapped: Decision Making in Students' Educational Careers* (Stanford, CA: Stanford University Press, 1986); and Russell J. Skiba, Ada B. Simmons, Shana Ritter, Ashley C. Gibb, M. Karega Rausch, Jason Cuadrado, and Choon-Geun Chung, "Achieving Equity in Special Education: History, Status, and Current Challenges," *Exceptional Children* 74, no. 3 (2008): 264–88.

53. U.S. Department of Education, "U.S. Department of Education Takes Action to Deliver Equity for Students with Disabilities," press release, February 23, 2016, available at http://www.ed.gov/news/press-releases/us-department-education-takes-action-deliver-equity-students-disabilities.

54. See, for instance, R. L'Heureux Lewis-McCoy, *Inequality in the Promised Land: Race, Resources, and Suburban Schooling* (Stanford, CA: Stanford University Press, 2014), chap. 2.

55. On this point, see Tyson, *Integration Interrupted*, chaps. 3 and 4. Also see Lewis-McCoy, *Inequality in the Promised Land*, chap. 6.

56. Prudence L. Carter, *Stubborn Roots: Race, Culture and Inequality in U.S. and South African Schools* (New York: Oxford University Press, 2012), chap. 5.

57. Ibid.; also see Tyson, *Integration Interrupted*, chap. 4, and Amanda Lewis, "Struggling with Dangerous Subjects: Language, and Power at Metro2," chap. 3 in *Race in the Schoolyard: Negotiating the Color Line in Classrooms and Communities* (New Brunswick, NJ: Rutgers University Press, 2003). These issues are also discussed in Lewis-McCoy, *Inequality in the Promised Land*, chap. 5.

58. Emily DeRuy, "In Wealthier School Districts, Students Are Farther Apart," *Atlantic*, May 3, 2016, http://www.theatlantic.com/education/archive/2016/05/in-wealthier-school-districts-students-are-farther-apart/481041/.

CHAPTER EIGHT

1. David P. Baker, *The Schooled Society: The Educational Transformation of Global Culture* (Palo Alto, CA: Stanford University Press, 2014).

2. Susan Yonezawa, Amy Stuart Wells, and Irene Serna, "Choosing Tracks: 'Freedom of Choice' in Detracking Schools," *American Educational Research Journal* 39, no. 1 (2002): 37–67; Karolyn Tyson, *Integration Interrupted: Tracking, Black Students, and Acting White after Brown* (New York: Oxford University Press, 2011).

3. James E. Rosenbaum, "Institutional Career Structures and the Social Construction of

Ability," in *Handbook of Theory and Research for the Sociology of Education*, ed. John G. Richardson (New York: Greenwood Press, 1986), pp. 139–71; Jeannie Oakes, *Keeping Track: How Schools Structure Inequality*, 2nd ed. (New Haven, CT: Yale University Press, 2005).

4. Jeannie Oakes and Gretchen Guiton, "Matchmaking: The Dynamics of High School Tracking Decisions," *American Educational Research Journal* 32, no. 1 (1995): 3–33.

5. National Center for Educational Statistics, *Curricular Differentiation in Public High Schools*, NCES 95360, December 1994, https://nces.ed.gov/surveys/frss/publications/95360/index.asp?sectionid=1.

6. Oakes and Guiton, "Matchmaking."

7. Maika Watanabe, "Tracking in the Era of High Stakes Accountability Reform: Case Studies of Classroom Instruction in North Carolina," *Teachers College Record* 110, no. 3 (2008): 489–534.

8. Oakes, *Keeping Track*.

9. Linn Posey-Maddox, *When Middle-Class Parents Choose Urban Schools: Class, Race, and the Challenge of Equity in Public Education* (Chicago: University of Chicago Press, 2014).

10. Sean Kelly and Heather Price, "The Correlates of Tracking Policy: Opportunity Hoarding, Status Competition, or a Technical-Functional Explanation?," *American Educational Research Journal* 48 (2011): 560–85; Charles Tilly, *Durable Inequality* (Berkeley: University of California Press, 1999).

11. Emily DeRuy, "In Wealthier School Districts, Students Are Farther Apart," *Atlantic*, May 3, 2016, http://www.theatlantic.com/education/archive/2016/05/in-wealthier-school-districts-students-are-farther-apart/481041/.

12. Samuel Bowles and Herbert Gintis, *Schooling in Capitalist America: Educational Reform and the Contradictions of Economic Life* (New York: Basic Books, 1976); Felicia Pratto, Jim Sidanius, and Shana Levin, "Social Dominance Theory and the Dynamics of Intergroup Relations: Taking Stock and Looking Forward," *European Review of Social Psychology* 17 (2006): 271–320.

13. Yonezawa, Wells, and Serna, "Choosing Tracks."

14. John L. Rury and Jeffrey E. Mirel, "The Political Economy of Urban Education," *Review of Research in Education* 22 (1997): 49–110; Kysa Nygreen, *These Kids: Identity, Agency, and Social Justice at a Last Chance High School* (Chicago: University of Chicago Press, 2013).

15. Signithia Fordham and John Ogbu, "Black Students' School Success: Coping with the 'Burden of "Acting White,"'" *Urban Review* 18 (1986): 176–206.

16. Eric McNamara Horvat and Kristine Lewis, "Reassessing the 'Burden of Acting White': The Importance of Peer Groups in Managing Academic Success," *Sociology of Education* 76, no. 4 (2003): 265–80; Karolyn Tyson, William Darity Jr., and Domini R. Castellino, "It's Not 'A Black Thing': Understanding the Burden of Acting White and Other Dilemmas of High Achievement," *American Sociological Review* 70, no. 4 (2005): 582–605.

17. Yonezawa, Wells, and Serna, "Choosing Tracks," 56.

18. Immanuel Kant, *Observations on the Feeling of the Beautiful and Sublime*, trans. John T. Goldthwait (Berkeley: University of California Press, 2004), pp. 110–11.

19. Emily Arcia, "Achievement and Enrollment Status of Suspended Students: Outcomes in a Large, Multicultural School District," *Education and Urban Society* 38, no. 3 (2006): 359–69.

20. Anne Gregory, Russell J. Skiba, and Pedro A. Noguera, "The Achievement Gap and the Discipline Gap: Two Sides of the Same Coin?," *Educational Researcher* 39, no. 1 (2010): 59–68.

21. James E. Davis and Will J. Jordan, "The Effects of School Context, Structure, and Experiences on African American Males in Middle and High School," *Journal of Negro Education* 63, no. 4 (1994): 570–87.

22. See Gregory, Skiba, and Noguera, "The Achievement Gap and the Discipline Gap"; Edward W. Morris, "'Tuck in That Shirt!': Race, Class, Gender, and Discipline in an Urban School," *Sociological Perspectives* 48, no. 1 (2005): 25–48; Ann A. Ferguson, *Bad Boys: Public Schools in the Making of Black Masculinity* (Ann Arbor: University of Michigan Press, 2000), and Kenneth B. Clark, *Dark Ghetto: Dilemma of Social Power* (New York: Harper Collins, 1967).

23. David J. Harding, "Collateral Consequences of Violence in Disadvantaged Neighborhoods," *Social Forces* 88, no. 2 (2009): 757–84; Patrick Sharkey, Amy Ellen Schwartz, Ingrid Gould Ellen, and Johanna Lacoe, "High Stakes in the Classroom, High Stakes on the Street: The Effects of Community Violence on Student's Standardized Test Performance," *Sociological Science* 1 (2014): 199–220.

24. Eric A. Stewart, Christopher J. Schreck, and Ronald L. Simons, "'I Ain't Gonna Let No One Disrespect Me': Does the Code of the Street Reduce or Increase Violent Victimization among African American Adolescents?," *Journal of Research in Crime and Delinquency* 43, no. 4 (2006): 427–58; Elijah Anderson, *Code of the Street: Decency, Violence, and the Moral Life of the Inner City* (New York: W. W. Norton, 2006).

25. Johanna R. Lacoe, "Unequally Safe: The Race Gap in School Safety," *Youth Violence and Juvenile Justice* 13, no. 2 (2015): 143–68.

26. Tara L. Kuther and Celia B. Fisher, "Victimization by Community Violence in Young Adolescents from a Suburban City," *Journal of Early Adolescence* 18, no. 1 (1998): 53–76.

27. Lacoe, "Unequally Safe."

28. John M. Wallace Jr., Sara Goodkind, Cynthia M. Wallace, and Jerald G. Bachman, "Racial, Ethnic, and Gender Differences in School Discipline among U.S. High School Students: 1991–2005," *Negro Educational Review* 59 (2008): 47–62; Gregory, Skiba, and Noguera, "The Achievement Gap and the Discipline Gap."

29. Sarah B. Miles and Deborah Stipek, "Contemporaneous and Longitudinal Associations between Social Behavior and Literacy Achievement in a Sample of Low-Income Elementary School Children," *Child Development* 77, no. 1 (2006): 103–17.

30. Gregory, Skiba, and Noguera, "The Achievement Gap and the Discipline Gap."

31. Gary G. Wehlage and Robert A. Rutter, "Dropping Out: How Much Do Schools Contribute to the Problem?," *Teachers College Record* 87 (1986): 374–92.

32. Aaron Kupchik and Geoff Ward, "Race, Poverty, and Exclusionary School Security: An Empirical Analysis of U.S. Elementary, Middle, and High Schools," *Youth Violence and Juvenile Justice* 12, no. 4 (2014): 332–54.

33. Khalil Gibran Muhammad, *The Condemnation of Blackness: Race, Crime, and the Making of Modern Urban America* (Cambridge, MA: Harvard University Press, 2010).

34. Russell J. Skiba, Robert S. Michael, Abra Carroll Nardo, and Reece L. Peterson, "The Color of Discipline: Sources of Racial and Gender Disproportionality in School Punishment," *Urban Review* 34, no. 4 (December 2002): 317–42; Wehlage and Rutter, "Dropping Out"; Rachel Dinkes, Emily Forrest Cataldi, and Wendy Lin-Kelly, "Indicators of School Crime and Safety: 2007" (Washington, DC: National Center for

Education Statistics, Institution of Education Sciences, U.S. Department of Education and Bureau of Justice, 2007).

35. Anna C. McFadden, George E. Marsh II, Barrie Jo Price, and Yunhan Hwang, "A Study of Race and Gender Bias in the Punishment of Handicapped School Children," *Education and Treatment of Children* 15, no. 2 (1992): 140–146.

36. Skiba et al., "The Color of Discipline."

37. Gary D. Gottfredson, Denise C. Gottfredson, Allison Ann Payne, and Nisha C. Gottfredson, "School Climate Predictors of School Disorder: Results from a National Study of Delinquency Prevention in Schools," *Journal of Research in Crime and Delinquency* 42, no. 4 (2005): 412–44.

38. Daniel J. Losen and Gary Orfield, eds., *Racial Inequity in Special Education* (Cambridge, MA: Harvard Education Press, 2002).

39. Colin Ong-Dean, *Distinguishing Disability: Parents, Privilege, and Special Education* (Chicago: University of Chicago Press, 2009).

40. Matthew Ladner and Christopher Hammons, "Special but Unequal: Race and Special Education," in *Rethinking Special Education for a New Century*, ed. Chester E. Finn Jr., Andrew J. Rotherham, and Charles R. Hokanson Jr. (Washington, DC: Progressive Policy Institute and Thomas B. Fordham Foundation, 2001), pp. 85–100.

41. James L. Moore III, Malik S. Henfield, and Delila Owens, "African American Males in Special Education: Their Attitudes and Perceptions toward High School Counselors and School Counseling Services," *American Behavioral Scientist* 51, no. 7 (2008): 907–27.

42. Beth Harry, *Cultural Diversity, Families, and the Special Education System: Communication for Empowerment* (New York: Teachers College Press, 1992).

43. John L. Hosp and Daniel J. Reschly, "Disproportionate Representation of Minority Students in Special Education: Academic, Demographic, and Economic Predictors," *Exceptional Children* 70, no. 2 (2004): 185–99.

44. Alfredo J. Artiles and Stanley C. Trent, "Overrepresentation of Minority Students in Special Education: A Continuing Debate," *Journal of Special Education* 27, no. 4 (1994): 410–37; Wanda J. Blanchett, "From Brown to the Resegregation of African Americans in Special Education—it Is Time to 'Go for Broke,'" *Urban Education* 44, no. 4 (2009): 370–88; Cecil R. Reynolds, Patricia A. Lowe, and Adam L. Saenz, "The Problem of Bias in Psychological Assessment," in *The Handbook of School Psychology*, ed. Cecil R. Reynolds and Terry B. Gutkin, 3rd ed. (New York: John Wiley and Sons, 1999), pp. 549–95.

45. William Julius Wilson, *More than Just Race: Being Black and Poor in the Inner City* (New York: Norton, 2009), chap. 1.

46. Donald L. MacMillian and Daniel J. Reschly, "Overrepresentation of Minority Students: The Case for Greater Specificity or Reconsideration of the Variables Examined," *Journal of Special Education* 32, no 1 (1998): 15–24.

47. Russell Skiba, Ada Simmons, Shana Ritter, Kristin Kohler, Michelle Henderson, and Tony Wu, "The Context of Minority Disproportionality: Practitioner Perspectives on Special Education Referral," *Teachers College Record* 108 (2006): 1424–59.

48. Douglas S. Massey and Nancy A. Denton, *American Apartheid* (Cambridge, MA: Harvard University Press, 1993).

49. Jeanne Brooks-Gunn and Greg J. Duncan, "The Effects of Poverty on Children," *Future of Children* 7, no. 2 (1997): 55–71.

50. Thomas Parrish, "Racial Disparities in the Identification, Funding, and Provision

of Special Education," in Losen and Orfield, *Racial Inequity in Special Education*, pp. 15–37.

51. Donald P. Oswald, Martha J. Coutinho, and Al M. Best, "Community and School Predictors of Overrepresentation of Minority Children in Special Education," in Losen and Orfield, *Racial Inequality in Special Education*, 1–13.

52. Russell J. Skiba, Lori Poloni-Staudinger, Ada B. Simmons, L. Renae Feggins-Azziz, and Choong-Geun Chung, "Unproven Links: Can Poverty Explain Ethnic Disproportionality in Special Education?," *Journal of Special Education* 39, no. 3 (2005): 130–44; Jacob Hibel, George Farkas, and Paul L. Morgan, "Who Is Placed into Special Education?," *Sociology of Education* 83, no. 4 (2010): 312–32.

53. Russell Skiba et al., "The Context of Minority Disproportionality," 1451.

CHAPTER NINE

1. John Rawls, *A Theory of Justice* (Cambridge, MA: Belknap Press of Harvard University Press, 1971); T. M. Scanlon, *What We Owe to Each Other* (Cambridge, MA: Belknap Press of Harvard University Press, 1998); and Ronald Dworkin, *Sovereign Virtue: The Theory and Practice of Equality* (Cambridge, MA: Harvard University Press, 2000).

2. Martin Luther King Jr., *Strength to Love* (Minneapolis: Fortress Press, 2010), p. 29.

3. Anderson, *The Imperative of Integration*, p. 103.

4. The argument summarized in this and the next several paragraphs has been adapted from ibid., pp. 16–22.

5. Ibid., p. 18.

6. Ibid.

7. Ibid., p. 19.

8. Ibid., p. 16. For a useful discussion of Anderson's linchpin thesis that disambiguates her formulation of it, see Tommie Shelby, "Integration, Inequality, and Imperatives of Justice: A Review Essay," *Philosophy and Public Affairs* 42, no. 3 (2014): 253–85, §4.

9. Anderson, *The Imperative of Integration*, pp. 19–20.

10. Jim Sidanius and Felicia Pratto, *Social Dominance: An Intergroup Theory of Social Hierarchy and Oppression* (Cambridge: Cambridge University Press, 1999).

11. Ibid., 45.

12. In addition to legitimizing racial dominance relations, historically this notion also supported informal and formal practices, processes, and institutions predicated on these relations. So apart from legitimating the dominance of whites over blacks, it also justified affording blacks education and educational institutions that were inferior to what was afforded whites. Whites represented themselves, and were represented by European Enlightenment philosophers, as superior to blacks in intellect, temperament, and character. In the United States, they used their power to deny blacks schooling or to provide it on highly unequal terms. While whites learned to read and do math and science, and accumulated knowledge of arts, letters, and history, blacks learned nothing or only what was necessary to make them better slaves or social subordinates. Black "ignorance," which was virtually guaranteed by these practices, was then used to justify giving them an inferior and unequal education. Thus, this mutually reinforcing interplay between racial ideology and social practices allowed whites to hoard opportunities to gain a superior education, to attend superior educational institutions, and to enjoy the many benefits of education. Here we expand on an observation Anderson makes in *The Imperative of Integration*, p. 8. She says: "U.S. whites have long hoarded opportunities by establishing school systems

that provide no, or an inferior, education to blacks, Latinos, and Native Americans." Our book combines a history of this phenomenon with philosophical reflections on justice to argue that contemporary examples of educational opportunity hoarding, such as tracking, discipline, and special education, which impact the racial achievement gap, are, like their predecessors, manifestly unjust.

13. Anderson, *The Imperative of Integration*, p. 20.
14. Ibid.
15. Derrick Darby and Richard E. Levy, "Postracial Remedies," *University of Michigan Journal of Law Reform* 50, no. 2 (2017): 387–488, contains the argument for why this is a virtue.
16. W. E. Burghardt Du Bois, "Does the Negro Need Separate Schools?," *Journal of Negro Education* 4, no. 3 (1935): 332.
17. See, for instance, Carol D. Lee, *Culture, Literacy and Learning: Blooming in the Midst of the Whirlwind* (New York: Teachers College Press, 2007), chaps. 3–5.
18. Carol Corbett Burris, *On the Same Track: How Schools Can Join the Twenty-First Century Struggle against Resegregation* (Boston: Beacon Press, 2014), pp. 74–77.
19. Quotes are from ibid., p. 93; and Carol Corbett Burris and Delia T. Garrity, *Detracking for Excellence and Equity* (Alexandria, VA: Association for Supervision and Curriculum Development [ASCD], 2008), p. 56.
20. Burris, *On the Same Track*, pp. 83–84.
21. For a somewhat more skeptical look at the tracking controversies, see Tom Loveless, *The Tracking Wars: State Reform Meets School Policy* (Washington, DC: Brookings Institution Press, 1999). This book emphasizes failures of the detracking movement of the 1990s, mostly due to the same sources of resistance that Burris describes.
22. Burris, *On the Same Track*, see especially chap. 5; Burris and Garrity, *Detracking for Excellence and Equity*, chaps. 7 and 8. In their account of changing teacher attitudes about student learning, Burris and Garrity briefly discuss the idea of "multiple intelligences," or the belief "that all students have gifts and talents" (pp. 37, 93–94, 106). We are concerned about this construct, as it may be considered quite compatible with the Color of Mind. Thomas Jefferson, for instance, believed that Africans were "generally more gifted than the whites" in musical ability, but that they lacked cognitive capacity. The labeling of other talents or propensities, such as bodily-kinesthetic or interpersonal, as psychologist Howard Gardener has done, potentially opens the door to the idea that blacks and other minority students lack verbal and logical intelligence, which are most highly rewarded in schools (and closely aligned with conventional conceptions of intelligence). Many racists, like Jefferson, are happy to concede that blacks have less-favored forms of ability, such as bodily kinesthetic in the case of football players. As a general point of consensus among psychologists, the empirical evidence to support Gardner's theory is weak; see Beth A. Visser, Michael C. Ashton, and Philip Vernon, "g and the Measurement of Multiple Intelligences: A Response of Gardner," *Intelligence* 34, no. 5 (2006): 507–10; on Jefferson's views, see his *Notes on the State of Virginia* (Boston: Lilly and Wait, 1832), p. 147.
23. Burris, *On the Same Track*, chap. 8.
24. George Theoharis, *The School Leaders Our Children Deserve: Seven Keys to Equity, Social Justice and School Reform* (New York: Teachers College Press, 2009), chaps. 1 and 2.
25. Ibid., chaps. 3 and 4.
26. Ibid., chaps. 6 and 7.
27. Ibid., chaps. 9 and 10.

28. Beth C. Rubin and Pedro Noguera, "Tracking Detracking: Sorting through the Dilemmas and Possibilities in Practice," *Equity and Excellence in Education* 37, no. 1 (2004): 92–101.

29. Our perspective is informed by David Tyack and Larry Cuban's *Tinkering toward Utopia: A Century of Public School Reform* (Cambridge, MA: Harvard University Press, 1995), conclusion, which holds that meaningful reform must resonate for teachers and building-level leaders.

30. On conservative views, see Michael W. Apple, *Educating the "Right" Way: Markets, Standards, God, and Inequality* (New York: Routledge, 2006), chaps. 1 and 7; for discussion of a leftist perspective, see Jean Anyon, *Radical Possibilities: Public Policy, Urban Education, and a New Social Movement* (New York: Routledge, 2014).

INDEX